ABSTRACTS
of
PASQUOTANK COUNTY NORTH CAROLINA
GUARDIAN BOND BOOKS
1798–1831

Compiled by

Jean Wood Paschal

HERITAGE BOOKS
2012

HERITAGE BOOKS
AN IMPRINT OF HERITAGE BOOKS, INC.

Books, CDs, and more—Worldwide

For our listing of thousands of titles see our website at
www.HeritageBooks.com

Published 2012 by
HERITAGE BOOKS, INC.
Publishing Division
100 Railroad Ave. #104
Westminster, Maryland 21157

Copyright © 2012 Jean Wood Paschal

Other Heritage Books by the author:
Abstracts of Pasquotank County, North Carolina Guardian Bond Books, 1798–1831
Abstracts of Pasquotank County, North Carolina Guardian Bond Books, 1832–1867

All rights reserved. No part of this book may be reproduced or transmitted in any form or by any means, electronic or mechanical, including photocopying, recording or by any information storage and retrieval system without written permission from the author, except for the inclusion of brief quotations in a review.

International Standard Book Numbers
Paperbound: 978-0-7884-5448-6
Clothbound: 978-0-7884-9242-6

Contents

Preface i

Introduction iii

Guardian Bond Book 1798 – 1801 1

Guardian Bond Book 1802 – 1805 15

Guardian Bond Book 1805 – 1808 25

Guardian Bond Book 1808 – 1811 35

Guardian Bond Book 1812 – 1816 49

Guardian Bond Book 1816 - 1822 63

Guardian Bond Book 1822 – 1824 91

Guardian Bond Book 1824 – 1827 125

Guardian Bond Book 1827 – 1831 153

Guardian Bond Book 1821 – 1831 181

Index 185

Preface

Guardian Bonds are essentially an untouched resource for most casual genealogical researchers due to the difficulty accessing the information they contain.

Prior to the 1850 census records, there were very few legal documents that listed the names of all the children that belonged within a family unit. If the child's father did not write a will that mentioned the child by name, it is hard to establish any type of official connection between them. Information found in the Guardian Bonds can help a researcher recreate the basic structure of their ancestor's family.

Between the years of 1798 and 1867, there were sixteen volumes of Guardian Bond books created by the Clerk of Court for the Pleas and Quarters Sessions for Pasquotank County, North Carolina. All guardian bonds issued in Pasquotank County during this period of time were recorded in these books with the exception of a three year gap from February 1862 to September 1865. Since these dates coincide with the Civil War, it is probably safe to assume that no official bonds were issued during those years. There is no missing bond book as the bonds issued before and after this gap were recorded in the same bond book.

The sixteen original Guardian Bond books are only available for viewing at the State Archives in Raleigh, North Carolina. *(Archive Call Numbers: C.R.075.511.1 - C.R.075.511.16)* Even though these books were microfilmed by the Genealogical Society of Utah in September of 1941, very few local libraries across the country have the microfilm reels available for immediate use.

Specific information within the individual bond books is also hard to locate. There is an incomplete index of names at the beginning of the earliest Guardian Bond books but these existing indexes have a lot of errors. Many of the later Guardian Bond books either had no index at all or were missing some of the index pages for the volume. There was also no consistency between the books on which names recorded on the bonds were used for the index. Some of the book indexes list just the name of the ward while others recorded the father's name with the general notation "orphans of" or "heirs of." The names that are recorded in the existing Guardian Bond book indexes are not in alphabetical order but, they are divided into groups by the first letter of the surname.

This volume is intended to serve as a comprehensive index for the first ten volumes of the Pasquotank County Guardian Bond books. The abstracted information for each bond contains the name of the father when identified, the name of the ward or wards, the name of the guardian, the bond number, the bond amount, and the names of the bondsmen who signed the document as sureties.

While the utmost care was taken to decipher the names on these bonds accurately, there will be some inconsistencies throughout this volume regarding spelling. The spelling of both surnames and given names on the bonds varied from year to year and some parts of the recorded names were simply unreadable or unrecognizable. Any additional information for the abstracted bond supplied by me or questionable translation of a name will be written in italics and encased by parenthesis.

Copies of these bonds can be obtained from the North Carolina State Archives in Raleigh, North Carolina. Requests for copies of specific Guardian Bonds from the Archives must be identified by the number of the bond as well as which Guardian Bond book it was recorded in. Additional information such as the ward's name or father's name should also be included in the request.

Jean Wood Paschal
Summerville, South Carolina
September 2012

Introduction

There is some confusion over what responsibilities a guardian had toward his ward in the late 1700's and early 1800's. A *ward* was simply any person who was considered to be under the protection of the local court system. For the most part a guardian was the person appointed by the court who was entrusted with managing the property and possessions of his ward. While this normally referred to property owned by children under the age of twenty one, it also applied to adults who were judged by the court to be too incompetent to handle their own affairs.

Although there were some instances where a child also lived with their appointed guardian, this was not always the case. The majority of these children were appointed a guardian only when they inherited property in their own name. If the property was inherited from a grandparent or other relative, it was not unusual to find that the child's father was named as the guardian for his own child. In cases where the child inherited property after the death of the father, most were assigned a male guardian even if their mother was still alive and the child lived with her. The majority of these guardians were usually related to the child in some way but not always. If the estimated value of the child's property was substantial, the court would sometimes choose an unrelated, but well trusted member of the community to act as the child's guardian.

The man chosen by the court to be the guardian of another person was expected to keep accurate records concerning their ward's finances and had to agree to an annual audit of their accounts by the court. They also had to post a bond to guarantee that they would faithfully perform their duties as a guardian, and protect their ward's property to the best of their abilities. Failure to administer their guardianship honestly would cause the guardian to forfeit the bond amount.

The amount of money each Guardian Bond represented varied depending on what property the ward actually owned when the guardian was chosen. Usually the bonds were issued at twice the estimated value of the ward's possessions. Payment of a Guardian Bond was guaranteed by the bondsmen who signed the document.

Introduction

There were usually a total of three bondsmen, the guardian and two additional men who also agreed to the payment of the bond if it was forfeited.

A Guardian Bond did not last forever nor was it issued for free. It had to be periodically renewed usually once a year at a cost of between six to eight shillings during the early years or one dollar when the monetary standard changed. However, any major changes of circumstances during the year such as the death of the guardian, marriage of a ward, or the death of a bondsman necessitated that a new bond was issued.

During the late 1600's to early 1700's there were no uniform laws to cover how an orphaned child's inheritance was handled. Even when a guardian was appointed by the court, many times the inheritance simply disappeared before the child came of age.

There is no doubt that the matter of Guardianship and how a ward's possessions could be protected was a major concern for all the inhabitants of North Carolina. This problem was addressed by the North Carolina General Assembly in 1755. A detailed law was passed on how those possessions were to be administered and the penalties involved when a guardian failed in his responsibilities. The following is an extract of the portions of this law that are directly concerned with Guardian Bonds:

> An Act for Regulating Orphans, their Guardians and Estates.
> *(Acts of the North Carolina General Assembly, Vol. 25, Pgs. 313-330, 1755)*
>
> *Whereas, for want of proper Laws for regulating Guardians, and the Management of Orphans, their Interests and Estates have been greatly Abused and their Education very much neglected; for prevention whereof for the future, Be it Enacted by the Governor, Council and Assembly, and it is hereby Enacted by the Authority of the Same, ...*
>
> *I. And be it further Enacted by the Authority aforesd., That the Supreme Courts and County Courts of this Province within their respective Jurisdictions, have and Shall have full power and Authority from time to time to take Cognizance of all matters Concerning Orphans and their Estates, and to appoint Guardians in Such Cases where to them it shall appear necessary and shall take good Security of all Guardians by them to be Appointed, for the Estates of the Orphans by them Committed; and if any Court shall Commit an Orphans Estate to the Guardianship of any person or persons without taking good and Sufficient Security for the Same, the Justice or Justices Appointing Such Guardian Shall be liable for all loss*

Introduction

and Damages Sustained by the Orphan for want of Such Security being taken, to be recovered by Action at the Common Law in any Court of Record in which the Same is Cognizable in the Suit of the Party grieved. Provided always, That where the Securities were good at the time of their being taken or Accepted, but afterwards became Insolvent, in Such case the Justice or Justices shall not be liable.

II. And be it further Enacted, That the Bond to be given by any person or persons appointed Guardian as aforesd.; shall be made payable to the Justice or Justices present in Court and Granting Such Guardianship, the Survivors or Survivor of them, their Executors and Administrators in trust for the benefit of the Child or Children Committed to the Tuition and Care of such Guardian, which Bond such Court shall cause to be Acknowledged before them and Recorded; and that in the Name of the Justice or Justices to whom the Same is made payable, the Survivors or Survivor of them, their Executors, and Administrators, any Person or Persons injured, may and shall at his, her or their Costs and Charges, Commence and prosecute a Suit against Such Guardian and his Securities, Executors or Administrators, and shall and may recover all damages which he, she or they have Sustained by reason of the breach of the Conditions hereof.......

XIII. And be it further Enacted by the Authority aforesd., That where any person who now is or hereafter shall be Security for the Estate of any Orphan, shall conceive himself in danger by reason thereof, and Petition the Court where such Security was entered into for Relief, it shall be lawful for such Court upon Petition to them Exhibited, forthwith to Order Summons to issue against the Party or Parties with and for whom the Petitioner Stands bound, returnable to the next Court, and thereupon to compel Such Party or Parties to give sufficient other or Counter Security, to be approved by the said Court or to Deliver to the Said Estate to the Petitioner or Such other person as the Court shall direct, or they may and are hereby empowered to make such other order or Rule therein for Relief of the Petitioner and better Securing such Orphan's Estate as to them shall appear just and equitable..........

Even though this law was only supposed to be in effect for five years, it remained in force until 1762 when "An Act for the better Care of Orphans, and Security and Management of their Estates" was passed by the North Carolina General Assembly. This law was basically an expanded version of the previous Act, but the portions of the law concerning guardian bonds remained the same.

By 1784, the North Carolina General Assembly realized that there was a portion of the adult population in the State who were

Introduction

incapable of managing their lives and possessions on their own. As shown by the following, a new law was passed which allowed the courts to place these people under the care of a guardian.

An Act to Prevent Unjust Appeals, and to Impower the County Courts in this State to Provide for the Safe Keeping the Estates of Ideots and Lunatics.
(Acts of the North Carolina General Assembly, Vol. 24, Pg. 678, 1784)

III. And, whereas, there are in divers parts of this State ideots and lunatics possessed of considerable property who waste and destroy the same, and make improvident dispositions thereof; Be it therefore Enacted, That it shall and may be lawful for every county court in this State wherever any such ideots or lunatics shall be within the jurisdiction thereof, to appoint him or her a guardian, taking bond for the faithful administration of the trust reposed in them, in the same manner as bonds are taken from the guardians of orphans; and such guardians when so appointed shall continue during the pleasure of the court, and shall have the same powers to all intents, constructions and purposes, and shall be subject to the same rules, orders and restrictions, as guardians of orphans appointed by the court, such ideotcy or lunacy to be ascertained by the inquisition of a jury by virtue of a writ to be issued by such court to the sheriff of the county for that purpose.

The laws concerning guardian bonds remained in effect and basically unchanged for the next one hundred years.

Although the earliest guardian bonds were simply hand written documents, by 1798, most guardian bonds were preprinted forms which were bound together as a book. Each of these forms had blank areas which were to be filled in by the Clerk of Court when a guardian was assigned to a ward. Any changes that needed to be made to the printed wording on the document were simply marked through and the new wording was written in by hand.

A new guardian bond book was not issued each year; it was used until each bond in the book had been assigned. This means that the bond books covered multiple years and rarely coincided with beginning a new book at the start of a year.

The guardian bonds were recorded in these books in the order that they were issued. The first bond in each new book was simply identified as bond number 1. No attempt was made to record the bonds in any type of alphabetical order.

Pasquotank County, North Carolina
Guardian Bonds
Book 1798 - 1801

STATE of NORTH-CAROLINA.

KNOW all Men by thefe Prefents, That We

are held and firmly bound unto

Efquires, and the reft of the Juftices affigned to keep
the peace for *County, in the full and juft fum of*
pounds: To the which
payment well and truly to be made, we bind ourfelves, our heirs, executors and
adminiftrators, jointly and feverally, firmly by thefe prefents. Sealed with our
feals, and dated this 179

WHEREAS the above bounden
hath been this day, by the worfhipful court of faid county appointed
guardian to orphan of
deceafed: Now the condition of the
above obligation is fuch, that if the faid
guardian as aforefaid, fhall well and truly difcharge his faid guardianfhip, by
taking care of and improving all the eftate belonging to the faid orphan ; and
fhall alfo fettle his guardianfhip accounts with the court of faid county, as is required by law ; and that he will deliver up to the faid
orphan, as aforefaid, when he fhall attain lawful age, all fuch
eftate as he ought of right to be poffeffed of, or fooner if required, agreeable to
the true intent and meaning of the act of the General Affembly in fuch cafe made
and provided ; then this obligation to be void, otherwife to remain in full force
and virtue.

Signed, Sealed and delivered
in the Prefence of

Pasquotank County, North Carolina

Bailey, Henry 6 March 1799 Bond No. 29
Ward: Sarah Bailey orphan of Henry Bailey deceased
Guardian: John Lane Bond amount: 200 pounds
Bondsmen: John Lane, Joseph Scott, John Shaw

Barnes, Thomas 30 December 1798 Bond No. 5
Ward: Silas Fountain Barnes illegitimate child of Thomas Barnes*
Guardian: Stephen Barnes Bond amount: 1000 pounds
Bondsmen: Stephen Barnes, James Barnes, Devotion Davis Jr.
*(*Note: the word orphan was scratched out)*

Brothers, Andrew 10 December 1801 Bond No. 90
Ward: Isaac C. Brothers orphan of Andrew Brothers deceased
Guardian: Miles Brothers Bond amount: 100 pounds
Bondsmen: Miles Brothers, Josiah Relfe, Benjamin Davis

Brothers, John 4 March 1801 Bond No. 71
Ward: Anna Brothers orphan of John Brothers deceased
Guardian: Micajah Chancy Bond amount: 250 pounds
Bondsmen: Micajah Chancy, Jesse Reding, Edward Chancy

Brothers, Jonathan 5 June 1799 Bond No. 33
Wards: Ruth & John Brothers orphans of Jonathan Brothers
Guardian: Bailey Davis Bond amount: 500 pounds
Bondsmen: Bailey Davis, Durant Davis, Joseph Davis

Brothers, Jonathan 5 June 1799 Bond No. 34
Wards: Samuel & Mabel Brothers orphans of Jonathan Brothers
Guardian: Bailey Davis Bond amount: 1000 pounds
Bondsmen: Bailey Davis, Durant Davis, Joseph Davis

Brothers, Joseph 6 December 1798 Bond No. 17
Wards: Enoch, Peggy, Robert, Micajah, Mary, & Joseph Brothers
    orphans of Joseph Brothers deceased
Guardian: Joshua Brothers Bond amount: 1000 pounds
Bondsmen: Joshua Brothers, John Smithson, Timothy Cotter

Guardian Bond Book 1798 - 1801   3

Clark, Micajah   4 December 1799   Bond No. 48
Ward: Ephraim Clark orphan of Micajah Clark deceased
Guardian: Isaac Overman   Bond amount: 200 pounds
Bondsmen: Isaac Overman, Joshua Trueblood & Abner Nichols

Cartwright, Ahaz   4 March 1800   Bond No. 55
Ward: Ahaz Cartwright orphan of Ahaz Cartwright deceased
Guardian: John Cartwright   Bond amount: 100 pounds
Bondsmen: John Cartwright, Job Brothers, Henry Brothers

Cartwright, John   2 June 1801   Bond No. 76
Wards: John & Enoch Cartwright children of John Cartwright*
Guardian: John Jones   Bond amount: 200 pounds
Bondsmen: John Jones, William S. Hinton, Samuel Spence
           *(*Note: the word orphan was scratched out)*

Carver, Job   8 December 1801   Bond No. 82
Ward: Evergan Carver orphan of Job Carver deceased
Guardian: James Carver   Bond amount: 500 pounds
Bondsmen: James Carver, William Wilson, William T. Muse

Carver, Job   9 December 1801   Bond No. 87
Ward: Mary Carver orphan of Job Carver deceased
Guardian: William Wilson   Bond amount: 500 pounds
Bondsmen: William Wilson, James Shannonhouse, William Muse

Carver, Job   10 December 1801   Bond No. 88
Ward: Alfred Carver orphan of Job Carver deceased
Guardian: William T. Muse   Bond amount: 500 pounds
Bondsmen: William Muse, William Wilson, James Shannonhouse

Carver, Job   10 December 1801   Bond No. 89
Ward: John Carver orphan of Job Carver deceased
Guardian: William T. Muse   Bond amount: 500 pounds
Bondsmen: William Muse, William Wilson, James Shannonhouse

Pasquotank County, North Carolina

Commander, Joseph   8 December 1798   Bond No. 18
Ward: Joseph Commander orphan of Joseph Commander deceased
Guardian: Joseph Banks   Bond amount: 5000 pounds
Bondsmen: Joseph Banks, Matthias E. Sawyer, Thomas Jordan

Connor, Cader   5 September 1799   Bond No. 47
Ward: John Connor orphan of Cader Connor deceased
Guardian: John MacDonald   Bond amount: 1000 pounds
Bondsmen: John MacDonald, Jos. Banks, Christopher Nicholson

Connor, Kader   3 March 1800   Bond No. 52
Ward: Crawford Connor orphan of Cader Connor deceased
Guardian: John Overman   Bond amount: 1000 pounds
Bondsmen: John Overman, Charles Overman, Aaron Lowe

Davis, Anthony   4 December 1799   Bond No. 50
Wards: Anthony & Joseph Davis orphans of Anthony Davis
Guardian: Ruth Davis   Bond amount: 500 pounds
Bondsmen: Ruth Davis, James Spence, Joseph Gray

Davis, David   3 June 1800   Bond No. 59
Ward: David Davis orphan of David Davis deceased
Guardian: Miles Davis   Bond amount: 1000 pounds
Bondsmen: Miles Davis, Bailey Davis, Joseph Davis

Davis, Samuel   6 March 1799   Bond No. 24
Ward: Lovey Davis orphan of Samuel Davis deceased
Guardian: John Crocker   Bond amount: 2000 pounds
Bondsmen: John Crocker, Joseph Banks, Archibald Davis

Davis, Samuel   6 March 1799   Bond No. 25
Ward: Lydia Davis orphan of Samuel Davis deceased
Guardian: John Crocker   Bond amount: 2000 pounds
Bondsmen: John Crocker, Joseph Banks, Archibald Davis

Davis, Samuel   4 December 1799   Bond No. 51
Wards: Lovey & Lydia Davis orphans of Samuel Davis deceased
Guardian: Thomas Palin   Bond amount: 500 pounds
Bondsmen: Thomas Palin, Thomas Jordan Jr., Joseph Scott

Guardian Bond Book 1798 - 1801

Davis, Thomas 4 December 1798 Bond No. 6
Ward: Thomas Davis orphan of Thomas Davis deceased
Guardian: Stephen Barnes Bond amount: 1000 pounds
Bondsmen: Stephen Barnes, Joseph Banks, Ruben Keaton

Davis, Thomas 4 December 1798 Bond No. 7
Ward: John Davis orphan of Thomas Davis deceased
Guardian: Stephen Barnes Bond amount: 1000 pounds
Bondsmen: Stephen Barnes, Joseph Banks, Ruben Keaton

George, David 5 December 1798 Bond No. 14
Ward: William George orphan of David George deceased
Guardian: John McDonald Bond amount: 2000 pounds
Bondsmen: John McDonald, Joseph Scott, Ruben Keaton

George, David 5 December 1798 Bond No. 15
Ward: John George orphan of David George deceased
Guardian: John McDonald Bond amount: 2000 pounds
Bondsmen: John McDonald, Joseph Scott, Ruben Keaton

Gilbert, Jeremiah 3 June 1800 Bond No. 58
Wards: Joel & Aaron Lancaster Gilbert sons of Jeremiah Gilbert *
Guardian: Josiah Gilbert Jr. Bond amount: 100 pounds
Bondsmen: Josiah Gilbert Jr., Jeremiah Gilbert
    (*Note: the word orphan was scratched out)

Gilbert, Jeremiah 8 September 1801 Bond No. 78
Wards: Joel Gilbert and Aaron Lancaster Gilbert his sons *
Guardian: Jeremiah Gilbert Bond amount: 40 pounds
Bondsmen: Jeremiah Gilbert, Nathan Morris
    (*Note: the word orphan was scratched out)

Graves, James 4 September 1799 Bond No. 42
Ward: Jeremiah Graves orphan of James Graves deceased
Guardian: Bailey Jackson Bond amount: 500 pounds
Bondsmen: Bailey Jackson, Timothy Cotter, John Lane

Pasquotank County, North Carolina

Gray, John   4 September 1799   Bond No. 41
Wards: Robert, Dorcas, Mary, Elizabeth & Jean Grey orphans of John Gray deceased
Guardian: Joseph Gray   Bond amount: 200 pounds
Bondsmen: Joseph Gray, James Spence, James Sawyer

Gray, John   3 March 1801   Bond No. 65
Wards: Robert Gray, Dorcas Gray, Mary Gray, Elizabeth Gray & Jean Grey orphans of John Gray deceased
Guardian: James Smith   Bond amount: 150 pounds
Bondsmen: James Smith, James Spence

Gray, Thomas   5 June 1799   Bond No. 31
Ward: Jean Grey orphan of Thomas Gray deceased
Guardian: James Spence   Bond amount: 500 pounds
Bondsmen: James Spence, Hollowell Sawyer, Joseph Draper

Henley, Joseph   6 September 1798   Bond No. 4
Ward: George R. Henley orphan of Joseph Henley deceased
Guardian: Joshua Trueblood   Bond amount: 1000 pounds
Bondsmen: Joshua Trueblood, Joseph Relfe, Jesse Redding

Howell, Rowan   4 March 1801   Bond No. 70
Ward: Benjamin Howell orphan of Rowan Howell deceased
Guardian: John Bailey   Bond amount: 200 pounds
Bondsmen: John Bailey, Joseph Banks

Jordan, John A.   3 June 1801   Bond No. 77
Ward: Elizabeth Jordan orphan of John A. Jordan deceased
Guardian: Willoughby Dozier   Bond amount: 1000 pounds
Bondsmen: Willoughby Dozier, John Lane, Demsey Nash

Kirby, Abraham   4 March 1801   Bond No. 67
Wards: Sarah Kirby, James Kirby, Betsy Kirby & Lucinda Kirby orphans of Abraham Kirby deceased
Guardian: Robert Bernard   Bond amount: 1000 pounds
Bondsmen: Robert Bernard, Gabriel Bailey, Frederick B. Sawyer

Guardian Bond Book 1798 - 1801

Lockwood, Armwell 5 June 1799   Bond No. 30
Wards: Elizabeth & Nancy Lockwood orphans of Armwel Lockwood
Guardian: Holland Lockwood   Bond amount: 250 pounds
Bondsmen: Holland Lockwood, Benjamin Jones

Lowry, John   12 December 1801   Bond No. 93
Wards: Polly Lowery & Benjamin Lowry orphans of John Lowery
Guardian: William Banks   Bond amount: 4000 pounds
Bondsmen: William Banks, Thaddeus Freshwater, Joseph Banks

Lufman, William   10 December 1801   Bond No. 92
Wards: John, Miles, & Wm. Lufman orphans of William Lufman
Guardian: Aaron Williams   Bond amount: 100 pounds
Bondsmen: Aaron Williams, Ebenezer Sawyer, Timothy Cotter

Mann, Thomas   4 December 1799   Bond No. 49
Ward: Sarah Mann orphan of Thomas Mann deceased
Guardian: William T. Relfe   Bond amount: 5000 pounds
Bondsmen: William T. Relfe, Rubin Keaton, John Smithson Jr.

Morris, Aaron   4 December 1798   Bond No. 8
Ward: Jehoshaphat Morris orphan of Aaron Morris Sr. deceased
Guardian: Aaron Morris Jr.   Bond amount: 600 pounds
Bondsmen: Aaron Morris Jr., Benjamin Prichard, John Bell

Morris, Aaron   4 December 1798   Bond No. 9
Ward: Sarah Morris orphan of Aaron Morris Sr. deceased
Guardian: Aaron Morris Jr.   Bond amount: 500 pounds
Bondsmen: Aaron Morris Jr., Benjamin Prichard, John Bell

Morris, Aaron   4 December 1798   Bond No. 10
Ward: John Morris orphan of Aaron Morris Sr. deceased
Guardian: Aaron Morris Jr.   Bond amount: 600 pounds
Bondsmen: Aaron Morris Jr., Benjamin Prichard, John Bell

Morris, Aaron   4 December 1798   Bond No. 11
Ward: Aaron Morris orphan of Aaron Morris Sr. deceased
Guardian: John Bell   Bond amount: 600 pounds
Bondsmen: John Bell, Aaron Morris Jr., Christopher Morris

Morris, Aaron 4 December 1798 Bond No. 12
Ward: Margaret Morris orphan of Aaron Morris Sr. deceased
Guardian: John Bell Bond amount: 600 pounds
Bondsmen: John Bell, Aaron Morris Jr., Christopher Morris

Morris, Aaron 4 December 1798 Bond No. 13
Ward: Pritchard Morris orphan of Aaron Morris Sr. deceased
Guardian: Benjamin Pritchard Bond amount: 600 pounds
Bondsmen: Benjamin Pritchard, Aaron Morris Jr.

Morris, Joseph 30 September 1799 Bond No. 37
Ward: Nathan Morris orphan of Joseph Morris Sr. deceased
Guardian: Joshua Morris Bond amount: 50 pounds
Bondsmen: Joshua Morris, John Morris, Joseph Turner

Morris, Joseph 30 September 1799 Bond No. 38
Ward: Anna Morris orphan of Joseph Morris Sr. deceased
Guardian: Joshua Morris Bond amount: 50 pounds
Bondsmen: Joshua Morris, John Morris, Joseph Turner

Morris, Joseph 30 September 1799 Bond No. 39
Ward: Penniah Morris orphan of Joseph Morris Sr. deceased
Guardian: Joshua Morris Bond amount: 50 pounds
Bondsmen: Joshua Morris, John Morris, Joseph Turner

Morris, Joseph 30 September 1799 Bond No. 40
Ward: Millicent Morris orphan of Joseph Morris Sr. deceased
Guardian: Joshua Morris Bond amount: 50 pounds
Bondsmen: Joshua Morris, John Morris, Joseph Turner

Nicholson, John 4 March 1800 Bond No. 56
Wards: George & Polly Nicholson orphans of John Nicholson
Guardian: Jerusha Nicholson Bond amount: 400 pounds
Bondsmen: Jerusha Nicholson, Ruben Keaton, John McDonald, William Wilson

Guardian Bond Book 1798 - 1801

Overman, Ruben   5 March 1799   Bond No. 20
Ward: Daniel Overman orphan of Ruben Overman deceased
Guardian: Thomas Banks   Bond amount: 1000 pounds
Bondsmen: Thomas Banks, William Banks, Jonathan Banks

Overman, Ruben   3 December 1800   Bond No. 64
Ward: Samuel Overman orphan of Ruben Overman deceased
Guardian: William Stott   Bond amount: 1000 pounds
Bondsmen: William Stott, Ruben Keaton, Jesse Reding

Overman, Thomas   5 June 1798   Bond No. 1
Ward: Thomas Overman was found by a jury to be insane *
Guardian: Ozier *(Ozias?)* Overman   Bond amount: 500 pounds
Bondsmen: Ozier *(Ozias?)* Overman, Thaddeus Freshwater
    (*Note: the word orphan was scratched out)

Overman, Thomas   3 March 1800   Bond No. 53
Wards: Charles, Thomas, Rhoda & John Overman orphans of
     Thomas Overman deceased
Guardian: Gabriel Bailey   Bond amount: 1000 pounds
Bondsmen: Gabriel Bailey, Charles Overman, Josiah Bundy

Palin, Lemuel   4 September 1799   Bond No. 46
Ward: Nancy Palin orphan of Lemuel Palin deceased
Guardian: Thomas Jordan Jr.   Bond amount: 1000 pounds
Bondsmen: Thomas Jordan Jr., Joseph Scott, Nehemiah Pendleton

Palin, Thomas   2 December 1800   Bond No. 63
Ward: Susannah Palin orphan of Thomas Palin deceased
Guardian: Benjamin Pritchard   Bond amount: 1000 pounds
Bondsmen: Benjamin Pritchard, Toms White

Pendleton, John F.   9 December 1801   Bond No. 84
Ward: Abner Pendleton orphan of John F. Pendleton deceased
Guardian: David Jennings   Bond amount: 500 pounds
Bondsmen: David Jennings, William Keaton, Frederick Davis

Pendleton, John F. 9 December 1801 Bond No. 86
Ward: John Pendleton orphan of John F. Pendleton deceased
Guardian: David Jennings Bond amount: 500 pounds
Bondsmen: David Jennings, William Keaton, Frederick Davis

Pool, Joseph 6 June 1798 Bond No. 2
Ward: Joshua Pool orphan of Joseph Pool deceased
Guardian: Joseph Turner Bond amount: 100 pounds
Bondsmen: Joseph Turner, John Commander & Devotion White

Pool, Joseph 6 September 1798 Bond No. 3
Ward: Tamer Pool orphan of Joseph Pool deceased
Guardian: Joseph Turner Bond amount: 50 pounds
Bondsmen: Joseph Turner, Benjamin Sawyer

Pool, Patrick 5 March 1799 Bond No. 22
Wards: James, Robert, Solomon and John Pool orphans of Patrick
 Pool deceased
Guardian: Joseph Kenyon Bond amount: 5000 pounds
Bondsmen: Joseph Kenyon, Isaac Overman, Devotion Davis

Pool, William 4 March 1800 Bond No. 54
Ward: Joshua Pool son of William Pool *
Guardian: John Lane Bond amount: 500 pounds
Bondsmen: John Lane, Bailey Jackson, David Pritchard
 (*Note: the word orphan was scratched out)

Poyenter, John 4 September 1799 Bond No. 43
Wards: Joseph & Thomas Poyenter orphans of John Poyenter
Guardian: Joseph Keaton Bond amount: 500 pounds
Bondsmen: Joseph Keaton, Matthias Sawyer, Frederick B. Sawyer

Proby, William 2 June 1801 Bond No. 72
Ward: William Proby who has been found by a jury to be in a state
 of lunacy *
Guardian: Sarah Proby Bond amount: 1000 pounds
Bondsmen: Sarah Proby, Jesse Reding, Joseph Relfe
 (*Note: the word orphan was scratched out)

Guardian Bond Book 1798 - 1801

Proby, William 11 September 1801 Bond No. 81
Ward: William Proby who has been found by a jury to be in a state of lunacy *
Guardian: Ciperan Sheppard Bond amount: 1000 pounds
Bondsmen: Ciperan Sheppard, Timothy Cotter, William Proby Jr.
*(*Note: the word orphan was scratched out)*

Reding, Thomas 7 March 1800 Bond No. 57
Ward: Henry Palin Reding orphan of Thomas Reding Esq.
Guardian: Thomas Reding Bond amount: 1000 pounds
Bondsmen: Thomas Reding, Benjamin Davis, Daniel Shirley

Reding, Thomas 10 December 1801 Bond No. 91
Ward: Henry Palin Reding orphan of Thomas Reding Esq.
Guardian: William T. Muse Bond amount: 500 pounds
Bondsmen: William T. Muse, Jesse Reding, William Wilson

Relfe, Enoch 4 September 1799 Bond No. 44
Ward: Anna Drew Relfe orphan of Enoch Relfe Esq. deceased
Guardian: Thomas T. Relfe Bond amount: 1000 pounds
Bondsmen: Thomas T. Relfe, John Pendleton, Joseph D_ Banks

Relfe, Enoch 4 September 1799 Bond No. 45
Ward: James Shaw Relfe orphan of Enoch Relfe Esq. deceased
Guardian: Thomas T. Relfe Bond amount: 1000 pounds
Bondsmen: Thomas T. Relfe, John Pendleton, Joseph D_ Banks

Relfe, Enoch 4 March 1801 Bond No. 68
Ward: Anna Drew Relfe orphan of Enoch Relfe Esq. deceased
Guardian: William T. Relfe Bond amount: 1000 pounds
Bondsmen: William T. Relfe, William T. Muse, Jesse Reding

Relfe, Enoch 4 March 1801 Bond No. 69
Ward: James Shaw Relfe orphan of Enoch Relfe Esq. deceased
Guardian: William T. Relfe Bond amount: 1000 pounds
Bondsmen: William T. Relfe, William T. Muse, Jesse Reding

Relfe, Nathan 5 March 1799   Bond No. 19
Ward: Nathan Relfe orphan of Nathan Relfe deceased
Guardian: Joseph Relfe   Bond amount: 1000 pounds
Bondsmen: Joseph Relfe, Joshua Trueblood, Peter Forbes

Relfe, Thomas 5 March 1799   Bond No. 23
Wards: John Relfe & Enoch Relfe orphans of Thomas Relfe
Guardian: Timothy Cotter   Bond amount: 5000 pounds
Bondsmen: Timothy Cotter, Samuel Cobb, Devotion Davis Jr.

Russell, Thomas 8 September 1801   Bond No. 79
Ward: Mary Russell orphan of Thomas Russell deceased
Guardian: James Russell   Bond amount: 200 pounds
Bondsmen: James Russell, Joseph Relfe, Robert McMorine

Sanders, Richard 9 September 1801   Bond No. 80
Ward: Hosea Sanders orphan of Richard Sanders deceased
Guardian: William Chalk   Bond amount: 250 pounds
Bondsmen: William Chalk, Thomas Banks, Devotion White

Sawyer, Lot 8 December 1801   Bond No. 83
Wards: Abel, Mary, Nancy & Martha Sawyer orphans of Lot Sawyer
Guardian: Nancy Sawyer   Bond amount: 2000 pounds
Bondsmen: Nancy Sawyer, James Spence, Mordecai Smith

Shakespeare, Samuel 4 September 1800   Bond No. 62
Ward: George Shakespeare orphan of Samuel Shakespeare
Guardian: Martha Shakespeare   Bond amount: 200 pounds
Bondsmen: Martha Shakespeare, Robert McMorine, William Muse

Simpson, Joab 5 March 1799   Bond No. 21
Ward: Caleb Simpson orphan of Joab Simpson deceased
Guardian: Samuel Scott   Bond amount: 300 pounds
Bondsmen: Samuel Scott, Timothy Cotter

Smithson, John 5 June 1800   Bond No. 61
Ward: Joseph Smithson orphan of John Smithson Esq. deceased
Guardian: Andrew Brothers   Bond amount: 500 pounds
Bondsmen: Andrew Brothers, William Stott, Briant Brothers

Guardian Bond Book 1798 - 1801

Smithson, Rubin 2 June 1801 Bond No. 75
Wards: Miles, Sally, Bathsheba, William & Polly Smithson
  orphans of Rubin Smithson deceased
Guardian: Ruben Davis Jr. Bond amount: 1000 pounds
Bondsmen: Ruben Davis Jr., Willis Davis, Ruben Davis Sr.

Stamp, Richard 20 September 1799 Bond No. 36
Ward: Thomas Stamp orphan of Richard Stamp deceased
Guardian: Jesse Reding Bond amount: 5000 pounds
Bondsmen: Jesse Reding, William Banks, Joshua Trueblood

Swann, John 5 December 1798 Bond No. 16
Ward: Rebecca Swann orphan of John Swann Esq. deceased
Guardian: Abraham Kirby Bond amount: 1000 pounds
Bondsmen: Abraham Kirby, Hugh Knox, Andrew Knox

Swann, John 4 March 1801 Bond No. 66
Ward: Rebecca Swann orphan of John Swann deceased
Guardian: Robert Bernard Bond amount: 1000 pounds
Bondsmen: Robert Bernard, Gabriel Bailey, Frederick B. Sawyer

Swann, John 2 June 1801 Bond No. 73
Ward: Rebecca Swann orphan of John Swann Esq. deceased
Guardian: Bailey Jackson Bond amount: 1000 pounds
Bondsmen: Bailey Jackson, John Lane, Ebenezer Sawyer

Symons, John 6 March 1799 Bond No. 26
Wards: William & Ferebee Symons orphans of John Symons Sr.
Guardian: John Nixon Bond amount: 200 pounds
Bondsmen: John Nixon, Zachariah Nixon, William P. Muse

Symons, John 6 March 1799 Bond No. 27
Wards: Sarah & John Symons orphans of John Symons Sr.
Guardian: John Nixon Bond amount: 200 pounds
Bondsmen: John Nixon, Zachariah Nixon, William P. Muse

Symons, John 6 March 1799 Bond No. 28
Wards: Thomas & Mary Symons orphans of John Symons Sr.
Guardian: John Nixon Bond amount: 200 pounds
Bondsmen: John Nixon, Zachariah Nixon, William P. Muse

Taylor, Joseph 5 June 1799 Bond No. 32
Ward: Nancy Taylor orphan of Joseph Taylor deceased
Guardian: John Burton Bond amount: 500 pounds
Bondsmen: John Burton, John Lane, Devotion Davis

Temple, Joseph 2 June 1801 Bond No. 74
Ward: James Temple orphan of Joseph Temple deceased
Guardian: Joseph Temple Bond amount: 1000 pounds
Bondsmen: Joseph Temple, Lodwick Williams, Joseph Gray

Trueblood, John 20 September 1799 Bond No. 35
Ward: James Trueblood orphan of John Trueblood deceased
Guardian: Joshua Trueblood Bond amount: 500 pounds
Bondsmen: Joshua Trueblood, Jesse Reding, Isaac Overman

White, Ann 5 June 1800 Bond No. 60
Ward: Susannah Davis alias Pritchard daughter of Ann White *
Guardian: Samuel Trueblood Bond amount: 300 pounds
Bondsmen: Saml. Trueblood, Ciperan Shepherd, Thos. Pendleton
  (*Note: the word orphan was scratched out)

Wilson, Stephen 8 December 1801 Bond No. 85
Ward: Ruth Wilson orphan of Stephen Wilson deceased
Guardian: Jeremiah Wilson Bond amount: 50 pounds
Bondsmen: Jeremiah Wilson, Andrew Pendleton

Pasquotank County, North Carolina
Guardian Bonds
Book 1802 - 1805

Allen, Thomas 8 March 1804 Bond No. 46
Ward: Thomas Allen orphan of Thomas Allen deceased
Guardian: William Allen Bond amount: 500 pounds
Bondsmen: William Allen, James Pool, Asa Jackson

Brothers, John 5 June 1804 Bond No. 51
Ward: Anne Brothers orphan of John Brothers deceased
Guardian: Andrew Brothers Bond amount: 500 pounds
Bondsmen: Andrew Brothers, Miles Brothers, David Shirley

Pasquotank County, North Carolina

Bundy, Josiah 5 September 1804 Bond No. 54
Ward: Miriam Bundy orphan of Josiah Bundy deceased
Guardian: Joshua Parisho Bond amount: 500 pounds
Bondsmen: Joshua Parisho, Charles Overman, Christopher Morris

Brent, Charles P. 4 June 1805 Bond No. 69
Wards: William, John & ___ Brent orphans of Charles P. Brent
Guardian: Phineas Albertson Bond amount: 500 pounds
Bondsmen: Phineas Albertson, Wm. Albertson, Robert McMorine

Cartwright, Ahaz 8 December 1803 Bond No. 40
Ward: Job Cartwright orphan of Ahaz Cartwright deceased
Guardian: Josiah Cartwright Bond amount: 400 pounds
Bondsmen: Josiah Cartwright, Thomas Jennings, James Clark

Commander, Aylsberry 3 September 1804 Bond No. 52
Ward: Jos. Commander orphan of Aylsberry Commander
Guardian: Thomas Commander Bond amount: 200 pounds
Bondsmen: Thomas Commander, Evan Evans, Joseph Banks

Connor, Demsey 7 December 1802 Bond No. 4
Ward: John L. Conner orphan of Demsey Conner deceased
Guardian: George A. Connor Bond amount: 5000 pounds
Bondsmen: George A. Connor, Charles Grandy, Robert McMorine

Connor, Demsey 7 December 1802 Bond No. 5
Ward: Fanny Conner orphan of Demsey Conner deceased
Guardian: George A. Connor Bond amount: 5000 pounds
Bondsmen: George A. Connor, Charles Grandy, Robert McMorine

Davis, Samuel 9 December 1802 Bond No. 9
Ward: Lydia Davis orphan of Samuel Davis deceased
Guardian: Joseph Banks Bond amount: 1000 pounds
Bondsmen: Joseph Banks, Andrew Knox, Benjamin Symons

Davis, Thomas 6 December 1804 Bond No. 58
Ward: Catharine Davis orphan of Thomas Davis deceased
Guardian: Malachi Jackson Bond amount: 500 pounds
Bondsmen: Malachi Jackson, Robert McMorine, Benjamin White

Guardian Bond Book 1802 - 1805

Gale, Cornelius 4 June 1804 Bond No. 50
Ward: Sarah Gale orphan of Cornelius Gale deceased
Guardian: Timothy Cotter Bond amount: 1000 pounds
Bondsmen: Timothy Cotter, Bailey Jackson, Marmaduke Scott

Gale, John 5 June 1805 Bond No. 72
Wards: William S., Elizabeth & Sarah Gale orphans of John Gale
Guardian: William Proby Bond amount: 500 pounds
Bondsmen: William Proby, Timothy Cotter, James Trueblood

Griffin, John 6 December 1803 Bond No. 34
Ward: Samuel Griffin orphan of John Griffin deceased
Guardian: Thomas Palmer Bond amount: 500 pounds
Bondsmen: Thomas Palmer, John McMorine, Willis Palmer

Henley, Joseph 10 March 1803 Bond No. 18
Ward: Nancy Henley orphan of Joseph Henley deceased
Guardian: Joshua Morris Bond amount: 200 pounds
Bondsmen: Joshua Morris, Samuel Trueblood

Halstead, John 8 December 1803 Bond No. 37
Ward: Benjamin Halstead orphan of John Halstead deceased
Guardian: William Hinton Bond amount: 500 pounds
Bondsmen: William S. Hinton, John Lane, Miles Richardson

Halstead, John 8 December 1803 Bond No. 38
Ward: Thomas Halstead orphan of John Halstead deceased
Guardian: William Hinton Bond amount: 500 pounds
Bondsmen: William S. Hinton, John Lane, Miles Richardson

Jennings, John 9 March 1803 Bond No. 13
Ward: Thomas Jennings orphan of John Jennings deceased
Guardian: Thaddeus Freshwater Bond amount: 200 pounds
Bondsmen: Thaddeus Freshwater, Benjamin Lowry

Jennings, John 9 June 1803 Bond No. 27
Ward: Mary Jennings orphan of John Jennings deceased
Guardian: William Banks Bond amount: 200 pounds
Bondsmen: William Banks, Joseph Banks, Jesse Reding

Koen, Caleb 7 June 1803 Bond No. 24
Wards: Joseph & Jonathan Koen orphans of Caleb Koen deceased
Guardian: James Blount Bond amount: 250 pounds
Bondsmen: James Blount, William S. Hinton, James Sawyer

Lister, Elisha 7 March 1804 Bond No. 44
Wards: Israel, Elisha, Polly, Thomas, Winifred & Jacob Lister
    orphans of Elisha Lister deceased
Guardian: Jacob Lister Bond amount: 500 pounds
Bondsmen: Jacob Lister, Jesse Reding, Miles Brothers

Meeds, Timothy 9 December 1802 Bond No. 11
Ward: Alfred Meeds orphan of Timothy Meeds deceased
Guardian: Aylesberry Commander Bond amount: 500 pounds
Bondsmen: Aylesberry Commander, John McDonald, Joseph Banks

Meeds, Timothy 9 June 1803 Bond No. 28
Ward: Alfred Meeds orphan of Timothy Meeds deceased
Guardian: Joseph Banks Bond amount: 300 pounds
Bondsmen: Joseph Banks, John Lane, Timothy Cotter

Meads, Timothy 9 December 1803 Bond No. 41
Wards: John, Robert, Thaddeus, Nancy, Deborah Meeds orphans
    of Timothy Meads deceased
Guardian: Thomas Banks Bond amount: 500 pounds
Bondsmen: Thomas Banks, William Banks, William F. Muse

Meads, Timothy 6 March 1805 Bond No. 65
Ward: Alfred Meads orphan of Timothy Meads deceased
Guardian: John McDonald Bond amount: 500 pounds
Bondsmen: John McDonald, John Boyd, William F. Muse

Morris, Aaron 5 June 1805 Bond No. 70
Ward: Jehoshaphat Morris orphan of Aaron Morris deceased
Guardian: Aaron Morris Jr. Bond amount: 200 pounds
Bondsmen: Aaron Morris Jr., Benj. White, Josiah White Jr. of Perq.

Morris, Aaron 5 June 1805 Bond No. 71
Ward: Sarah Morris orphan of Aaron Morris deceased

Guardian Bond Book 1802 - 1805

Guardian: Aaron Morris Jr.   Bond amount: 1000 pounds
Bondsmen: Aaron Morris Jr., Benj. White, Josiah White Jr. of Perq.

Morris, Thomas   8 March 1804   Bond No. 47
Wards: Margaret, Mary, Elizabeth & Thomas Morris orphans of
    Thomas Morris deceased
Guardian: William F. Muse   Bond amount: 500 pounds
Bondsmen: William F. Muse, Robert McMorine, Joseph Banks

Murden, Jeremiah   7 December 1802   Bond No. 6
Ward: Silvanus Murden orphan of Jeremiah Murden deceased
Guardian: Robert Murden   Bond amount: 1000 pounds
Bondsmen: Robert Murden, Bailey Jackson, William T. Relfe

Murden, Jeremiah   6 March 1805   Bond No. 64
Ward: Silvanus Murden orphan of Jeremiah Murden deceased
Guardian: Jeremiah Murden   Bond amount: 1000 pounds
Bondsmen: Jeremiah Murden, Fred. B. Sawyer, Demsey Sawyer

Murden, Robert   5 September 1804   Bond No. 55
Ward: Robert Murden who is in a State of Lunacy *
Guardian: Demsey & Griffith Sawyer   Bond amount: 2000 pounds
Bondsmen: Demsey Sawyer, Griffith Sawyer, William Muse
    (*Note: the word orphan was scratched out)

Nichols, Benjamin   8 December 1803   Bond No. 39
Wards: Polly, Elizabeth & Keziah orphans of Benjamin Nichols
Guardian: Noah McPherson   Bond amount: 300 pounds
Bondsmen: Noah McPherson, Thomas Jennings, Wilson Blount

Nichols, Joseph   8 March 1804   Bond No. 45
Wards: David & Kiddy Nichols orphans of Joseph Nichols deceased
Guardian: Jacob Richardson   Bond amount: 1000 pounds
Bondsmen: Jacob Richardson, James Chamberlin, Noah McPherson

Nicholson, Christopher   7 December 1803   Bond No. 36
Ward: Jane Nicholson orphan of Christopher Nicholson deceased
Guardian: James McAdams   Bond amount: 1000 pounds
Bondsmen: James McAdams, Thos. Jordan Sr., Benjamin Symons

Overman, Nathan   5 December 1804   Bond No. 57
Ward: Mordicai Overman orphan of Nathan Overman deceased
Guardian: Henry P. Overman   Bond amount: 1000 pounds
Bondsmen: Henry P. Overman, Joseph Parker, Nathan Overman

Overman, *(Othniel?)* 7 December 1804   Bond No. 59
Wards: Wm., Joshua, Lewis & Sally orphans of Othniel Overman
Guardian: Nathan Overman   Bond amount: 1000 pounds
Bondsmen: Nathan Overman, Thomas Banks, William Gaskins

Padrick, Jonathan   6 March 1804   Bond No. 43
Ward: Jonathan Padrick orphan of Jonathan Padrick deceased
Guardian: John Simpson   Bond amount: 500 pounds
Bondsmen: John Simpson, William Albright, Timothy Cotter

Pendleton, John F.   10 June 1802   Bond No. 2
Ward: Abner Pendleton orphan of John F. Pendleton deceased
Guardian: Andrew Knox   Bond amount: 1000 pounds
Bondsmen: Andrew Knox, William T. Muse, Steven Barnes

Pendleton, John F.   10 June 1802   Bond No. 3
Ward: John Pendleton orphan of John F. Pendleton deceased
Guardian: Andrew Knox   Bond amount: 1000 pounds
Bondsmen: Andrew Knox, William T. Muse, Steven Barnes

Pendleton, Joseph   5 March 1805   Bond No. 62
Wards: Henry & Samuel Pendleton orphans of Joseph Pendleton
Guardian: Job Cartwright   Bond amount: 1000 pounds
Bondsmen: Job Cartwright, John Pendleton, John Russell

Pendleton, Robert   9 December 1802   Bond No. 10
Ward: Elcey Pendleton orphan of Robert Pendleton deceased
Guardian: William Albertson   Bond amount: 500 pounds
Bondsmen: William Albertson, Robert McMorine, P. Albertson

Pendleton, Robert   10 March 1803   Bond No. 19
Ward: John Pendleton orphan of Robert Pendleton deceased
Guardian: Joseph Banks   Bond amount: 200 pounds
Bondsmen: Joseph Banks, John Nixon, James Sawyer

Guardian Bond Book 1802 - 1805

Pendleton, Robert 10 March 1803 Bond No. 20
Ward: Elizabeth Pendleton orphan of Robert Pendleton deceased
Guardian: Joseph Banks Bond amount: 200 pounds
Bondsmen: Joseph Banks, John Nixon, James Sawyer

Pool, Patrick 8 June 1803 Bond No. 25
Wards: Solomon & John Pool orphans of Patrick Pool deceased
Guardian: James Pool Bond amount: 300 pounds
Bondsmen: James Pool, Benjamin S. Overman, Josiah Relfe

Price, John 6 September 1803 Bond No. 29
Ward: John Price orphan of John Price deceased
Guardian: Joseph Parker Bond amount: 200 pounds
Bondsmen: Joseph Parker, Wm. Robinson, James L. Shannonhouse

Price, John 8 September 1803 Bond No. 32
Ward: Samuel Price orphan of John Price deceased
Guardian: Thomas Jordan Sr. Bond amount: 2000 pounds
Bondsmen: Thomas Jordan Sr., Benjamin Pritchard, Joshua Morris

Price, John 6 December 1803 Bond No. 33
Ward: Sarah Price orphan of John Price deceased
Guardian: Joseph Parker Bond amount: 1000 pounds
Bondsmen: Joseph Parker, Thomas Jordan, Benjamin Pritchard

Pritchard, Thomas 6 March 1805 Bond No. 66
Ward: Isaac Pritchard orphan of Thomas Pritchard deceased
Guardian: Hezekiah Cartwright Bond amount: 1000 pounds
Bondsmen: Hezekiah Cartwright, Samuel Pritchard, John Rowe

Pritchard, Thomas 6 March 1805 Bond No. 67
Ward: Thomas Pritchard orphan of Thomas Pritchard deceased
Guardian: Samuel Pritchard Bond amount: 1000 pounds
Bondsmen: Samuel Pritchard, Hezekiah Cartwright, John Rowe

Proby, William 7 March 1805 Bond No. 68
Ward: Paul Proby orphan of William Proby deceased
Guardian: Timothy Cotter Bond amount: 500 pounds
Bondsmen: Timothy Cotter, John McDonald, William F. Muse

Sanders, Richard   8 June 1803   Bond No. 26
Wards: Anne & Abi Sanders orphans of Richard Sanders deceased
Guardian: John L. Broshir   Bond amount: 200 pounds
Bondsmen: John L. Broshir, Joseph L. Brooks, Thomas Warrington

Sawyer, Benjamin   5 March 1805   Bond No. 61
Ward: Joseph Sawyer orphan of Benjamin Sawyer deceased
Guardian: John Russell   Bond amount: 500 pounds
Bondsmen: John Russell, John Pendleton, Job Cartwright

Scarborough, Jehu   9 March 1803   Bond No. 16
Wards: John & Joseph Scarborough orphans of Jehu Scarborough
Guardian: Mark Spence   Bond amount: 400 pounds
Bondsmen: Mark Spence, Samuel Spence, James Spence Jr.

Scarborough, Jehu   9 March 1803   Bond No. 17
Wards: David & Jehu Scarborough orphans of Jehu Scarborough
Guardian: Mark Spence   Bond amount: 400 pounds
Bondsmen: Mark Spence, Samuel Spence, James Spence Jr.

Sharborough, Jehu   6 September 1803   Bond No. 30
Wards: John & Joseph Sharborough orphans of Jehu Sharborough
Guardian: Noah McPherson   Bond amount: 1000 pounds
Bondsmen: Noah McPherson, Isaac Stokely, Wilson Sanderlin

Scarborough, Jehu   6 September 1803   Bond No. 31
Wards: David & Jehu Sharborough orphans of Jehu Sharborough
Guardian: Noah McPherson   Bond amount: 1000 pounds
Bondsmen: Noah McPherson, Isaac Stokely, Wilson Sanderlin

Small, Obadiah   9 June 1802   Bond No. 1
Wards: Elizabeth, Joshua & Nathan orphans of Obadiah Small
Guardian: John Pike   Bond amount: 100 pounds
Bondsmen: John Pike, Benjamin Pritchard

Snowden, William   9 March 1803   Bond No. 14
Ward: Lemuel Snowden orphan of William Snowden deceased
Guardian: Thaddeus Freshwater   Bond amount: 200 pounds
Bondsmen: Thaddeus Freshwater, Benjamin Lowry

Guardian Bond Book 1802 - 1805

Snowden, William 9 March 1803 Bond No. 15
Ward: Thaddeus Snowden orphan of William Snowden deceased
Guardian: Thaddeus Freshwater Bond amount: 200 pounds
Bondsmen: Thaddeus Freshwater, Benjamin Lowry

Spence, Mark 7 June 1803 Bond No. 22
Wards: Edward, Wilson & Wm. Spence orphans of Mark Spence
Guardian: Samuel Spence Bond amount: 1000 pounds
Bondsmen: Samuel Spence, James Jones, Lodwick Williams

Spence, Mark 7 June 1803 Bond No. 23
Wards: Miles & Nancy Spence orphans of Mark Spence deceased
Guardian: Samuel Spence Bond amount: 500 pounds
Bondsmen: Samuel Spence, James Jones, Lodwick Williams

Symons, John 6 March 1804 Bond No. 42
Ward: Penelope Symons orphan of John Symons deceased
Guardian: Robert White Bond amount: 100 pounds
Bondsmen: Robert White, Francis White, Benjamin Davis

Symons, John 4 December 1804 Bond No. 56
Wards: Sarah, John, Thos. & Mary Symons orphans of John Symons
Guardian: William Symons Bond amount: 1000 pounds
Bondsmen: William Symons, William Wilson, Joseph Banks

Taylor, Joseph 8 December 1802 Bond No. 8
Ward: Nancy Taylor orphan of Joseph Taylor deceased
Guardian: Joab Jackson Bond amount: 200 pounds
Bondsmen: Joab Jackson, Thomas Jackson, James Jackson

Tooley, Adam 7 March 1803 Bond No. 12
Wards: Elizabeth, Sarah, John & Wm. orphans of Adam Tooley
Guardian: Benjamin Overman Bond amount: 500 pounds
Bondsmen: Benjamin Overman, Joseph Banks, Robert McMorine

Trueblood, John 7 December 1802 Bond No. 7
Ward: Rebecca Trueblood orphan of John Trueblood deceased
Guardian: Charles Overman Bond amount: 300 pounds
Bondsmen: Charles Overman, James Overman, John Overman

Weymouth, Amos   7 June 1803   Bond No. 21
Ward: Miriam Weymouth orphan of Amos Weymouth deceased
Guardian: Isaac Clark   Bond amount: 200 pounds
Bondsmen: Isaac Clark, Josiah Cartwright, Claudius Morgan

White, Francis   4 June 1804   Bond No. 48
Ward: Elizabeth White orphan of Francis White deceased
Guardian: John White   Bond amount: 1500 pounds
Bondsmen: John White, James White, Josiah White

White, Francis   4 June 1804   Bond No. 49
Ward: Sarah White orphan of Francis White deceased
Guardian: Thomas Jordan Jr.   Bond amount: 300 pounds
Bondsmen: Thos. Jordan Jr., Benjamin Overman, Job Cartwright

White, James   5 March 1805   Bond No. 63
Wards: Benjamin & John White orphans of James White deceased
Guardian: Thomas Morris Sr.   Bond amount: 1000 pounds
Bondsmen: Thomas Morris Sr, John Overman, Joseph Commander

Winberry, William   3 September 1804   Bond No. 53
Ward: Milly Winberry orphan of William Winberry deceased
Guardian: Enoch Winbury   Bond amount: 100 pounds
Bondsmen: Enoch Winbury, John Halstead, Timothy Cotter

Wood, John   6 December 1803   Bond No. 35
Ward: James Wood orphan of John Wood deceased
Guardian: William Wood   Bond amount: 300 pounds
Bondsmen: William Wood, Joseph Wood, James Spence

Young, David   5 March 1805   Bond No. 60
Ward: William Proby Young his son *
Guardian: David Young   Bond amount: 500 pounds
Bondsmen: David Young, Charles Grice
        (*Note: the word orphan was scratched out)

Pasquotank County, North Carolina
Guardian Bonds
Book 1805 - 1808

Banks, James 5 September 1805 Bond No. 5
Wards: *(Luook?)*, Susannah & Rebecca orphans of James Banks
Guardian: Joseph Banks Bond amount: 600 pounds
Bondsmen: Joseph Banks, John Pendleton, Jesse Reding

Barnes, Thomas 9 March 1808 Bond No. 67
Ward: Silas Fountain Barnes orphan of Thomas Barns deceased
Guardian: William Wilson Bond amount: 1000 pounds
Bondsmen: William Wilson, John McDonald, Gabriel Bailey

Bray, John 8 September 1807 Bond No. 48
Wards: William, Mary, James & Sarah Bray orphans of John Bray
Guardian: Jonathan Humphries Bond amount: 500 pounds
Bondsmen: Jonathan Humphries, Daniel McPherson,
    Thomas Humphries

Brothers, Jesse 5 September 1806 Bond No. 29
Wards: Benjamin, Millicent, James & Jesse Brothers orphans of
    Jesse Brothers deceased
Guardian: Benjamin S. Overman Bond amount: 500 pounds
Bondsmen: Benjamin Overman, Wm. Shepherd, Frederick Sawyer

Brothers, Jonathan 6 March 1806 Bond No. 22
Ward: Polly Brothers orphan of Jonathan Brothers deceased
Guardian: Miles Davis Bond amount: 500 pounds
Bondsmen: Miles Davis, Bailey Davis, Briant Brothers

Brothers, Jonathan 3 September 1806 Bond No. 28
Ward: John Brothers orphan of Jonathan Brothers deceased
Guardian: John Casse Bond amount: 500 pounds
Bondsmen: John Casse, Samuel Scott, Willis Simpson

Bundy, Josiah 3 December 1805 Bond No. 9
Ward: Charles Bundy orphan of Josiah Bundy deceased
Guardian: William Robinson Bond amount: 100 pounds
Bondsmen: William Robinson, Mordicai Morris, Isaac Overman

Bundy, Josiah 3 March 1806 Bond No. 17
Ward: Miriam Bundy orphan of Josiah Bundy deceased
Guardian: Josiah Griffin Bond amount: 500 pounds
Bondsmen: Josiah Griffin, Joshua Parisho, Isaac Overman

Bundy, Josiah 2 June 1807 Bond No. 39
Ward: Charles Bundy orphan of Josiah Bundy deceased
Guardian: Joshua Morris Bond amount: 200 pounds
Bondsmen: Joshua Morris, Mordicai Morris, Phinehas Albertson

Bundy, Josiah 10 December 1807 Bond No. 62
Ward: Miriam Bundy orphan of Josiah Bundy deceased

Guardian Bond Book 1805 - 1808

Guardian: Isaac Overman Bond amount: 200 pounds
Bondsmen: Isaac Overman, James Trueblood, Jonathan Trueblood

Butt, James 3 December 1805 Bond No. 8
Wards: Christopher, Barshaba & Wilson orphans of James Butt
Guardian: James Jones Bond amount: 200 pounds
Bondsmen: James Jones, Owen Williams

Cartwright, John 2 December 1806 Bond No. 31
Wards: Job, Deborah, Rebecca & Malachi Cartwright orphans of
       John Cartwright deceased
Guardian: Hezekiah Cartwright Bond amount: 1000 pounds
Bondsmen: Hezekiah Cartwright, John Rowe, Robert Scott

Cartwright, Thomas 7 March 1808 Bond No. 64
Wards: Miriam, James & Nancy orphans of Thomas Cartwright
Guardian: Marmaduke Scott Bond amount: 300 pounds
Bondsmen: Marmaduke Scott, Gabriel Bailey, Bailey Jackson

Cartwright, Thomas 7 March 1808 Bond No. 65
Wards: Marmaduke & Susannah orphans of Thomas Cartwright
Guardian: Marmaduke Scott Bond amount: 300 pounds
Bondsmen: Marmaduke Scott, Gabriel Bailey, Bailey Jackson

Carver, Job 3 September 1806 Bond No. 24
Ward: Alfred Carver orphan of Job Carver deceased
Guardian: James Carver Bond amount: 1000 pounds
Bondsmen: James Carver, William S. Hinton, William T. Muse

Carver, Job 3 September 1806 Bond No. 25
Ward: John Carver orphan of Job Carver deceased
Guardian: James Carver Bond amount: 1000 pounds
Bondsmen: James Carver, William S. Hinton, William T. Muse

Commander, Aylesbury 2 December 1806 Bond No. 32
Ward: Joseph Commander orphan of Aylesbury Commander
Guardian: John Commander Jr. Bond amount: 300 pounds
Bondsmen: John Commander Jr., McKeel Cartwright,
          John Pendleton

Commander, Joseph Sr. 5 December 1805   Bond No. 15
Ward: Joseph Commander orphan of Joseph Commander Sr.
Guardian: Joseph Commander   Bond amount: 3000 pounds
Bondsmen: Joseph Commander, Samuel Price, Josiah Relfe

Cory, Davidson   2 June 1807   Bond No. 40
Wards: Benjamin & Eleanor Cory orphans of Davidson Cory
Guardian: Jacob Lister   Bond amount: 200 pounds
Bondsmen: Jacob Lister, Jesse Reding, Joseph Banks

Drapor, Joseph   8 December 1807   Bond No. 57
Wards: Mary & Lovey Drapor orphans of Joseph Drapor deceased
Guardian: Sarah Drapor   Bond amount: 200 pounds
Bondsmen: Sarah Drapor, James Carver, Frederick B. Sawyer

Forehand, Anthony   9 March 1808   Bond No. 70
Wards: James, Esther, Rebecca & Partheana Forehand orphans of
    Anthony Forehand deceased
Guardian: William S. Hinton   Bond amount: 100 pounds
Bondsmen: William S. Hinton, William T. Muse, Timothy Cotter

Gordon, Joseph   3 December 1805   Bond No. 10
Wards: William & John Gordon orphans of Joseph Gordon deceased
Guardian: Sarah Gordon   Bond amount: 500 pounds
Bondsmen: Sarah Gordon, Asa Sanderlin, Nehimiah Pendleton

Gordon, Joseph   3 September 1806   Bond No. 27
Wards: William, John & Mary Gordon orphans of Joseph Gordon
Guardian: Nehemiah Pendleton   Bond amount: 1000 pounds
Bondsmen: Nehemiah Pendleton, Wm. Wilson, William Gordon

Gray, Joseph   8 September 1807   Bond No. 46
Ward: Polly Gray orphan of Joseph Gray deceased
Guardian: Isaac Stokeley   Bond amount: 500 pounds
Bondsmen: Isaac Stokeley, Frederick Blount, James Spence Sr.

Gray, Joseph   8 September 1807   Bond No. 47
Ward: Thomas Gray orphan of Joseph Gray deceased

Guardian Bond Book 1805 - 1808   29

Guardian: Robert Gray   Bond amount: 500 pounds
Bondsmen: Robert Gray, James Spence Sr., Abner Whitney

Griffin, James   9 September 1807   Bond No. 54
Ward: James Griffin orphan of James Griffin deceased
Guardian: William Wilson   Bond amount: 100 pounds
Bondsmen: William Wilson, John Boyd, William T. Muse

Hinley, Abraham   4 September 1805   Bond No. 3
Wards: James, Sarah, Elizabeth & Lucinda Hinley orphans of
          Abraham Hinley deceased
Guardian: Cyprian Shepard   Bond amount: 1000 pounds
Bondsmen: Cyprian Shepard, William B. Shepard, Timothy Cotter

Jarvis, John   3 June 1807   Bond No. 41
Wards: Elizabeth, Penelope & Caty Jarvis orphans of John Jarvis
Guardian: John McDonald   Bond amount: 200 pounds
Bondsmen: John McDonald, Benjamin Symons, Joseph L. Broshir

Jennings, Joseph   2 June 1807   Bond No. 37
Ward: Elizabeth Jennings orphan of Joseph Jennings deceased
Guardian: William Wilson   Bond amount: 2000 pounds
Bondsmen: William Wilson, John McDonald, Joseph Banks

Jordan, Isaac   4 December 1805   Bond No. 14
Wards: Richard & Thomas Jordan orphans of Isaac Jordan deceased
Guardian: John Boyd   Bond amount: 250 pounds
Bondsmen: John Boyd, Thomas Jordan, Joseph Banks

Keaton, Reuben   9 December 1807   Bond No. 59
Wards: Elizabeth & Winnifred Keaton orphans of Reuben Keaton
Guardian: John McDonald   Bond amount: 2000 pounds
Bondsmen: John McDonald, William Muse, Frederick B. Sawyer

Lacy, Josiah   2 December 1806   Bond No. 35
Ward: Anne Lacy orphan of Josiah Lacy deceased
Guardian: Benjamin White   Bond amount: 500 pounds
Bondsmen: Benjamin White, Joseph Banks, Jonathan Banks

Lockwood, Holland 10 December 1807 Bond No. 63
Wards: John, Abner & James orphans of Holland Lockwood
Guardian: George J. Hain Bond amount: 2000 pounds
Bondsmen: George J. Hain, Jesse Reding, John Boyd

Lowry, Robert 9 March 1808 Bond No. 68
Ward: Patsey Lowry orphan of Robert Lowry deceased
Guardian: Thomas Banks Bond amount: 1000 pounds
Bondsmen: Thomas Banks, William Banks, Jonathan Banks

Luton, Constantine 8 September 1807 Bond No. 52
Wards: Constantine, John & William Luton orphans of
    Constantine Luton deceased
Guardian: Harvey Luton Bond amount: 500 pounds
Bondsmen: Harvey Luton, Benjamin Lowery, Christopher Morris

Luton, Constantine 8 September 1807 Bond No. 53
Wards: Nancy, Milly, Susannah & Polly Luton orphans of
    Constantine Luton deceased
Guardian: Harvey Luton Bond amount: 500 pounds
Bondsmen: Harvey Luton, Benj. Lowery, Christopher Cartwright

Meeds, Timothy 4 June 1807 Bond No. 44
Ward: Alfred Meeds orphan of Timothy Meeds deceased
Guardian: Benjamin Davis Bond amount: 1000 pounds
Bondsmen: Benjamin Davis, Timothy Cotter, Josiah Relfe

Mitchell, John 4 June 1807 Bond No. 42
Ward: Elizabeth Mitchell orphan of John Mitchell deceased
Guardian: Timothy Cotter Bond amount: 500 pounds
Bondsmen: Timothy Cotter, William Carter

Morgan, Claudius 5 December 1805 Bond No. 16
Ward: Chloe Morgan an Illegitimate Child
Guardian: Claudius Morgan Bond amount: 250 pounds
Bondsmen: Claudius Morgan, Malachi Smithson, Miles Smithson

Guardian Bond Book 1805 - 1808

Murden, Jeremiah 5 December 1805 Bond No. 12
Ward: Sylvanus Murden orphan of Jeremiah Murden deceased
Guardian: William Gregory Bond amount: 500 pounds
Bondsmen: William Gregory, Francis Grice, William L. Hinton

Murden, Robert 10 September 1807 Bond No. 56
Ward: Robert Murden who is in a State of Lunacy deceased
Guardian: James Chamberlain Bond amount: 1000 pounds
Bondsmen: James Chamberlin, Jacob Richardson, Timothy Cotter

Nichols, Benjamin 4 June 1806 Bond No. 23
Wards: Betsey, Polly & Heziakia orphans of Benjamin Nichols
Guardian: Charles Brite Bond amount: 1000 pounds
Bondsmen: Charles Brite, David Scaff, Josiah Cartwright

Nicholson, John 4 December 1805 Bond No. 11
Wards: Nancy, George & Polly orphans of John Nicholson
Guardian: John McDonald Bond amount: 400 pounds
Bondsmen: John McDonald, George A. S. Conner

Overman, Berey 8 September 1807 Bond No. 50
Ward: Matthew Overman orphan of Berey Overman deceased
Guardian: Mark Morris Bond amount: 200 pounds
Bondsmen: Mark Morris, John Overman, Isaac Morris

Overman, *(Jas. or Jos.)* 1 December 1806 Bond No. 30
Ward: Elizabeth Overman orphan of *(Jas. or Jos.)* Overman
Guardian: Nathan Trueblood Bond amount: 500 pounds
Bondsmen: Nathan Trueblood, Joseph Relfe, John Trueblood

Palin, Thomas 4 March 1806 Bond No. 18
Ward: Keziah Palin orphan of Thomas Palin deceased
Guardian: William Wilson Bond amount: 500 pounds
Bondsmen: William Wilson, William T. Muse, John McDonald

Palin, Thomas 4 March 1806 Bond No. 19
Ward: Mary Palin orphan of Thomas Palin deceased
Guardian: William Wilson Bond amount: 500 pounds
Bondsmen: William Wilson, William T. Muse, John McDonald

Palin, Thomas   4 March 1806   Bond No. 20
Ward: Thomas Palin orphan of Thomas Palin deceased
Guardian: William Wilson   Bond amount: 500 pounds
Bondsmen: William Wilson, William T. Muse, John McDonald

Pendleton, Joseph   2 June 1807   Bond No. 38
Ward: Henry Pendleton orphan of Joseph Pendleton deceased
Guardian: William Wilson   Bond amount: 600 pounds
Bondsmen: William Wilson, John McDonald, Joseph Banks

Pendleton, Joseph   9 December 1807   Bond No. 58
Ward: Thaddeus Pendleton orphan of Joseph Pendleton deceased
Guardian: Joseph L. Broshir   Bond amount: 500 pounds
Bondsmen: Joseph L. Broshir, Stephen Barns, James Jackson

Pritchard, Malachi   2 December 1805   Bond No. 7
Wards: Peggy & Malachi Pritchard orphans of Malachi Pritchard
Guardian: James Harris   Bond amount: 300 pounds
Bondsmen: James Harris, Joseph Cartwright, William *(Ca__u?)*

Richardson, Stephen   4 December 1805   Bond No. 13
Ward: Stephen Richardson orphan of Stephen Richardson deceased
Guardian: Jacob Richardson   Bond amount: 250 pounds
Bondsmen: Jacob Richardson, Josiah Richardson, John Pritchard

Robinson, William   8 September 1807   Bond No. 45
Wards: Elizabeth Matilda Robinson, Martha Jane Robinson &
        Margaret Anne Robinson orphans of William Robinson
Guardian: William T. Muse   Bond amount: 5000 pounds
Bondsmen: William T. Muse, Aaron Morris Sr., Fred. B. Sawyer

Sanders, Evan   8 March 1808   Bond No. 66
Wards: Elizabeth, Mary & Simson orphans of Evan Sanders
Guardian: Nehemiah Pendleton   Bond amount: 100 pounds
Bondsmen: Nehemiah Pendleton, Henry P. Overman, Wm. Wilson

Scott, Simpson   9 December 1807   Bond No. 61
Ward: Dorcas Scott orphan of Simpson Scott deceased

Guardian Bond Book 1805 - 1808

Guardian: Cornelus Clark   Bond amount: 200 pounds
Bondsmen: Cornelus Clark, Hezikah Cartwright, Isaac Cartwright

Scott, Simpson   9 March 1808   Bond No. 69
Ward: Edward Scott orphan of Simpson Scott deceased
Guardian: John Casse   Bond amount: 500 pounds
Bondsmen: John Casse, Thomas Cartwright, Lemuel Jackson

Simpson, Joab   9 December 1807   Bond No. 60
Ward: Caleb Simpson orphan of Joab Simpson deceased
Guardian: John Casse   Bond amount: 500 pounds
Bondsmen: John Casse, Robert Scott, Thomas Harkins

Small, Samuel   5 September 1805   Bond No. 4
Wards: Joseph, Nancy & Samuel Small orphans of Samuel Small
Guardian: Thomas Jordan Sr.   Bond amount: 300 pounds
Bondsmen: Thomas Jordan Sr., William F. Muse, William Spence

Smithson, John   6 March 1806   Bond No. 21
Wards: John, Penelope & Milly orphans of John Smithson deceased
Guardian: Daniel Shirley   Bond amount: 1000 pounds
Bondsmen: Daniel Shirley, James Chamberlain, Josiah Relfe

Smithson, John   3 September 1806   Bond No. 26
Wards: Caleb, Lovey & Meriam orphans of John Smithson
Guardian: Miriam Smithson   Bond amount: 500 pounds
Bondsmen: Miriam Smithson, William Kote, Job Cartwright

Spence, Mark   8 September 1807   Bond No. 49
Wards: Edmond, Wilson, William & Miles Spence orphans of
        Mark Spence deceased
Guardian: Frederick Blount   Bond amount: 500 pounds
Bondsmen: Frederick Blount, James Spence Sr., Senith Jones

Stokeley, Joseph   4 September 1805   Bond No. 1
Wards: Susannah, Sally & Joseph orphans of Joseph Stokeley
Guardian: Abner Whitney   Bond amount: 900 pounds
Bondsmen: Abner Whitney, William S. Hinton, James Carver

Stokeley, Joseph   4 September 1805   Bond No. 2
Wards: Elizabeth & Polly Stokeley orphans of Joseph Stokeley
Guardian: Abner Whitney   Bond amount: 600 pounds
Bondsmen: Abner Whitney, William S. Hinton, James Carver

Stokeley, Joseph   8 September 1807   Bond No. 51
Ward: Harvey Stokeley orphan of Joseph Stokeley deceased
Guardian: Matthias Smithson   Bond amount: 500 pounds
Bondsmen: Matthias Smithson, James Spence Sr., Robert Gray

Taylor, Joseph   3 December 1806   Bond No. 36
Ward: Nancy Taylor orphan of Joseph Taylor deceased
Guardian: Stephen Scott Jr.   Bond amount: 300 pounds
Bondsmen: Stephen Scott Jr., Robert Scott, Stephen Scott Sr.

Tooley, Adam   2 December 1806   Bond No. 33
Ward: Elizabeth Tooley orphan of Adam Tooley deceased
Guardian: Timothy Cotter   Bond amount: 200 pounds
Bondsmen: Timothy Cotter, Robert McMorine, Joseph Banks

Tooley, Adam   2 December 1806   Bond No. 34
Wards: John, William & Sarah Tooley orphans of Adam Tooley
Guardian: Robert McMorine   Bond amount: 500 pounds
Bondsmen: Robert McMorine, Timothy Cotter, William T. Muse

Tooley, Adam   9 September 1807   Bond No. 55
Ward: Elizabeth Tooley orphan of Adam Tooley deceased
Guardian: Robert McMorine   Bond amount: 200 pounds
Bondsmen: Robert McMorine, Wm. Muse, Frederick B. Sawyer

White, Nehemiah   4 June 1807   Bond No. 43
Wards: Mary, Reuben, Martha & Peggy orphans of Nehemiah White
Guardian: Josiah White   Bond amount: 1000 pounds
Bondsmen: Josiah White, Benjamin Symons, Samuel Price

Wood, Evan   5 September 1805   Bond No. 6
Ward: Molly Wood orphan of Evan Wood deceased
Guardian: William Stott   Bond amount: 500 pounds
Bondsmen: William Stott, Robert Pool, Josiah Relfe

Pasquotank County, North Carolina
Guardian Bonds
Book 1808 - 1811

Ackiss, Thomas　　　　2 December 1811　　　Bond No. 88
Ward: Margaret Ackiss orphan of Thomas Ackiss deceased
Guardian: John McDonald　　　　Bond amount: 500 pounds
Bondsmen: John McDonald, John Davis, William Wilson

Aydlett, Thomas　　　　8 June 1808　　　Bond No. 6
Ward: _____* orphan of Thomas Aydlett deceased
Guardian: John McDonald　　　　Bond amount: 2000 pounds
Bondsmen: John McDonald, William Wilson, John Rowe
(*Note: no name was entered)

Aydlett, Thomas 4 March 1811 Bond No. 75
Wards: Wilson, Eliza, *(Sedima or Dedima?)*, Polly & Sarah
    Aydlett orphans of Thomas Aydlett deceased
Guardian: James Chamberlain   Bond amount: 1000 pounds
Bondsmen: James Chamberlain, Timothy Cotter, Josiah Relfe

Bailey, Thomas 3 June 1811 Bond No. 79
Wards: Polly, William, Sally & David Bailey orphans of Thomas
    Bailey deceased
Guardian: John Bailey   Bond amount: 1000 pounds
Bondsmen: John Bailey, John Overman, Joseph Relfe

Barns, Stephen 3 September 1811 Bond No. 84
Ward: Anna Barns orphan of Stephen Barns deceased
Guardian: Malachi Jackson   Bond amount: 2000 pounds
Bondsmen: Malachi Jackson, Miles Davis, John Davis

Barns, Stephen 3 September 1811 Bond No. 85
Ward: Clarkey Barns alias Davis orphan of Stephen Barns deceased
Guardian: John Davis   Bond amount: 2000 pounds
Bondsmen: John Davis, Malachi Jackson, Bailey Davis

Boswell, Isaac 7 June 1808 Bond No. 3
Ward: Isaac Boswell orphan of Isaac Boswell deceased
Guardian: Joseph Pritchard   Bond amount: 300 pounds
Bondsmen: Joseph Pritchard, Joseph Jordan, Benjamin Pritchard

Brite, Charles 5 March 1811 Bond No. 78
Wards: Polly & Charles Brite orphans of Charles Brite deceased
Guardian: John Jennings Jr.   Bond amount: 500 pounds
Bondsmen: John Jennings Jr, Frederick Whitehurst, Arthur Pritchard

Broshir, John L. 8 June 1809 Bond No. 43
Wards: Joseph, John, Anne & William Broshir orphans of John L.
    Broshir deceased
Guardian: Simon L. Broshir   Bond amount: 2000 pounds
Bondsmen: Simon L. Broshir, Harvey Luton, Thomas Palmer

Guardian Bond Book 1808 - 1811

Broshir, Joseph S. 8 June 1809 Bond No. 42
Wards: Elizabeth Broshir & Polly Broshir orphans of Joseph S. Broshir deceased
Guardian: Simon L. Broshir Bond amount: 2000 pounds
Bondsmen: Simon L. Broshir, Harvey Luton, Thomas Palmer

Brothers, Jonathan 5 March 1811 Bond No. 77
Ward: Samuel Brothers orphan of Jonathan Brothers deceased
Guardian: Thomas Davis Bond amount: 500 pounds
Bondsmen: Thomas Davis, Benjamin Bailey, Edmund Davis

Bundy, Benjamin 5 June 1810 Bond No. 64
Wards: John, Peninah, Caleb, Jonathan, Elias, Jesse & Rix Bundy orphans of Benjamin Bundy deceased
Guardian: George Bundy Bond amount: 1000 pounds
Bondsmen: George Bundy, Josiah Bundy, Joshua Morris

Cartwright, Darias 7 June 1808 Bond No. 2
Ward: Miriam Cartwright orphan of Darias Cartwright deceased
Guardian: John McDonald Bond amount: 300 pounds
Bondsmen: John McDonald, John Boyce, James L. Shannonhouse

Cartwright, Joseph 6 December 1808 Bond No. 16
Ward: Nancy Cartwright orphan of Joseph Cartwright deceased
Guardian: Francis Wilson Bond amount: 300 pounds
Bondsmen: Francis Wilson, James Carver, William Nicholson

Cartwright, Joseph 6 June 1809 Bond No. 40
Ward: Wilson Cartwright orphan of Joseph Cartwright deceased
Guardian: Harvey Luton Bond amount: 500 pounds
Bondsmen: Harvey Luton, Thaddeus Freshwater, Christopher Cartwright

Cartwright, McKeel 5 September 1809 Bond No. 51
Ward: John Cartwright orphan of McKeel Cartwright deceased
Guardian: John Madren Bond amount: 500 pounds
Bondsmen: John Madren, Nathan Trueblood, John Rowe

Chancey, Edmund 7 March 1810 Bond No. 61
Wards: Polly & Micajah Chancey orphans of Edmund Chancey
Guardian: Josiah Relfe Bond amount: 3000 pounds
Bondsmen: Josiah Relfe, Malachi Sawyer, Joseph Relfe

Commander, Aylesbury 5 March 1810 Bond No. 58
Ward: Joseph Commander orphan of Aylesbury Commander
Guardian: John Mullen Bond amount: 250 pounds
Bondsmen: John Mullen, Joshua Morris, William Spence

Commander, Joseph 7 December 1809 Bond No. 56
Ward: Joseph Commander orphan of Joseph Commander [lame]
Guardian: Joshua Morris Bond amount: 1000 pounds
Bondsmen: Joshua Morris, Thomas Morris, Mordicai Morris Jr.

Commander, Joseph 5 December 1811 Bond No. 91
Ward: Joseph Commander orphan of Joseph Commander [lame]
Guardian: Thomas Jordan Sr. Bond amount: 500 pounds
Bondsmen: Thomas Jordan, William T. Muse, John Mullen

Davis, Durant 4 December 1810 Bond No. 70
Wards: John, Miles & Martha Davis orphans of Durant Davis
Guardian: John McDonald Bond amount: 1000 pounds
Bondsmen: John McDonald, Benjamin Bailey, John Pool

Davis, Durant 5 March 1811 Bond No. 76
Ward: Durant Davis orphan of Durant Davis deceased
Guardian: Miles Davis Bond amount: 500 pounds
Bondsmen: Miles Davis, Thomas Davis, Benjamin Bailey

Davis, Isaac 8 June 1809 Bond No. 46
Wards: Mabel, John & Rebecca Davis orphans of Isaac Davis
Guardian: Willis Davis Bond amount: 500 pounds
Bondsmen: Willis Davis, Charles Brite, Fredrick Davis

Guardian Bond Book 1808 - 1811

Davis, Thomas   5 June 1809   Bond No. 38
Ward: William H. Davis orphan of Thomas Davis deceased
Guardian: Thomas Davis   Bond amount: 1000 pounds
Bondsmen: Thomas Davis, Gabriel Bailey, Bailey Davis

Delon, Mark   7 December 1808   Bond No. 20
Ward: Penelope Delon orphan of Mark Delon deceased
Guardian: Simon Delon   Bond amount: 100 pounds
Bondsmen: Simon Delon, John McDonald, Miles Davis

Delon, Mark   7 December 1808   Bond No. 21
Ward: Miriam Delon orphan of Mark Delon deceased
Guardian: Simon Delon   Bond amount: 100 pounds
Bondsmen: Simon Delon, John McDonald, Miles Davis

Delon, Mark   7 December 1808   Bond No. 22
Ward: Margaret Delon orphan of Mark Delon deceased
Guardian: Simon Delon   Bond amount: 100 pounds
Bondsmen: Simon Delon, John McDonald, Miles Davis

Delon, Mark   7 December 1808   Bond No. 23
Ward: Anne Delon orphan of Mark Delon deceased
Guardian: Simon Delon   Bond amount: 100 pounds
Bondsmen: Simon Delon, John McDonald, Miles Davis

Delon, William   7 December 1808   Bond No. 24
Wards: Enoch, Mark, Miriam, Francis & Nancy Delon orphans of
     William Delon deceased
Guardian: Simon Delon   Bond amount: 100 pounds
Bondsmen: Simon Delon, John McDonald, Miles Davis

Glasgow, Caleb   6 June 1811   Bond No. 83
Ward: Keziah Glasgow orphan of Caleb Glasgow deceased
Guardian: Thomas Weymouth   Bond amount: 60 pounds
Bondsmen: Thomas Weymouth, Charles Grice, Gabriel Bailey

Pasquotank County, North Carolina

Grice, Francis 5 June 1810 Bond No. 63
Wards: Harriet, Francis, Charles, William, Sarah, Mary & Joseph
  Grice orphans of Francis Grice deceased
Guardian: Charles Grice Bond amount: 500 pounds
Bondsmen: Charles Grice, William Carter, Timothy Cotter

Griffin, Joseph 7 December 1808 Bond No. 25
Wards: Joseph, David & Sarah Griffin orphans of Joseph Griffin
Guardian: Francis White Bond amount: 500 pounds
Bondsmen: Francis White, Benjamin Pritchard, Benjamin White
  (*of*) Up River

Harvey, Thomas 6 December 1808 Bond No. 17
Wards: Benjamin Hardy Harvey & Thomas Harvey orphans of
  Thomas Harvey Esq. deceased
Guardian: William M. Harvey Bond amount: 1000 pounds
Bondsmen: William M. Harvey, Robert McMorine, James Carver

Hooker, Stephen 7 June 1808 Bond No. 4
Wards: Milly & Anne Hooker orphans of Stephen Hooker deceased
Guardian: John Boyd Bond amount: 200 pounds
Bondsmen: John Boyd, John McDonald, William T. Muse

Jackson, Arthur 5 December 1810 Bond No. 72
Wards: appointed guardian to his children Mary, Polly, Milley &
  Louisa Jackson *
Guardian: Arthur Jackson Bond amount: 2000 pounds
Bondsmen: Arthur Jackson, Noah McPherson, Bailey Jackson
  (*note: the words orphan and deceased were scratched out)*

Jackson, Joab 11 March 1809 Bond No. 36
Wards: Tamer, Elizabeth, Benjamin, James, Joseph & Penny
  Jackson orphans of Joab Jackson deceased
Guardian: Andrew Davis* Bond amount: 1000 pounds
Bondsmen: Reuben Jackson, Thomas Jackson
  (*Note: Andrew Davis was named Guardian but Reuben Jackson was
    identified as the Guardian in a different spot and signed as
    bondsman.)*

Guardian Bond Book 1808 - 1811

Jarvis, John 7 March 1809 Bond No. 30
Wards: Elizabeth & Penelope Jarvis orphans of John Jarvis deceased
Guardian: William Gaskins Bond amount: 300 pounds
Bondsmen: William Gaskins, Thomas Banks, Nathan Overman

Jennings, John 8 March 1809 Bond No. 32
Ward: Polly Jennings orphan of John Jennings deceased
Guardian: John Boyd Bond amount: 500 pounds
Bondsmen: John Boyd, John McDonald

Leonard, Benjamin 4 December 1811 Bond No. 90
Ward: Benjamin Leonard orphan of Benjamin Leonard deceased
Guardian: Josiah White Bond amount: 500 pounds
Bondsmen: Josiah White, Malachi Jackson, John Pool

Lister, Elisha 5 June 1811 Bond No. 82
Wards: Polly, Elisha, Thomas & Jacob orphans of Elisha Lister
Guardian: William T. Relfe* Bond amount: 500 pounds
Bondsmen: John Coppersmith, Richard Hewitt, Benjamin Hewitt
   (*note: William T. Relfe was named guardian but his name was scratched out as a bondsman and he did not sign the bond)

Low, Thomas 5 December 1809 Bond No. 54
Wards: Priscilla Low, Patsey Low, Zachariah Low, Joshua Low & Nancy Low orphans of Thomas Low deceased
Guardian: Benjamin White Bond amount: 1000 pounds
Bondsmen: Benjamin White, John Lane, Gabriel Bailey

Lowry, John 7 March 1809 Bond No. 31
Ward: Benjamin Lowry orphan of John Lowry deceased
Guardian: Thomas Banks Bond amount: 1000 pounds
Bondsmen: Thomas Banks, William Gaskins, Nathan Overman

Lucas, George 6 December 1808 Bond No. 15
Ward: William Lucas orphan of George Lucas deceased
Guardian: Francis Wilson Bond amount: 300 pounds
Bondsmen: Francis Wilson, James Carver, William Nicholson

Madrin, Matthias　　　　8 June 1809　　　　Bond No. 44
Wards: Mary, Thomas & Rebecca orphans of Matthias Madrin
Guardian: David Pritchard Jr.　　　Bond amount: 500 pounds
Bondsmen: David Pritchard Jr., Marmaduke Scott, Charles Brite

Madrin, Matthias　　　　8 June 1809　　　　Bond No. 45
Wards: Miriam Madrin, Nancy Madrin & Matthias Madrin
　　　orphans of Matthias Madrin deceased
Guardian: David Pritchard　　　Bond amount: 500 pounds
Bondsmen: David Pritchard Jr., Marmaduke Scott, Charles Brite

Meeds, Benjamin　　　　8 June 1808　　　　Bond No. 8
Ward: Rhoda Meeds orphan of Benjamin Meeds deceased
Guardian: John McDonald　　　Bond amount: 100 pounds
Bondsmen: John McDonald, William Wilson, James Carver

Milby, Zadock　　　　8 December 1809　　　　Bond No. 57
Wards: Polly Milby & Susanna Milby orphans of Zadock Milby
Guardian: Joel Sawyer　　　Bond amount: 1000 pounds
Bondsmen: Joel Sawyer, Fredrick B. Sawyer, Noah Sawyer

Morris, Aaron Sr.　　　　7 March 1809　　　　Bond No. 29
Ward: Sarah Morris orphan of Aaron Morris Sr. deceased
Guardian: Jehoshaphat Morris　　　Bond amount: 1000 pounds
Bondsmen: Jehoshaphat Morris, Joseph Parker, Mark Morris

Nash, Dundly　　　　3 December 1810　　　　Bond No. 67
Ward: John Nash orphan of Dundly Nash deceased
Guardian: Bailey Jackson　　　Bond amount: 100 pounds
Bondsmen: Bailey Jackson, Charles Grice

Newbold, Samuel　　　　2 December 1811　　　　Bond No. 87
Wards: *(Grizzle?)*, William, John & Elizabeth Newbold orphans of
　　　Samuel Newbold deceased
Guardian: Elizabeth Newbold　　　Bond amount: 1000 pounds
Bondsmen: Elizabeth Newbold, Thos. Newbold, Thos. Nicholson

Guardian Bond Book 1808 - 1811   43

Nichols, John　　　　7 December 1809　　Bond No. 55
Ward: David Nichols orphan of John Nichols deceased
Guardian: Levy Richardson　　　Bond amount: 1000 pounds
Bondsmen: Levy Richardson, Daniel Richardson, Jacob Richardson

Nixon, James　　　　6 June 1809　　Bond No. 41
Wards: Mary Nixon, Thomas Nixon, Samuel Nixon & Margaret
　　　Nixon orphans of James Nixon deceased
Guardian: Kader Perry　　　Bond amount: 2000 pounds
Bondsmen: Kader Perry, Benjamin White, Gabriel Bailey

Overman, Charles　　　5 December 1808　　Bond No. 9
Ward: Miriam Overman orphan of Charles Overman deceased
Guardian: John Overman　　　Bond amount: 500 pounds
Bondsmen: John Overman, Gabriel Bailey, Nathan Overman

Overman, Charles　　　5 December 1808　　Bond No. 10
Ward: Benjamin Overman orphan of Charles Overman deceased
Guardian: John Overman　　　Bond amount: 500 pounds
Bondsmen: John Overman, Gabriel Bailey, Nathan Overman

Overman, Charles　　　5 December 1808　　Bond No. 11
Ward: Elizabeth Overman orphan of Charles Overman deceased
Guardian: John Overman　　　Bond amount: 500 pounds
Bondsmen: John Overman, Gabriel Bailey, Nathan Overman

Overman, Charles　　　5 December 1808　　Bond No. 12
Ward: Eli Overman orphan of Charles Overman deceased
Guardian: John Overman　　　Bond amount: 500 pounds
Bondsmen: John Overman, Gabriel Bailey, Nathan Overman

Overman, Charles　　　5 December 1808　　Bond No. 13
Ward: Susannah Overman orphan of Charles Overman deceased
Guardian: Benjamin Albertson　　　Bond amount: 500 pounds
Bondsmen: Benjamin Albertson, Nathan Trueblood, George Bundy

Overman, Charles 5 December 1808 Bond No. 14
Ward: Anne Overman orphan of Charles Overman deceased
Guardian: Benjamin Albertson Bond amount: 500 pounds
Bondsmen: Benjamin Albertson, Nathan Trueblood, George Bundy

Pendleton, Joseph 8 March 1809 Bond No. 33
Ward: Thaddeus Pendleton orphan of Joseph Pendleton deceased
Guardian: William Wilson Bond amount: 500 pounds
Bondsmen: William Wilson, William T. Relfe, Simon L. Broshir

Pendleton, Joshua 7 September 1809 Bond No. 52
Wards: Elizabeth Pendleton & Clarky Pendleton orphans of
 Joshua Pendleton deceased
Guardian: William Wilson Bond amount: 500 pounds
Bondsmen: William Wilson, Simon L. Brosher, Gabriel Bailey

Pool, Patrick 7 December 1808 Bond No. 19
Wards: Nancy Pool, Tamer Pool & Elizabeth Pool orphans of
 Patrick Pool deceased
Guardian: Margaret Pool Bond amount: 200 pounds
Bondsmen: Margaret Pool, Miles Davis, Bailey Davis

Pritchard, Benjamin 9 June 1809 Bond No. 50
Ward: Susanna Evans WIDOW* of Benjamin Pritchard deceased
Guardian: Joseph Banks Bond amount: 500 pounds
Bondsmen: Joseph Banks, Gabriel Bailey, John Bailey
 (*Note: the word orphan was scratched out)

Raper, David 5 December 1809 Bond No. 53
Ward: Bailey Raper his son*
Guardian: David Raper Bond amount: 250 pounds
Bondsmen: David Raper, Nathaniel Gordon, Cornelius Raper
 (*Note: the word orphan was scratched out)

Reding, Jesse 6 June 1809 Bond No. 39
Ward: Keziah Reding orphan of Jesse Reding Esquire deceased
Guardian: William T. Relfe Bond amount: 5000 pounds
Bondsmen: William T. Relfe, Thomas Davis, William Banks

Guardian Bond Book 1808 - 1811   45

Richardson, John   4 December 1810   Bond No. 69
Wards: John Richardson & Winifred Richardson orphans of John
       Richardson deceased
Guardian: Fearebey Richardson   Bond amount: 1000 pounds
Bondsmen: Fearebey Richardson, James McBride, Jonathan Brite

Russell, James   3 September 1810   Bond No. 66
Ward: James Russell orphan of James Russell deceased
Guardian: Francis Grice   Bond amount: 500 pounds
Bondsmen: Francis Grice, Charles Grice, Timothy Cotter

Russell, James   4 December 1811   Bond No. 89
Wards: Malachi Russell & Elizabeth Russell orphans of James
       Russell deceased
Guardian: Josiah Relfe   Bond amount: 1000 pounds
Bondsmen: Josiah Relfe, Joseph Relfe, Andrew Brothers

Sawyer, Caleb   5 December 1810   Bond No. 74
Wards: Mary Sawyer & Thomas Sawyer orphans of Caleb Sawyer
Guardian: Josiah Relfe   Bond amount: 500 pounds
Bondsmen: Josiah Relfe, Miles Brothers, Malachi Sawyer

Sawyer, Hollowell   6 March 1810   Bond No. 60
Ward: Ira Sawyer orphan of Hollowell Sawyer deceased
Guardian: Jonathan Brite   Bond amount: 500 pounds
Bondsmen: Jonathan Brite, Arthur Jackson, Lancelot Richardson

Sawyer, John   3 December 1811   Bond No. 86
Ward: Ebenezar Sawyer orphan of John Sawyer deceased
Guardian: Noah Sawyer   Bond amount: 1000 pounds
Bondsmen: Noah Sawyer, Jonathan Humphries, Joel Sawyer

Sawyer, Malachi   4 June 1811   Bond No. 81
Wards: James Sawyer, Ferebee Sawyer & Susannah orphans of
       Malachi Sawyer deceased
Guardian: James Chamberlain   Bond amount: 500 pounds
Bondsmen: James Chamberlain, Josiah Relfe, Thomas Sawyer

Sawyer, Nichols　　　　4 March 1811　　　Bond No. 71
Wards: Wilson & Kiddy Sawyer orphans of Nichols Sawyer
Guardian: Joseph Gray　　　　　Bond amount: 500 pounds
Bondsmen: Joseph Gray, James Carver, Joel Sawyer

Scott, Samuel　　　　9 March 1809　　　Bond No. 34
Wards: Jesse, Peggy and Enoch Scott orphans of Samuel Scott
Guardian: Elizabeth Scott　　　Bond amount: 1000 pounds
Bondsmen: Elizabeth Scott, John Casse, Thomas Haskins

Scott, Samuel　　　　9 March 1809　　　Bond No. 35
Wards: Charity & James Scott orphans of Samuel Scott deceased
Guardian: Elizabeth Scott　　　Bond amount: 1000 pounds
Bondsmen: Elizabeth Scott, John Casse, Thomas Haskins

Scott, Simpson　　　　9 June 1809　　　Bond No. 47
Wards: Dorcas & Edward Scott orphans of Simpson Scott deceased
Guardian: John Hamilton　　　Bond amount: 500 pounds
Bondsmen: John Hamilton, Timothy Cotter

Sharbrough, John　　　7 March 1809　　　Bond No. 27
Wards: John, Joseph, Jehu & David Sharbrough orphans of John
　　　　Sharbrough deceased
Guardian: Miles Smithson　　　Bond amount: 1000 pounds
Bondsmen: Miles Smithson, Reuben Davis, Cornelius Clark

Sharbrough, Luke　　　3 September 1810　　Bond No. 65
Ward: Hillgrove Sharbrough orphan of Luke Sharbrough deceased
Guardian: Jarvis Jennings　　　Bond amount: 500 pounds
Bondsmen: Jarvis Jennings, Cornelius Clark, Malachi Scott

Smith, William　　　　4 December 1810　　Bond No. 68
Ward: William Smith orphan of William Smith deceased
Guardian: Timothy Cotter　　　Bond amount: 50 pounds
Bondsmen: Timothy Cotter, Bailey Jackson

Guardian Bond Book 1808 - 1811   47

Stamp, Richard   6 March 1809   Bond No. 26
Ward: Thomas A. Stamp orphan of Richard Stamp deceased
Guardian: John Shaw   Bond amount: 3000 pounds
Bondsmen: John Shaw, John Boyd

Stokeley, Joseph   5 December 1810   Bond No. 73
Wards: Sally, Betsey, Polly & Joseph orphans of Joseph Stokeley
Guardian: Mathias Smithson   Bond amount: 2000 pounds
Bondsmen: Mathias Smithson, Malachi Smithson, Miles Smithson

Tooley, Adam   9 June 1809   Bond No. 48
Wards: Elizabeth, William & John Tooley orphans of Adam Tooley
Guardian: Gabriel Bailey   Bond amount: 1000 pounds
Bondsmen: Gabriel Bailey, Robert McMorine, Timothy Cotter

Trueblood, Jesse   9 June 1809   Bond No. 49
Wards: Mary, Nancy & Millicent orphans of Jesse Trueblood
Guardian: William Wilson   Bond amount: 1000 pounds
Bondsmen: William Wilson, John McDonald, Benjamin Symons

Turner, John H.   7 December 1808   Bond No. 18
Wards: Agathy, Peggy, John & *(Janug?)* Turner orphans of John
       H. Turner deceased
Guardian: Gabriel Bailey   Bond amount: 300 pounds
Bondsmen: Gabriel Bailey, John Lane, William Wilson

Warnier, *(Auget?)*   6 March 1810   Bond No. 59
Wards: Caroline & Lydia _*_ orphans of *(Auget?)* Warnier
Guardian: Thomas Brownrigg   Bond amount: 200 pounds
Bondsmen: Thomas Brownrigg, Joseph Parker, William T. Muse
       (* note: possibly & Wm. written after Lydia)

White, Benjamin   4 June 1811   Bond No. 80
Wards: Joshua, Henry, Nancy, Benjamin & Abraham White
       orphans of Benjamin White deceased
Guardian: Josiah White   Bond amount: 1000 pounds
Bondsmen: Josiah White, Abraham Symons, William T. Muse

White, Devotion　　　　　8 June 1808　　　　Bond No. 7
Wards: Anne & Mary White orphans of Devotion White deceased
Guardian: Jesse Reding　　　　　Bond amount: 500 pounds
Bondsmen: Jesse Reding, Thomas Pool, Isaac Overman

White, Devotion　　　　　7 March 1809　　　Bond No. 28
Wards: Anne & Mary White orphans of Devotion White deceased
Guardian: Josiah Relfe　　　　　Bond amount: 500 pounds
Bondsmen: Josiah Relfe, Malachi Sawyer, Thomas Harkins

White, Francis　　　　　7 June 1808　　　　Bond No. 1
Wards: Francis & Martha White orphans of Francis White deceased
Guardian: Josiah White　　　　　Bond amount: 500 pounds
Bondsmen: Josiah White, Benjamin Symons, James McAdams

White, Jordan　　　　　7 June 1808　　　　Bond No. 5
Ward: William White orphan of Jordan White deceased
Guardian: Henry Brothers　　　　Bond amount: 250 pounds
Bondsmen: Henry Brothers, Thomas Jordan Sr., Jonathan
　　　　Trueblood

White, Jordan　　　　　11 March 1809　　　Bond No. 37
Wards: Richard & John White orphans of Jordan White deceased
Guardian: Josiah White　　　　　Bond amount: 500 pounds
Bondsmen: Josiah White, Gabriel Bailey, Benjamin Symons

Wyatt, Isaac　　　　　8 March 1810　　　　Bond No. 62
Ward: Richard Wyatt orphan of Isaac Wyatt deceased
Guardian: Robert H. Smith　　　　Bond amount: 1000 pounds
Bondsmen: Robert H. Smith, Thomas Pool, William Shaw

Pasquotank County, North Carolina
Guardian Bonds
Book 1812 - 1816

Ackiss, Thomas　　　3 March 1813　　　Bond No. 17
Wards: Nancy and Margaret Ackiss orphans of Thomas Ackiss
Guardian: Henry Raper　　　Bond amount: 4000 pounds
Bondsmen: Henry Raper, John Rowe, John Overman

Ackiss, Thomas　　　4 March 1816　　　Bond No. 82
Ward: Francis Ackiss orphan of Thomas Ackiss deceased
Guardian: Rowan Barclift　　　Bond amount: 3000 pounds
Bondsmen: Rowan Barclift, Kader Perry, John Pool

Aydlett, Thomas 6 December 1814 Bond No. 47
Wards: Wilson Aydlett, Betsy Aydlett, Polly Aydlett & Sally
   Aydlett orphans of Thomas Aydlett deceased
Guardian: John Taylor Bond amount: 500 pounds
Bondsmen: John Taylor, Gabriel Taylor, Caleb Pritchard

Bailey, David 6 December 1814 Bond No. 46
Wards: Manyard & Ann Bailey orphans of David Bailey deceased
Guardian: Josiah White Bond amount: 500 pounds
Bondsmen: Josiah White, William T. Muse, John Pool

Banks, Thomas 4 December 1815 Bond No. 70
Ward: Jonathan Banks orphan of Thomas Banks deceased
Guardian: William T. Muse Bond amount: 2000 pounds
Bondsmen: William T. Muse, Henry P. Overman, James Pool

Banks, Thomas 4 December 1815 Bond No. 71
Ward: Thomas Banks orphan of Thomas Banks deceased
Guardian: William T. Muse Bond amount: 2000 pounds
Bondsmen: William T. Muse, James Pool, Henry P. Overman

Banks, Thomas 4 December 1815 Bond No. 72
Ward: Reding Banks orphan of Thomas Banks deceased
Guardian: William T. Muse Bond amount: 2000 pounds
Bondsmen: William T. Muse, James Pool, Henry P. Overman

Banks, Thomas 4 December 1815 Bond No. 73
Ward: William G. Banks orphan of Thomas Banks deceased
Guardian: William T. Muse Bond amount: 2000 pounds
Bondsmen: William T. Muse, James Pool, Henry P. Overman

Barns, Stephen 8 March 1814 Bond No. 36
Ward: Anne Barns orphan of Stephen Barns deceased
Guardian: John Davis Bond amount: 2000 pounds
Bondsmen: John Davis, Thomas Davis, Malachi Jackson

Guardian Bond Book 1812 - 1816

Broshir, John　　　　3 June 1812　　　　Bond No. 3
Wards: Joseph R.Broshir, John Broshir, Ann Broshir & William
　　　Broshir orphans of John Broshir deceased
Guardian: Thomas Banks　　　　Bond amount: 2000 pounds
Bondsmen: Thomas Banks, William C. Banks, Simon L. Broshir

Broshir, John L.　　　　7 March 1815　　　　Bond No. 55
Wards: John Broshir, Nancy Broshir & William Broshir orphans
　　　of John L. Broshir deceased
Guardian: Harvey Luton　　　　Bond amount: 300 pounds
Bondsmen: Harvey Luton, William Gaskins, Peter McPerson

Broshir, Joseph L.　　　　7 March 1815　　　　Bond No. 54
Wards: Betty Broshir & Polly Broshir orphans of Joseph L.
　　　Broshir deceased
Guardian: William Gaskins　　　　Bond amount: 1000 pounds
Bondsmen: William Gaskins, Henry P. Overman, Harvey Luton

Brothers, Jonathan　　　　8 March 1815　　　　Bond No. 57
Ward: Polly Brothers orphan of Jonathan Brothers deceased
Guardian: Bailey Davis　　　　Bond amount: 500 pounds
Bondsmen: Bailey Davis, Thomas Davis, John Brothers - [son
　　　of Jonathan]

Bundy, Benjamin　　　　3 March 1813　　　　Bond No. 16
Wards: Milly Bundy, Jonathan Bundy, Elias Bundy, Jesse Bundy
　　　& Rix Bundy orphans of Benjamin Bundy deceased
Guardian: John Bundy　　　　Bond amount: 100 pounds
Bondsmen: John Bundy, Caleb Morris, John Newby

Bundy, Joseph　　　　5 March 1816　　　　Bond No. 85
Ward: William Bundy orphan of Joseph Bundy deceased
Guardian: Thomas Morris　　　　Bond amount: 200 pounds
Bondsmen: Thomas Morris, Caleb Morris, Mordicai Morris Jr.

Bundy, Joseph　　　　5 March 1816　　　　Bond No. 86
Wards: Joseph Bundy, Thomas Bundy, Rix Bundy & Nancy
　　　Bundy orphans of Joseph Bundy deceased

Guardian: Jacob Symons   Bond amount: 1000 pounds
Bondsmen: Jacob Symons, Thomas Morris, Mordicai Morris Jr.

Cartwright, John   9 March 1814   Bond No. 37
Wards: Deborah Cartwright, Rebecca Cartwright & Malachi
       Cartwright orphans of John Cartwright deceased
Guardian: Jobe Cartwright   Bond amount: 200 pounds
Bondsmen: Jobe Cartwright, Lazarus Gambling, Jesse Gambling

Cartwright, McKeal   6 December 1813   Bond No. 29
Ward: John M. Cartwright orphan of McKeal Cartwright deceased
Guardian: Lemuel Snowden   Bond amount: 500 pounds
Bondsmen: Lemuel Snowden, Benjamin M. Jackson, Harvey Luton

Cartwright, Thomas   9 March 1814   Bond No. 38
Wards: Mariam Cartwright, James Cartwright & Marmaduke
       Cartwright orphans of Thomas Cartwright deceased
Guardian: John Cartwright   Bond amount: 1000 pounds
Bondsmen: John Cartwright, Samuel Cartwright, Thos. Cartwright

Cartwright, Thomas   9 March 1814   Bond No. 39
Wards: Susannah Cartwright & Nancy Cartwright orphans of
       Thomas Cartwright deceased
Guardian: John Cartwright   Bond amount: 500 pounds
Bondsmen: John Cartwright, Samuel Cartwright, Thos. Cartwright

Chamberlain, James   6 June 1815   Bond No. 60
Wards: Margaret Chamberlain & Mary Chamberlain orphans of
       James Chamberlain deceased
Guardian: Sarah Chamberlain   Bond amount: 1000 pounds
Bondsmen: Sarah Chamberlain, Thomas Jordan Jr., Ambrose Knox

Chamberlain, James   7 June 1815   Bond No. 64
Ward: Nancy Chamberlain orphan of James Chamberlain deceased
Guardian: Frederick Whitehurst   Bond amount: 500 pounds
Bondsmen: Frederick Whitehurst, Reuben Brothers, Lazerous
          Gamberling

Guardian Bond Book 1812 - 1816

Chamberlain, James   5 March 1816   Bond No. 84
Wards: Margaret Chamberlain & Mary Chamberlain orphans of
   James Chamberlain deceased
Guardian: William Crutch   Bond amount: 2000 pounds
Bondsmen: William Crutch, Thomas Jordan, Ambrose Knox

Cotter, Timothy   10 December 1812   Bond No. 12
Ward: Hamilton Cotter orphan of Timothy Cotter deceased
Guardian: Hannah Cotter   Bond amount: 100 pounds
Bondsmen: Hannah Cotter, William T. Muse, John McDonald

Davis, Shadrack   7 March 1814   Bond No. 32
Wards: Christian and Elizabeth Davis orphans of Shadrack Davis
Guardian: Daniel McPherson   Bond amount: 3000 pounds
Bondsmen: Daniel McPherson, Lazarus Gambling, John Pritchard

Davis, Shadrack   7 March 1814   Bond No. 33
Ward: Shadrack Davis orphan of Shadrack Davis deceased
Guardian: Jesse Davis   Bond amount: 1000 pounds
Bondsmen: Jesse Davis, Fred. R. Whitehurst, David McPherson

Gale, John   6 March 1816   Bond No. 89
Wards: William S. Gale, Elizabeth Gale & Sarah Gale orphans of
   John Gale deceased
Guardian: William Thomas   Bond amount: 200 pounds
Bondsmen: William Thomas, Samuel Nash, Frederick Whitehurst

Gordon, William   7 December 1814   Bond No. 49
Wards: Dozier, William & Joseph Gordon orphans of William
   Gordon deceased
Guardian: Lydia Gordon   Bond amount: 1000 pounds
Bondsmen: Lydia Gordon, Thomas Jordan Jr., Thomas Barnard

Harris, Thomas   8 June 1814   Bond No. 42
Wards: Martha Harris & Davis Harris orphans of Thomas Harris
Guardian: Isaac Harris   Bond amount: 500 pounds
Bondsmen: Isaac Harris, Hezekiah Cartwright, Malachi Davis

Hoffmire, Alex 7 June 1814 Bond No. 41
Wards: George W., Sally, Joseph, Penniah & Franny Hoffmire
  orphans of Alex Hoffmire deceased
Guardian: Joseph Jordan Bond amount: 500 pounds
Bondsmen: Joseph Jordan, Thomas Jordan Sr., William Barns

Hoffmire, Alexander 5 December 1815 Bond No. 75
Wards: Sarah, Joseph, Fanny, Washington & Penny Hoffmire
  orphans of Alexander Hoffmire deceased
Guardian: Thomas Dailey Bond amount: 500 pounds
Bondsmen: Thomas Dailey, Joseph Jordan, John Lowry

Jackson, Arthur 2 June 1812 Bond No. 2
Wards: Mary, Polly, Milly & Louise Jackson his children *
Guardian: Arthur Jackson Bond amount: 500 pounds
Bondsmen: Arthur Jackson, Bailey Jackson Esq., Noah Sawyer
  (*note: the words orphan and deceased were scratched out)

Jackson, Peleg 2 June 1812 Bond No. 1
Ward: Joseph Jackson orphan of Peleg Jackson deceased
Guardian: Labray Jackson Bond amount: 1000 pounds
Bondsmen: Labray Jackson, Hezekiah Cartwright, Edmund Davis

Jackson, Seth 4 March 1813 Bond No. 22
Wards: Susanna & Polly Jackson orphans of Seth Jackson deceased
Guardian: Corbin Jackson Bond amount: 500 pounds
Bondsmen: Corbin Jackson, David Pritchard, Hezekiah Cartwright

Jackson, Seth 8 September 1813 Bond No. 28
Wards: Peggy & Penny Jackson orphans of Seth Jackson deceased
Guardian: Zachariah Jackson Bond amount: 500 pounds
Bondsmen: Zachariah Jackson, William Scott, William Jackson

James, Benjamin 6 December 1814 Bond No. 48
Ward: William James orphan of Benjamin James deceased
Guardian: John Davis Bond amount: 500 pounds
Bondsmen: John Davis, Thomas Davis, Ambrose Knox

Guardian Bond Book 1812 - 1816

Keaton, William 4 December 1815 Bond No. 74
Wards: Reuben & Anthony Keaton orphans of William Keaton
Guardian: William Snowden Bond amount: 400 pounds
Bondsmen: William Snowden, Benoni Cartwright, Henry P. Overman

Keaton, William 6 December 1815 Bond No. 78
Ward: Polly Keaton orphan of William Keaton deceased
Guardian: Harvey Luton Bond amount: 200 pounds
Bondsmen: Harvey Luton, John Pool, Gabriel Bailey

Lowry, Robert 4 March 1813 Bond No. 20
Ward: Patsey Knox alias Lowry orphan of Robert Lowry deceased
Guardian: Hugh Knox Bond amount: 5000 pounds
Bondsmen: Hugh Knox, Thomas Jordan, William T. Relfe

Markham, Charles 2 March 1813 Bond No. 14
Wards: Margaret Markham & Benjamin Markham orphans of
 Charles Markham deceased
Guardian: William Rose Bond amount: 500 pounds
Bondsmen: William Rose, Benjamin M. Jackson, Benjamin Powers

Markham, Thomas 7 June 1815 Bond No. 66
Wards: Marlen Markham & (_uckey) Markham orphans of
 Thomas Markham Jr. deceased
Guardian: John McDonald Bond amount: 500 pounds
Bondsmen: John McDonald, Thomas Jordan, Thomas Markham

Markham, Thomas 7 June 1815 Bond No. 67
Ward: Keziah Markham orphan of Thomas Markham Jr. deceased
Guardian: John McDonald Bond amount: 250 pounds
Bondsmen: John McDonald, Thomas Jordan, Thomas Markham

Markham, Thomas 7 June 1815 Bond No. 68
Ward: Millicent Markham orphan of Thos. Markham Jr. deceased
Guardian: John McDonald Bond amount: 200 pounds
Bondsmen: John McDonald, Thomas Jordan, Thomas Markham

Morgan, James 8 December 1812 Bond No. 6
Ward: Samuel Morgan orphan of James Morgan deceased
Guardian: Benjamin White Bond amount: 500 pounds
Bondsmen: Benjamin White, Miles Davis, Stephen White

Morris, Christopher 6 September 1814 Bond No. 43
Wards: Josiah Morris & Margaret Morris orphans of Christopher
    Morris deceased
Guardian: Thomas Pritchard Bond amount: 200 pounds
Bondsmen: Thomas Pritchard, Benjamin Pritchard, Caleb Pritchard

Morris, Joshua 7 March 1815 Bond No. 51
Wards: Nathan Morris, Mordicai Morris, Joseph Morris & Hannah
    Morris orphans of Joshua Morris deceased
Guardian: Thomas Morris Bond amount: 500 pounds
Bondsmen: Thos. Morris, Mordicai Morris Sr., Mordicai Morris Jr.

Morris, Mark 7 March 1815 Bond No. 52
Wards: Sarah and Mark Morris orphans of Mark Morris deceased
Guardian: Thomas Morris Bond amount: 200 pounds
Bondsmen: Thos. Morris, Mordicai Morris Sr., Mordicai Morris Jr.

Morris, Thomas 8 December 1812 Bond No. 7
Wards: Penelope Morris, Nathan Morris, Margaret Morris & James
    Morris orphans of Thomas Morris deceased
Guardian: Aaron Morris Jr. Bond amount: 500 pounds
Bondsmen: Aaron Morris Jr., Thomas Elliot, Jehoshaphat Symons

Nash, Dempsey 7 December 1814 Bond No. 50
Ward: John Nash orphan of Dempsey Nash deceased
Guardian: James Nash Bond amount: 200 pounds
Bondsmen: James Nash, Isaac Harrington, Malachi Davis

Nicholson, Henley 10 December 1812 Bond No. 13
Wards: Mary & Eliza Nicholson children of Henley Nicholson*
Guardian: George R. Henley Bond amount: 500 pounds
Bondsmen: George Henley, Joshua Trueblood, Thomas Overman Jr.
    (*note: the word orphan was scratched out)

Guardian Bond Book 1812 - 1816   57

Nicholson, Henley   9 June 1813   Bond No. 23
Wards: Mary Nicholson & Eliza Nicholson children of Henley
    Nicholson*
Guardian: John McDonald   Bond amount: 500 pounds
Bondsmen: John McDonald, William Wilson, John Pool
    (*note: the word orphan was scratched out)

Nixon, John   7 June 1815   Bond No. 62
Ward: Morris Nixon orphan of John Nixon deceased
Guardian: William T. Muse   Bond amount: 1000 pounds
Bondsmen: William T. Muse, William Wilson, Thomas Jordan

Nixon, John   7 June 1815   Bond No. 63
Ward: Samuel R. Nixon orphan of John Nixon deceased
Guardian: William T. Muse   Bond amount: 1000 pounds
Bondsmen: William T. Muse, William Wilson, Thomas Jordan

Nixon, John   6 December 1815   Bond No. 79
Ward: William Muse Nixon orphan of John Nixon deceased
Guardian: Joseph Parker   Bond amount: 2000 pounds
Bondsmen: Joseph Parker, Joseph Mullen, William T. Muse

Nixon, William   7 September 1813   Bond No. 26
Ward: Sarah Nixon orphan of William Nixon deceased
Guardian: John Cock   Bond amount: 500 pounds
Bondsmen: John Cock, Benjamin Hewett, Richard Hewett

Nixon, William   6 December 1815   Bond No. 81
Ward: Sarah Nixon orphan of William Nixon deceased
Guardian: Ambrose Knox   Bond amount: 500 pounds
Bondsmen: Ambrose Knox, William T. Muse, Thomas Davis

Overman, Charles   9 December 1812   Bond No. 11
Ward: Miriam Overman orphan of Charles Overman deceased
Guardian: Nathan Trueblood   Bond amount: 1000 pounds
Bondsmen: Nathan Trueblood, Joshua Trueblood, Benoni Morris

Overman, Charles   3 March 1813   Bond No. 18
Wards: Eli & Benjamin Overman orphans of Charles Overman
Guardian: Joshua Morris   Bond amount: 1000 pounds
Bondsmen: Joshua Morris, Aaron Morris Jr., Benjamin Albertson

Overman, Thomas   8 December 1815   Bond No. 80
Wards: Charles & Grandy Overman orphans of Thomas Overman
Guardian: Isaac Overman   Bond amount: 300 pounds
Bondsmen: Isaac Overman, John Pool, Richard Muse

Palin, Thomas   3 March 1813   Bond No. 19
Ward: Thomas Palin orphan of Thomas Palin deceased
Guardian: Robert Chancy   Bond amount: 500 pounds
Bondsmen: Robert Chancy, Josiah Relfe, Thomas Barnard

Pike, John   6 September 1814   Bond No. 44
Wards: Jonathan Pike & Wilson Pike orphans of John Pike deceased
Guardian: Joseph Pike of Wilson   Bond amount: 600 pounds
Bondsmen: Joseph Pike, Jesse Pike, Benjamin Pike

Pipen, Thomas   7 March 1814   Bond No. 31
Ward: Nathaniel Pipen orphan of Thomas Pipen deceased
Guardian: Edward B. Trueblood   Bond amount: 100 pounds
Bondsmen: Edward B. Trueblood, Charles Grice, Joshua Trueblood

Pritchard, James   7 December 1813   Bond No. 30
Wards: Benjamin, William, Peggy, Mary, Ann & Sally Pritchard
       orphans of James Pritchard deceased
Guardian: Gabriel Bailey   Bond amount: 1500 pounds
Bondsmen: Gabriel Bailey, Charles Grice, John McDonald

Pritchard, John   4 March 1813   Bond No. 21
Wards: William Pritchard, Peggy Pritchard & Sally Pritchard
       orphans of John Pritchard deceased
Guardian: David Pritchard   Bond amount: 100 pounds
Bondsmen: David Pritchard Jr., Hezekiah Cartwright, Corbin
         Jackson

Guardian Bond Book 1812 - 1816

Raper, John 6 December 1815 Bond No. 77
Wards: Rebecca Raper, John Raper, (_olrey) Raper & Robert Raper orphans of John Raper deceased
Guardian: Henry Raper Bond amount: 2000 pounds
Bondsmen: Henry Raper, John Pool, Gabriel Bailey

Rayner, John 8 March 1814 Bond No. 34
Wards: Sally Rayner, William Rayner & Elizabeth Rayner orphans of John Rayner deceased
Guardian: David Pritchard Jr. Bond amount: 250 pounds
Bondsmen: David Pritchard Jr., James Harris, David Harrell

Scott, Samuel 5 March 1816 Bond No. 87
Wards: Enoch, Charles & Jarvis Scott orphans of Samuel Scott
Guardian: John Casse Bond amount: 500 pounds
Bondsmen: John Casse, John Rowe, Jesse Gambling

Shirley, David 6 September 1815 Bond No. 69
Wards: John & Ann Shirley orphans of David Shirley deceased
Guardian: Thomas Jordan Jr. Bond amount: 400 pounds
Bondsmen: Thomas Jordan Jr., William T. Muse, Ambrose Knox

Smith, Robert 8 September 1812 Bond No. 5
Wards: Joseph, Lydia & Sally Smith orphans of Robert Smith
Guardian: Tamer Smith Bond amount: 500 pounds
Bondsmen: Tamer Smith, John Sexton, David Scaff

Smith, Robert 6 June 1815 Bond No. 61
Wards: Joseph, Lydia & Sally Smith orphans of Robert Smith
Guardian: David Scaff Bond amount: 200 pounds
Bondsmen: David Scaff, John Scaff, George F. Overman

Snowden, Thaddeus 9 September 1813 Bond No. 27
Wards: William Snowden & Thaddeus Snowden orphans of Thaddeus Snowden deceased
Guardian: Harvey Luton Bond amount: 300 pounds
Bondsmen: Harvey Luton, Benjamin M. Jackson, Lemuel James

Spence, Mark   7 September 1813   Bond No. 25
Wards: Betsy Spence, Patsey Spence, William Spence & Nancy
    Spence orphans of Mark Spence deceased
Guardian: Parthenia Spence   Bond amount: 100 pounds
Bondsmen: Parthenia Spence, Fred. B. Sawyer, John C. Robinson

Spence, Samuel   8 December 1812   Bond No. 8
Ward: Reuben Spence orphan of Samuel Spence deceased
Guardian: Abel Sawyer   Bond amount: 100 pounds
Bondsmen: Abel Sawyer, William Wood, Thornton Spence

Spence, Samuel   8 December 1812   Bond No. 9
Ward: Elizabeth Spence orphan of Samuel Spence deceased
Guardian: William Wood   Bond amount: 100 pounds
Bondsmen: William Wood, Abel Sawyer, Thornton Spence

Spence, Samuel   8 December 1812   Bond No. 10
Ward: Joseph Spence orphan of Samuel Spence deceased
Guardian: Thornton Spence   Bond amount: 100 pounds
Bondsmen: Thornton Spence, William Wood, Abel Sawyer

Spence, Samuel   7 September 1813   Bond No. 24
Ward: Susannah Spence orphan of Samuel Spence deceased
Guardian: Abel Sawyer   Bond amount: 200 pounds
Bondsmen: Abel Sawyer, Joseph Gray, John C. Robinson

Stokeley, Isaac   7 March 1815   Bond No. 56
Wards: *(Alford or Alfred?)* Stokeley, Rhoda Stokeley, Joshua
    Stokeley, Jeremiah Stokeley, Peggy Stokeley & Emmy
    Stokeley orphans of Isaac Stokeley deceased
Guardian: Lydia Stokeley   Bond amount: 100 pounds
Bondsmen: Lydia Stokeley, Noah McPherson, Frederick B. Sawyer

Stott, Thomas   5 June 1815   Bond No. 58
Ward: Elizabeth Stott orphan of Thomas Stott deceased
Guardian: James Pool Jr.   Bond amount: 1000 pounds
Bondsmen: James Pool Jr., Richard Pool, John Pool Sr.

Guardian Bond Book 1812 - 1816

Stott, William   5 June 1815   Bond No. 59
Ward: William Stott orphan of William Stott deceased
Guardian: Thomas Markham   Bond amount: 1000 pounds
Bondsmen: Thomas Markham, Anthony Markham, William Relfe

Symons, John   7 June 1814   Bond No. 40
Ward: Mary Symons orphan of John Symons deceased
Guardian: Stephen White   Bond amount: 500 pounds
Bondsmen: Stephen White, Benjamin White, Henry Raper

Temple, James   7 March 1815   Bond No. 53
Ward: James Temple orphan of James Temple deceased
Guardian: Thomas Temple   Bond amount: 500 pounds
Bondsmen: Thomas Temple, Fred. B. Sawyer, Joseph Gray

Trueblood, Timothy   3 June 1812   Bond No. 4
Wards: Alfred Trueblood & Manyard Trueblood orphans of
    Timothy Trueblood deceased
Guardian: William Allen   Bond amount: 1000 pounds
Bondsmen: William Allen, Josiah White, Jonathan Trueblood

Warner, Samuel   5 March 1816   Bond No. 88
Wards: *(Sally or Sully)*, Samuel, Paloey, Peggy, Polly & Priscilla
    Warner orphans of Samuel Warner deceased
Guardian: William Wilson   Bond amount: 5000 pounds
Bondsmen: William Wilson, Harvey Luton, Henry P. Overman

White, Benjamin   6 December 1814   Bond No. 45
Ward: Benjamin White orphan of Benjamin White deceased
Guardian: Thomas Gaskins   Bond amount: 3000 pounds
Bondsmen: Thomas Gaskins, Thomas Banks, Henry P. Overman

White, Benjamin   4 March 1816   Bond No. 83
Wards: Abraham & Benjamin White orphans of Benjamin White
Guardian: Henry White   Bond amount: 200 pounds
Bondsmen: Henry White, John Pool, Robert White

Williams, Elisha 3 March 1813 Bond No. 15
Wards: Maxwell Williams, Shadrack Owen Williams & Lurana
    Williams orphans of Elisha Williams deceased
Guardian: Owen Williams Bond amount: 300 pounds
Bondsmen: Owen Williams, David Harrell, Abraham Smith

Williams, Elisha 8 March 1814 Bond No. 35
Wards: Maxy Williams, Shadrack Owen Williams & Lurana
    Williams orphans of Elisha Williams deceased
Guardian: Seth Williams Bond amount: 500 pounds
Bondsmen: Seth Williams, Owen Williams, Abraham Smith

Williams, Elisha 7 June 1815 Bond No. 65
Wards: Maxy Williams, Shadrack Owen Williams & Lurana
    Williams orphans of Elisha Williams deceased
Guardian: Samuel Sexton Bond amount: 500 pounds
Bondsmen: Samuel Sexton, Thomas Madren, John R. Warrington

Williams, Elisha 5 December 1815 Bond No. 76
Wards: Elisha Maxy Williams, Owen Williams & Lurana
    Williams orphans of Elisha Williams deceased
Guardian: Seth Williams Bond amount: 500 pounds
Bondsmen: Seth Williams, James Barns, Noah Sawyer

Pasquotank County, North Carolina
Guardian Bonds
Book 1816 - 1822

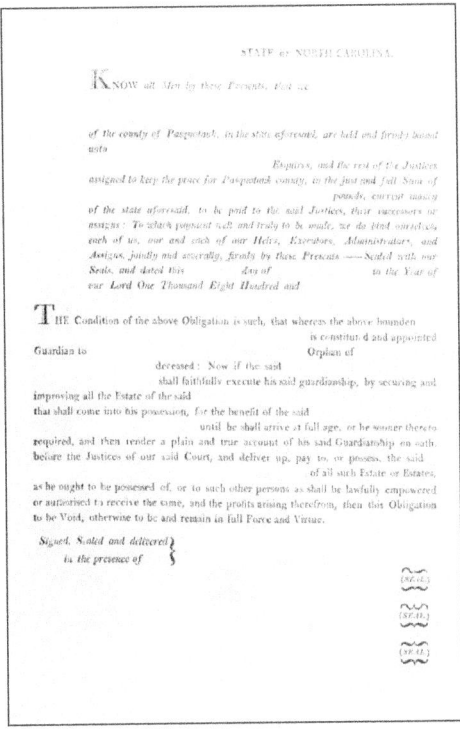

Ackiss, Thomas   4 December 1820   Bond No. 143
Ward: Francis Ackiss orphan of Thomas Ackiss deceased
Guardian: Stephen Mullen   Bond amount: 4000 pounds
Bondsmen: Stephen Mullen, Jos. Pritchard, William Allen

Ackiss, Thomas   4 February 1822   Bond No. 185
Ward: Francis Ackiss orphan of Thomas Ackiss deceased
Guardian: George Bailey   Bond amount: 6000 dollars*
Bondsmen: George Bailey, John Bailey, Benjamin Bailey,
         Robert Bailey
   (*Note: the word pounds was scratched out)

Adams, Thomas 5 December 1821 Bond No. 169
Wards: Elizabeth, Mary, Letty, Nancy & Andrew Adams orphans
 of Thomas Adams deceased
Guardian: Willoughby Adams Bond amount: 3000 pounds
Bondsmen: Willoughby Adams, Henry P. Overman, John Tooley

Albertson, William 8 March 1820 Bond No. 129
Wards: Benjamin, Penelope & Emmaline Albertson children of
 the said William Albertson*
Guardian: William Albertson Bond amount: 2000 pounds
Bondsmen: William Albertson, Robert H. Smith, William T. Muse
(*Note: the word orphan was scratched out)

Bailey, Benjamin 3 December 1816 Bond No. 21
Wards: Joseph Bailey, Rebecca Bailey, Jack Bailey & Clarkey
 Bailey orphans of Benjamin Bailey deceased
Guardian: John Davis Bond amount: 1000 pounds
Bondsmen: John Davis, William Barns, Malachi Jackson

Bailey, Benjamin 3 June 1818 Bond No. 63
Wards: Jos. Bailey, Rebecca Bailey, John Bailey & Clarky Bailey
 orphans of Benjamin Bailey deceased
Guardian: William H. Davis Bond amount: 500 pounds
Bondsmen: William H. Davis, Ambrose Knox, William Muse

Bailey, Charles 5 September 1821 Bond No. 163
Ward: Alexander Bailey orphan of Charles Bailey deceased
Guardian: Miles Elliott Bond amount: 150 pounds
Bondsmen: Miles Elliott, John Pool Sr., Exum Newby

Bailey, Charles 5 September 1821 Bond No. 164
Ward: Charles Harvey Bailey orphan of Charles Bailey deceased
Guardian: Miles Elliott Bond amount: 750 pounds
Bondsmen: Miles Elliott, John Pool Sr., Exum Newby

Bailey, David 5 June 1816 Bond No. 1
Ward: Nancy Bailey orphan of David Bailey deceased
Guardian: Malachi Jackson Bond amount: 500 pounds
Bondsmen: Malachi Jackson, Bailey Davis, Ambrose Knox

Guardian Bond Book 1816 - 1822

Bailey, Thomas 2 September 1817 Bond No. 36
Wards: Mary, William & David Bailey orphans of Thomas Bailey
Guardian: John Bailey Bond amount: 2000 pounds
Bondsmen: John Bailey, Robert Bailey, George Bailey

Banks, Jonathan 3 September 1816 Bond No. 12
Wards: Ana Banks, William Banks & Thaddeus Banks orphans of
  Jonathan Banks deceased
Guardian: Aaron Fletcher Bond amount: 2000 pounds
Bondsmen: Aaron Fletcher, Henry P. Overman, Thomas Jordan Jr.

Banks, Jonathan 3 September 1816 Bond No. 13
Wards: Patsey & Jonathan Banks orphans of Jonathan Banks
Guardian: Aaron Fletcher Bond amount: 1000 pounds
Bondsmen: Aaron Fletcher, Henry P. Overman, Thomas Jordan Jr.

Banks, Jonathan 7 March 1821 Bond No. 153
Wards: William, Patsy, Thaddeus & Jonathan Banks orphans of
  Jonathan Banks deceased
Guardian: Thaddeus Freshwater Bond amount: 2000 pounds
Bondsmen: Thaddeus Freshwater, H. P. Overman, Benjamin Davis

Banks, Thomas 5 September 1820 Bond No. 140
Ward: William G. Banks orphan of Thomas Banks deceased
Guardian: Nathan Overman Bond amount: 1000 pounds
Bondsmen: Nathan Overman, Henry Overman, Benoni Cartwright

Barns, Stephen 3 June 1818 Bond No. 80
Ward: Ann Barns orphan of Stephen Barns deceased
Guardian: Malachi Jackson Bond amount: 1000 pounds
Bondsmen: Malachi Jackson, William H. Davis, Ambrose Knox

Broshir, Fernon L. 7 January 1822 Bond No. 171
Ward: Simon Broshir orphan of Fernon L. Broshir deceased
Guardian: Edmund H. Perkins Bond amount: 1000 pounds
Bondsmen: Edmund H. Perkins, L. B. Pool Jr., W. W. Freshwater

Broshir, John 2 March 1819 Bond No. 97
Ward: William Broshir orphan of John Broshir deceased
Guardian: Thaddeus Freshwater Bond amount: 3000 pounds
Bondsmen: Thaddeus Freshwater, William Freshwater,
 Christopher Cartwright

Broshir, Joseph L. 2 December 1817 Bond No. 45
Ward: Elizabeth Broshir orphan of Joseph Broshir deceased
Guardian: George W. Pendleton Bond amount: 1000 pounds
Bondsmen: George Pendleton, William Gaskins, William T. Muse

Broshir, Joseph L. 2 December 1817 Bond No. 46
Ward: Mary Broshir orphan of Joseph Broshir deceased
Guardian: George W. Pendleton Bond amount: 1000 pounds
Bondsmen: George Pendleton, William Gaskins, William Muse

Broshir, Jos. L. 7 March 1820 Bond No. 123
Wards: Benjamin & Ann Broshir orphans of Jos. L. Broshir
Guardian: Thaddeus Freshwater Bond amount: 400 pounds
Bondsmen: Thaddeus Freshwater, William W. Freshwater, Henry
 P. Overman

Broshir, Jos. L. 5 December 1820 Bond No. 144
Ward: Mary Broshir orphan of Jos. L. Broshir deceased
Guardian: Henry P. Overman Bond amount: 5000 pounds
Bondsmen: Henry P. Overman, William W. Freshwater, Thaddeus
 Freshwater

Broshir, Joseph L. 6 March 1821 Bond No. 151
Ward: Polly Broshir orphan of Joseph L. Broshir deceased
Guardian: Edmund H. Perkins Bond amount: 6000 pounds
Bondsmen: Edmund H. Perkins, Joseph Perkins, Caleb Perkins

Broshir, Simon L. 7 January 1822 Bond No. 173
Wards: Thos., John, Elizabeth & Joseph orphans of Simon L. Broshir
Guardian: Simon B. Pool Bond amount: 4000 pounds
Bondsmen: Simon B. Pool, Edmund H. Perkins, William W.
 Freshwater

Guardian Bond Book 1816 - 1822   67

Brothers, Job   3 June 1817   Bond No. 30
Wards: Susannah & Durant Brothers orphans of Job Brothers
Guardian: Jehu Cartwright   Bond amount: 500 pounds
Bondsmen: Jehu Cartwright, Benjamin Bundy, Caleb Brothers

Brothers, Louis   6 June 1820   Bond No. 138
Ward: Tamer Brothers orphan of Louis Brothers deceased
Guardian: John C. Ehringhaus   Bond amount: 300 pounds
Bondsmen: John C. Ehringhaus, Ambrose Knox, Lemuel C. Moore

Brothers, Richard   6 June 1820   Bond No. 135
Wards: Clarky, Betsy, Nancy & Jas. orphans of Richard Brothers
Guardian: William Fletcher   Bond amount: 1000 pounds
Bondsmen: William Fletcher, Aaron Fletcher, Francis Fletcher

Bundy, Benjamin   7 December 1819   Bond No. 113
Wards: Elias, Jesse & Rix Bundy orphans of Benjamin Bundy
Guardian: Caleb Morris   Bond amount: 150 pounds
Bondsmen: Caleb Morris, Aaron White, Nathan Morris

Bundy, John   8 June 1819   Bond No. 106
Wards: Mary & Martha Bundy orphans of John Bundy deceased
Guardian: Nathan Bundy   Bond amount: 150 pounds
Bondsmen: Nathan Bundy, Benjamin Morgan, Richard Muse

Bundy, John   4 February 1822   Bond No. 183
Ward: Mary Bundy orphan of John Bundy deceased
Guardian: Nathan Bundy   Bond amount: 250 pounds
Bondsmen: Nathan Bundy, Thomas Pritchard, Nathan Morgan

Bundy, John   4 February 1822   Bond No. 184
Ward: Martha Bundy orphan of John Bundy deceased
Guardian: Nathan Bundy   Bond amount: 250 pounds
Bondsmen: Nathan Bundy, Thomas Pritchard, Nathan Morgan

Bundy, Joseph   4 March 1818   Bond No. 70
Ward: William Bundy orphan of Joseph Bundy deceased
Guardian: Jacob Symons   Bond amount: 200 pounds
Bondsmen: Jacob Symons, Benjamin Pritchard Jr., Asa Sanderlin

Burnham, Thomas 7 March 1820 Bond No. 127
Wards: Sabra and Nancy Burnham orphans of Thomas Burnham
Guardian: Thomas Temple Bond amount: 400 pounds
Bondsmen: Thomas Temple, Joseph Harrell, Abel Sawyer

Cartwright, John 3 June 1818 Bond No. 58
Wards: Rebecca Cartwright, Deborah Cartwright & Malachi
    Cartwright orphans of John Cartwright deceased
Guardian: Abner Williams Bond amount: 1000 pounds
Bondsmen: Abner Williams, John Casse, Jesse Gambling

Cartwright, Jos. 8 December 1819 Bond No. 116
Ward: Nancy Cartwright orphan of Jos. Cartwright deceased
Guardian: John McDonald Bond amount: 500 pounds
Bondsmen: John McDonald, William T. Muse, Richard Muse

Cartwright, Jos. 8 March 1820 Bond No. 130
Ward: Nancy Cartwright orphan of Jos. Cartwright deceased
Guardian: Hugh B. Knox Bond amount: 500 pounds
Bondsmen: Hugh B. Knox, William T. Muse, William C. George

Cartwright, Joseph 5 December 1821 Bond No. 170
Ward: Nancy Cartwright orphan of Joseph Cartwright deceased
Guardian: Carter Barnard Bond amount: 300 pounds
Bondsmen: Carter Barnard, Henry P. Overman, John Jennings

Cartwright, Thomas 5 June 1816 Bond No. 3
Ward: Miriam Cartwright orphan of Thomas Cartwright deceased
Guardian: James Cartwright Bond amount: 1000 pounds
Bondsmen: James Cartwright the younger, James Cartwright Sr.,
    John Cartwright

Cartwright, Thomas 5 June 1816 Bond No. 4
Wards: Marmaduke Cartwright and Nancy Cartwright orphans of
    Thomas Cartwright deceased
Guardian: James Cartwright Bond amount: 1000 pounds
Bondsmen: James Cartwright the younger, James Cartwright Sr.,
    John Cartwright

Guardian Bond Book 1816 - 1822

Cartwright, Thomas   5 June 1816   Bond No. 5
Wards: James Cartwright & Susannah Cartwright orphans of
    Thomas Cartwright deceased
Guardian: James Cartwright   Bond amount: 1000 pounds
Bondsmen: James Cartwright the younger, James Cartwright Sr.,
    John Cartwright

Carver, Alfred   8 September 1818   Bond No. 83
Wards: Eliza and Mary Carver orphans of Alfred Carver deceased
Guardian: John McDonald   Bond amount: 1000 pounds
Bondsmen: John McDonald, Henry P. Overman, William Wilson

Carver, Elias   7 March 1820   Bond No. 125
Wards: Polly & Betsy Carver orphans of Elias Carver deceased
Guardian: Abel Sawyer   Bond amount: 1000 pounds
Bondsmen: Abel Sawyer, Thomas Temple, Jos. Harrell

Chamberlain, James   4 March 1818   Bond No. 69
Wards: Mary Chamberlain & Peggy Chamberlain orphans of
    James Chamberlain deceased
Guardian: Stephen Mullen   Bond amount: 3000 pounds
Bondsmen: Stephen Mullen, William Crutch, Rowan Barclift

Copeland, Ira   5 June 1817   Bond No. 31
Wards: Martha Nancy Copeland & John Andrew Copeland
    orphans of Ira Copeland deceased
Guardian: Leonard Martin   Bond amount: 200 pounds
Bondsmen: Leonard Martin, John Pool, Thomas Jordan

Cotter, Timothy   4 June 1816   Bond No. 17
Wards: Hamilton, Timothy & Wilson orphans of Timothy Cotter
Guardian: John Carver   Bond amount: 1500 pounds
Bondsmen: John Carver, Charles Sawyer, William T. Muse

Cotter, Timothy   4 December 1816   Bond No. 24
Ward: Margaret Cotter orphan of Timothy Cotter deceased
Guardian: William Wilson   Bond amount: 500 pounds
Bondsmen: William Wilson, Henry P. Overman, William T. Muse

Davis, Bailey 5 December 1820 Bond No. 147
Wards: Mary Clark Davis & Sally Davis children of the said
    Bailey Davis*
Guardian: Bailey Davis Bond amount: 500 pounds
Bondsmen: Bailey Davis, William H. Davis, Malachi Jackson
    (*Note: the word orphan was scratched out)

Davis, Benjamin 3 March 1818 Bond No. 51
Wards: Benjamin & Rubin Davis orphans of Benjamin Davis
Guardian: William T. Muse Bond amount: 1000 pounds
Bondsmen: Wm. T. Muse, William Wilson, Thomas Shannonhouse

Davis, Durant 7 March 1820 Bond No. 126
Wards: Jno., Patsey & Davis Davis orphans of Durant Davis
Guardian: Carter Bernard Bond amount: 2000 pounds
Bondsmen: Carter Bernard, William Allen, Joseph Commander

Davis, Malachi 3 June 1818 Bond No. 59/60*
Ward: Joseph Davis orphan of Malachi Davis deceased
Guardian: William T. Muse Bond amount: 500 pounds
Bondsmen: William T. Muse, William Wilson, Ambrose Knox
    (*Note: the number 59 is overwritten with 60)

Etheridge, James 9 December 1818 Bond No. 96
Ward: Matthias Etheridge orphan of James Etheridge deceased
Guardian: Thomas J. Newbold Bond amount: 500 pounds
Bondsmen: Thomas J. Newbold, John Bailey, Nathan Small

Etheridge, Richard 3 September 1816 Bond No. 15
Wards: Richard, Harriot & Seth orphans of Richard Etheridge
Guardian: Thomas Markham Bond amount: 1500 pounds
Bondsmen: Thomas Markham, Aaron Fletcher, Henry P.
    Overman, Thomas Jordan

Etheridge, Richard 3 September 1816 Bond No. 16
Wards: William & Morris Etheridge orphans of Richard Etheridge
Guardian: Thomas Markham Bond amount: 1000 pounds
Bondsmen: Thomas Markham, Aaron Fletcher, Henry P.
    Overman, Thomas Jordan

Guardian Bond Book 1816 - 1822

Evans, Benjamin 3 June 1817 Bond No. 27
Wards: Mary & Ana Evans orphans of Benjamin Evans deceased
Guardian: James Palmer Bond amount: 500 pounds
Bondsmen: James Palmer, Henry Overman, William Freshwater

Evans, Evan 4 September 1816 Bond No. 18
Wards: Elizabeth Evans, Sarah Evans & Rebecka Evans orphans
 of Evan Evans deceased
Guardian: John Pool Bond amount: 150 pounds
Bondsmen: John Pool, Richard Pool, James Pool

Fox, George 7 September 1819 Bond No. 111
Wards: Mary & William Fox orphans of George Fox
Guardian: Joseph Fox Bond amount: 500 pounds
Bondsmen: Joseph Fox, Ambrose Knox, William W. Freshwater

Gambling, Lazarus 8 December 1819 Bond No. 117
Ward: Polly Gambling orphan of Lazarus Gambling
Guardian: Jesse Gambling Bond amount: 1000 pounds
Bondsmen: Jesse Gambling, Abner Williams, John R. Warrington

Gaskins, Thomas 2 December 1817 Bond No. 43
Ward: Nancy Gaskins orphan of Thomas Gaskins
Guardian: William W. Freshwater Bond amount: 1000 pounds
Bondsmen: William W. Freshwater, Thaddeus Freshwater,
 Richard Jordan

Gaskins, Thomas 2 December 1817 Bond No. 44
Ward: Patsey Gaskins orphan of Thomas Gaskins
Guardian: William W. Freshwater Bond amount: 1000 pounds
Bondsmen: William W. Freshwater, Thaddeus Freshwater,
 Richard Jordan

Gordon, William 8 September 1818 Bond No. 67
Wards: Dozier, William & Joseph orphans of William Gordon
Guardian: William Crutch Bond amount: 1000 pounds
Bondsmen: William Crutch, Richard Muse, John McDonald

Griffin, Thomas 7 September 1818 Bond No. 64
Ward: Moses H. Griffin orphan of Thomas Griffin
Guardian: James Morgan Bond amount: 100 pounds
Bondsmen: James Morgan, Eli White, Hezekiah Simpson

Harris, Isaac 5 September 1821 Bond No. 162
Ward: Grandy Harris orphan of Isaac Harris
Guardian: David Jennings Bond amount: 500 pounds
Bondsmen: David Jennings, Ruben T. Harris, David Sharborough

Herring, _____ 7 March 1820 Bond No. 120
Ward: Patsy Herrin orphan of ___ Herrin
Guardian: Thos. S. Jordan Bond amount: 1000 pounds
Bondsmen: Thos. S. Jordan, William W. Freshwater, John Jennings

Herring, John 7 January 1822 Bond No. 178
Ward: Patsy orphan of John Herring
Guardian: Timothy Pendleton Bond amount: 500 pounds
Bondsmen: Timothy Pendleton, Edmund Perkins, William Muse

Hoffmire, Alexander 9 June 1819 Bond No. 109
Wards: Washington, Sally, Penelope, Joseph & Fanny Hoffmire
 orphans of Alexander Hoffmire
Guardian: Thomas Dailey Bond amount: 1000 pounds
Bondsmen: Thomas Dailey, Frederick Pendleton, Richard Pool

Hollowell, Samuel 4 December 1821 Bond No. 168
Wards: Ambrose & John Hollowell orphans of Samuel Hollowell
Guardian: Samuel Brothers Bond amount: 500 pounds
Bondsmen: Samuel Brothers, Will T. Relfe, Nathan O. Morris

Hornett, Benjamin 5 December 1820 Bond No. 148
Ward: Benjamin Hornett orphan of Benjamin Hornett
Guardian: Demsey B. Pendleton Bond amount: 1000 pounds
Bondsmen: Demsey B. Pendleton, Frederick Pendleton,
 Christopher Cartwright

Jackson, Arthur 5 March 1818 Bond No. 75
Wards: Maxy, Polly, Milly & Louise orphans of Arthur Jackson

Guardian Bond Book 1816 - 1822

Guardian: Jacob Richardson   Bond amount: 1000 pounds
Bondsmen: Jacob Richardson, William T. Muse, John Pool Sr.

Jackson, James   7 March 1820   Bond No. 124
Ward: Jos. Jackson orphan of James Jackson deceased
Guardian: Thaddeus Freshwater   Bond amount: 1000 pounds
Bondsmen: Thaddeus Freshwater, William W. Freshwater,
    Henry P. Overman

Jackson, Malachi   6 December 1820   Bond No. 149
Wards: Barns B., Stephen B. & Palin children of Malachi Jackson*
Guardian: Malachi Jackson   Bond amount: 5000 pounds
Bondsmen: Malachi Jackson, William T. Relf, William H. Davis
    (*note: the word Orphan was scratched out)

James, Benjamin   3 June 1818   Bond No. __*
Ward: William James orphan of Benjamin James deceased
Guardian: Henry P. Overman   Bond amount: 500 pounds
Bondsmen: Henry P. Overman, William T. Muse, Harvey Luton
    (*Note: the bond is recorded between bond number 63 & 64)

Jennings, James   8 December 1818   Bond No. 93
Ward: Mary Jennings orphan of James Jennings deceased
Guardian: James Whidbee   Bond amount: 2000 pounds
Bondsmen: James Whidbee, Stephen Mullen, William T. Muse

Keaton, Benoni   4 September 1816   Bond No. 19
Wards: Joseph Keaton & Winifred Keaton children of Benoni*
Guardian: John McDonald   Bond amount: 200 pounds
Bondsmen: John McDonald, Thaddeus Freshwater, Thomas Jordan
    (*note: the word Orphan was scratched out)

Keaton, William   4 December 1821   Bond No. 166
Ward: Anthony M. Keaton orphan of William Keaton deceased
Guardian: Lemuel Snowden*   Bond amount: 200 pounds
Bondsmen: Lemuel Overton,* Henry P. Overman, John Cartwright
    (*Note: Lemuel Snowden was named Guardian and signed the
    bond. Lemuel Overton did not sign the document.)

Knox, Hugh 8 March 1820 Bond No. 132
Ward: Thomas D. Knox orphan of Captain Hugh Knox deceased
Guardian: William C. Brooks Bond amount: 5000 pounds
Bondsmen: William C. Brooks, William H. Davis, Lemuel Moore

Knox, Hugh 8 March 1820 Bond No. 134
Wards: Andrew & Margaret Knox orphans of Captain Hugh Knox
Guardian: Ambrose Knox Bond amount: 3000 pounds
Bondsmen: Ambrose Knox, John C. Ehringhaus, William T. Muse

Lowry, Jno. 5 December 1820 Bond No. 146
Wards: Benjamin Lowry, William Lowry & Jno. Lowry orphans
    of Jno. Lowry deceased
Guardian: William Trueblood Bond amount: 1000 pounds
Bondsmen: William Trueblood, Nathan O. Morris, Anderson Morris

Lowry, Thomas 2 September 1817 Bond No. 35
Ward: William Lowry orphan of Thomas Lowery deceased
Guardian: Aaron Fletcher Bond amount: 100 pounds
Bondsmen: Aaron Fletcher, William T. Muse

Luton, Harvey 7 September 1819 Bond No. 110
Ward: Thaddeus Luton orphan of Harvey Luton deceased
Guardian: Thaddeus Freshwater Bond amount: 1000 pounds
Bondsmen: Thaddeus Freshwater, William W. Freshwater,
    Frederick Pendleton

Madrin, ____ 8 September 1818 Bond No. 65
Ward: Matthias Madrin orphan of ____*(Blank)*____ deceased
Guardian: Edmund Trueblood Bond amount: 500 pounds
Bondsmen: Edmund Trueblood, John Casse, Stephen Stafford

Madrin, Matthias 4 March 1819 Bond No. 103
Ward: Miriam Madrin orphan of Matthias Madrin deceased
Guardian: Edmund Trueblood Bond amount: 500 pounds
Bondsmen: Edmund Trueblood, Abner Williams, Enoch Pritchard

Guardian Bond Book 1816 - 1822

Markham, Thomas   4 March 1818   Bond No. 74
Wards: William, Penny, Anthony, Thomas & John Markham
    orphans of Thomas Markham
Guardian: John Tooley   Bond amount: 500 pounds
Bondsmen: John Tooley, John Shannon, Demsey Brothers

Markham, Thomas   7 December 1819   Bond No. 114
Wards: William Markham, Penelope Markham & Anthony
    Markham orphans of Thomas Markham deceased
Guardian: Anthony Markham   Bond amount: 1000 pounds
Bondsmen: Anthony Markham, James Leonard, William T. Muse

Markham, Thomas   7 December 1819   Bond No. 115
Wards: Thomas & John Markham orphans of Thomas Markham
Guardian: Anthony Markham   Bond amount: 750 pounds
Bondsmen: Anthony Markham, James Leonard, William T. Muse

McDonald, John   7 January 1822   Bond No. 174
Wards: Nancy McDonald, *(Grizzle?)* McDonald, Elizabeth
    McDonald & John orphans of John McDonald deceased
Guardian: William C. George   Bond amount: 10,000 pounds
Bondsmen: William C. George, John McDonald, Hugh B. Knox

Miller, William   5 December 1816   Bond No. 26
Wards: John & James Miller orphans of William Miller deceased
Guardian: Jesse Gambling   Bond amount: 3000 pounds
Bondsmen: Jesse Gambling, Willis Simpson, Hezekiah Simpson

Miller, William   7 March 1820   Bond No. 128
Wards: Jno. & Jas. Miller orphans of William Miller deceased
Guardian: Daniel McPherson   Bond amount: 500 pounds
Bondsmen: Daniel McPherson, Robert Simpson, William Scott

Morgan, Charles   8 September 1818   Bond No. 68
Ward: Urih Morgan orphan of Charles Morgan deceased
Guardian: Nathan Morgan   Bond amount: 500 pounds
Bondsmen: Nathan Morgan, H. Perry, James Morgan

Pasquotank County, North Carolina

Morgan, Charles   4 February 1822   Bond No. 182
Ward: Urih Morgan orphan of Charles Morgan deceased
Guardian: Nathan Morgan   Bond amount: 200 dollars*
Bondsmen: Nathan Morgan, Benjamin Bailey, Matthew Overman
(*Note: the word pounds was scratched out)

Morgan, James   3 September 1816   Bond No. 10
Ward: Lamuel Morgan orphan of James Morgan deceased
Guardian: Nathan Morgan   Bond amount: 500 pounds
Bondsmen: Nathan Morgan, William Wood, Robertson White

Morris, Joshua   2 September 1817   Bond No. 38
Wards: Nathan Morris & Mordecai Morris orphans of Joshua Morris deceased
Guardian: Anderson Morris   Bond amount: 1000 pounds
Bondsmen: Anderson Morris, Mordecai Morris, Matthew Overman

Morris, Joshua   2 September 1817   Bond No. 39
Wards: Hannah Morris & Joseph Morris orphans of Joshua Morris
Guardian: Anderson Morris   Bond amount: 1000 pounds
Bondsmen: Anderson Morris, Mordecai Morris, Matthew Overman

Morris, Mark   2 September 1817   Bond No. 40
Wards: Mark & Sarah Morris orphans of Mark Morris deceased
Guardian: Matthew Overman   Bond amount: 500 pounds
Bondsmen: Matthew Overman, Mordecai Morris, Anderson Morris

Morris, Thomas   2 December 1817   Bond No. 47
Wards: Penniah & Nathan Morris orphans of Thomas Morris
Guardian: Matthew Overman   Bond amount: 1000 pounds
Bondsmen: Matthew Overman, John Lowry, Anderson Morris

Morris, Thomas   2 December 1817   Bond No. 48
Wards: Margaret Morris & James Morris orphans of Thomas Morris deceased
Guardian: Matthew Overman   Bond amount: 1000 pounds
Bondsmen: Matthew Overman, John Lowry, Anderson Morris

Guardian Bond Book 1816 - 1822

Morris, Thomas 7 March 1820 Bond No. 119
Wards: Margaret Morris, Joshua Morris & Sarah Ann Morris
orphans of Thomas Morris deceased
Guardian: Anderson Morris Bond amount: 2000 pounds
Bondsmen: Anderson Morris, Mordecai Morris, William Trueblood

Newby, James 3 December 1821 Bond No. 165
Wards: Mary Ann & James Newby orphans of James Newby
Guardian: Ann Newby Bond amount: 500 pounds
Bondsmen: Ann Newby, Benjamin Pritchard, Thomas Jordan

Nicholson, Christopher 8 December 1818 Bond No. 94
Ward: Jean Nicholson orphan of Christopher Nicholson deceased
Guardian: Stephen Mullen Bond amount: 1000 pounds
Bondsmen: Stephen Mullen, James Whidbee, Rowan Barclift

Nicholson, Henley 8 March 1820 Bond No. 131
Wards: Polly & Elizabeth Nicholson children of Henley Nicholson*
Guardian: Richard Muse Bond amount: 1000 pounds
Bondsmen: Richard Muse, Ambrose Knox William T. Muse
*(*Note: the word orphan was scratched out)*

Nicholson, Henley 4 February 1822 Bond No. 188
Wards: Mary & Elizabeth Nicholson children of Henley Nicholson*
Guardian: Joshua A. Pool Bond amount: 1500 pounds
Bondsmen: Joshua A. Pool, William Trueblood, Abner Williams
*(*Note: the word orphan was scratched out)*

Nixon, James 8 December 1818 Bond No. 90
Wards: Margaret & Samuel Nixon orphans of James Nixon deceased
Guardian: Sarah Perry Bond amount: 200 pounds
Bondsmen: Sarah Perry, John Winslow, Richard Pool

Overman, Charles 4 March 1818 Bond No. 53
Ward: Susannah Overman orphan of Charles Overman deceased
Guardian: Joseph Parker Bond amount: 500 pounds
Bondsmen: Joseph Parker, Thomas Shannonhouse, William Muse

Overman, Charles 4 March 1818 Bond No. 54
Ward: Ann Overman orphan of Charles Overman deceased
Guardian: Joseph Parker Bond amount: 500 pounds
Bondsmen: Joseph Parker, Thomas Shannonhouse, William Muse

Overman, Charles 4 March 1818 Bond No. 55
Ward: Elizabeth Overman orphan of Charles Overman deceased
Guardian: Joseph Parker Bond amount: 500 pounds
Bondsmen: Joseph Parker, Thomas Shannonhouse, William Muse

Overman, Mordecai 7 December 1819 Bond No. 112
Ward: George Overman orphan of Mordecai Overman deceased
Guardian: Henry P. Overman Bond amount: 1000 pounds
Bondsmen: Henry P. Overman, William W. Freshwater,
    Thaddeus Freshwater

Overman, Mordecai 7 January 1822 Bond No. 179
Ward: George *(H. or M.)* orphan of Mordecai Overman deceased
Guardian: Nathan Overman Bond amount: 1500 pounds
Bondsmen: Nathan Overman, Thaddeus Freshwater, Benoni
    Cartwright

Overman, Nathan 8 June 1819 Bond No. 107
Wards: Mary Overman, Martha Overman & Elizabeth Overman
    orphans of Nathan Overman deceased
Guardian: Benjamin Morgan Bond amount: 300 pounds
Bondsmen: Benjamin Morgan, Nathan Bundy, Robert Perry

Overman, Nathan 7 March 1821 Bond No. 154
Ward: Martha Overman orphan of Nathan Overman deceased
Guardian: Charles Overman Bond amount: 150 pounds
Bondsmen: Charles Overman, David Griffin, John Weeks

Overman, Nathan 7 March 1821 Bond No. 155
Ward: Elizabeth Overman orphan of Nathan Overman deceased
Guardian: Charles Overman Bond amount: 150 pounds
Bondsmen: Charles Overman, David Griffin, John Weeks

Guardian Bond Book 1816 - 1822

Overman, Nathan   7 March 1821   Bond No. 156
Ward: Polly Overman orphan of Nathan Overman deceased
Guardian: Charles Overman   Bond amount: 150 pounds
Bondsmen: Charles Overman, David Griffin, John Weeks

Overman, Robert   3 June 1818   Bond No. 62
Ward: Robert Overman orphan of Robert Overman deceased
Guardian: William Wilson   Bond amount: 300 pounds
Bondsmen: William Wilson, Thomas Shannonhouse, William Muse

Overman, Robert   4 March 1818   Bond No. 73
Ward: Samuel Overman orphan of Robert Overman deceased
Guardian: Benjamin Bailey   Bond amount: 500 pounds
Bondsmen: Benjamin Bailey, William Allen, Charles Bailey

Overman, Thomas   3 June 1817   Bond No. 28
Ward: Sarah Overman orphan of Thomas Overman deceased
Guardian: George Bailey   Bond amount: 100 pounds
Bondsmen: George Bailey, Hezekiah Jackson, John Bailey

Overman, Thomas   2 December 1817   Bond No. 42
Wards: Thomas Overman & Demsey Overman orphans of Thomas
       Overman deceased
Guardian: Benjamin Bailey   Bond amount: 500 pounds
Bondsmen: Benjamin Bailey, Charles Bailey, James Ackiss

Overman, Thomas   4 February 1822   Bond No. 186
Ward: Thomas Overman orphan of Thomas Overman deceased
Guardian: Benjamin Bailey   Bond amount: 250 pounds
Bondsmen: Benjamin Bailey, Robert Bailey, George Bailey

Overman, Thomas   4 February 1822   Bond No. 187
Ward: Demsey Overman orphan of Thomas Overman deceased
Guardian: Benjamin Bailey   Bond amount: 250 pounds
Bondsmen: Benjamin Bailey, Matthew Morgan, George Bailey

Overton, Archibald 6 June 1821 Bond No. 158
Wards: Mary, Betty, John, Lucy & Delilah Overton orphans of
 Archibald Overton deceased
Guardian: Samuel Brothers Bond amount: 500 pounds
Bondsmen: Samuel Brothers, Wm. Muse, Captain Stephen Charles

Palin, Thomas 4 March 1818 Bond No. 71
Wards: Joseph Palin, Sarah Palin, Henry Palin, John Palin &
 Nancy Palin orphans of Thomas Palin deceased
Guardian: Abner Pendleton Bond amount: 500 pounds
Bondsmen: Abner Pendleton, Henry Overman, Timothy Pendleton

Palmer, Willis 3 June 1818 Bond No. 61
Wards: Asena & *(Grizzy?)* Palmer orphans of Willis Palmer
Guardian: Willis Simpson Bond amount: 500 pounds
Bondsmen: Willis Simpson, Nathan Brite, Reuben Brothers

Parr, Noah 4 June 1818 Bond No. 77
Ward: Millie Parr orphan of Noah Parr deceased
Guardian: Leonard Martin Bond amount: 500 pounds
Bondsmen: Leonard Martin, John Casse, Abner Williams

Pendleton, George 4 February 1822 Bond No. 180
Ward: Nancy Pendleton orphan of George Pendleton deceased
Guardian: Edmund H. Perkins Bond amount: 6000 dollars*
Bondsmen: Edmund H. Perkins, Simon B. Pool, Timothy Pendleton
 (*Note: the word pounds was scratched out)

Pendleton, George 4 February 1822 Bond No. 181
Ward: Maranda Pendleton orphan of George Pendleton deceased
Guardian: Edmund H. Perkins Bond amount: 6000 dollars*
Bondsmen: Edmund H. Perkins, Simon B. Pool, Timothy Pendleton
 (*Note: the word pounds was scratched out)

Pendleton, John T. 3 September 1816 Bond No. 11
Ward: John Pendleton orphan of John T. Pendleton deceased
Guardian: Abner Pendleton Bond amount: 500 pounds
Bondsmen: Abner Pendleton, John Cartwright, Thomas Markham

Guardian Bond Book 1816 - 1822

Perry, Cader 6 March 1820 Bond No. 118
Wards: Cader Perry, Robinson Perry & Sarah Perry orphans of
  Cader Perry deceased
Guardian: Sarah Perry Bond amount: 1000 pounds
Bondsmen: Sarah Perry, John B. Perry, William Perry

Pike, Jesse 3 December 1817 Bond No. 50
Wards: Jesse Pike, Pharibe Pike & Wilson Pike orphans of Jesse
  Pike deceased
Guardian: Jehu Cartwright Bond amount: 1000 pounds
Bondsmen: Jehu Cartwright, Thomas Pool, John Casse

Pike, Jesse 6 December 1820 Bond No. 150
Wards: Jesse Pike, Ferbee Pike & Wilson Pike orphans of Jesse Pike
Guardian: Steven Taylor Bond amount: 5000 pounds
Bondsmen: Steven Taylor, John Morris, Robert Simpson

Pike, Jesse 4 February 1822 Bond No. 189
Ward: Jesse Pike orphan of Jesse Pike deceased
Guardian: Abner Williams Bond amount: 1500 pounds
Bondsmen: Abner Williams, Joshua A. Pool, John Casse

Pike, Jesse 4 February 1822 Bond No. 190
Wards: Fereby & Wilson Pike orphans of Jesse Pike deceased
Guardian: Abner Williams Bond amount: 1500 pounds
Bondsmen: Abner Williams, Joshua A. Pool, John Casse

Pool, Isaac 1 December 1817 Bond No. 41
Ward: Patrick Pool orphan of Isaac Pool deceased
Guardian: Thomas Pool Jr. Bond amount: 1000 pounds
Bondsmen: Thomas Pool Jr., John Pool Sr., Richard Pool

Pritchard, Caleb 7 March 1821 Bond No. 152
Ward: Benjamin Pritchard orphan of Caleb Pritchard deceased
Guardian: Benjamin Pritchard Bond amount: 200 pounds
Bondsmen: Benjamin Pritchard, Joseph Pritchard, Aaron White

Pritchard, James 5 June 1816 Bond No. 6
Ward: William Pritchard orphan of James Pritchard deceased
Guardian: John Pool Bond amount: 1000 pounds
Bondsmen: John Pool Sr., James Pool, Richard Pool

Pritchard, James 5 June 1816 Bond No. 7
Wards: Mary & Margaret Pritchard orphans of James Pritchard
Guardian: John Pool Sr. Bond amount: 2000 pounds
Bondsmen: John Pool Sr., James Pool, Richard Pool

Pritchard, James 5 June 1816 Bond No. 8
Wards: Ann & Sarah Pritchard orphans of James Pritchard deceased
Guardian: John Pool Bond amount: 2000 pounds
Bondsmen: John Pool Sr., James Pool, Richard Pool

Pritchard, John 9 September 1818 Bond No. 85
Wards: William Pritchard, Peggy Pritchard & Sally Pritchard
      orphans of John Pritchard deceased
Guardian: John Casse Bond amount: 500 pounds
Bondsmen: John Casse, Willis Simpson, William Scott

Pritchard, Richard 5 September 1821 Bond No. 161
Wards: Josiah Pritchard, Peter Pritchard & Philip Pritchard
      orphans of Richard Pritchard deceased
Guardian: Lemuel Jennings Bond amount: 1000 pounds
Bondsmen: Lemuel Jennings, Robert Weymouth, Jeremiah Sawyer

Pritchard, Richard 8 September 1818 Bond No. 84
Wards: Josiah Pritchard, Peter Pritchard & Philip Pritchard
      orphans of Richard Pritchard deceased
Guardian: Samuel Jennings Bond amount: 1500 pounds
Bondsmen: Samuel Jennings, Robert Weymouth, Jeremiah Sawyer

Proby, Paul 8 September 1818 Bond No. 66
Ward: Sarah Proby orphan of Paul Proby deceased
Guardian: Thomas Pritchard Bond amount: 200 pounds
Bondsmen: Thos. Pritchard, Rubin Brothers, Benjamin Pritchard Jr.

Guardian Bond Book 1816 - 1822

Raper, Cornelius 8 June 1819 Bond No. 105
Wards: Franny Raper, Samuel Raper & Robert Raper orphans of
　　Cornelius Raper deceased
Guardian: Benjamin Bailey Bond amount: 500 pounds
Bondsmen: Benjamin Bailey, Charles Bailey, Robert Bailey

Raper, Henry 4 March 1818 Bond No. 52
Wards: Joshua Raper & Ann Raper orphans of Henry Raper
Guardian: Richard Pool Bond amount: 1000 pounds
Bondsmen: Richard Pool, James Pool, John Pool

Raper, John 3 September 1816 Bond No. 14
Wards: John Robert Raper & Patsey Raper orphans of John Raper
Guardian: Caleb Raper Bond amount: 1000 pounds
Bondsmen: Caleb Raper, William Allen, Rowan Barclift

Relfe, Joseph 7 June 1820 Bond No. 139
Wards: Stephen Relfe, Joseph Relfe, Malachi Relfe & Josiah Relfe
　　orphans of Joseph Relfe deceased
Guardian: William Wilson Bond amount: 1000 pounds
Bondsmen: William Wilson, William T. Muse

Relfe, Josiah 6 June 1816 Bond No. 9
Ward: Nancy Relfe orphan of Josiah Relfe deceased
Guardian: Joseph Relfe Bond amount: 1000 pounds
Bondsmen: Joseph Relfe, William T. Muse, Matthias Smithson

Richardson, Miles 8 December 1818 Bond No. 91
Wards: Elizabeth Richardson, Polly Richardson & Miles
　　Richardson orphans of Miles Richardson deceased
Guardian: George Ferebee Bond amount: 200 pounds
Bondsmen: George Ferebee, Stephen Charles, Thomas Temple

Richardson, Miles 8 December 1818 Bond No. 92
Wards: Sally Richardson & Benjamin Richardson orphans of
　　Miles Richardson deceased
Guardian: George Ferebee Bond amount: 500 pounds
Bondsmen: George Ferebee, Stephen Charles, Thomas Temple

Riggs, Samuel   7 January 1822   Bond No. 177
Wards: Reddick Riggs & James Riggs orphans of Samuel Riggs
Guardian: David Jennings   Bond amount: 100 pounds
Bondsmen: David Jennings, Joseph Harris, Iara Davis

Roberts, Joshua   4 September 1816   Bond No. 20
Ward: Patsey Roberts child of Joshua Roberts*
Guardian: John McDonald   Bond amount: 200 pounds
Bondsmen: John McDonald, Thomas Jordan, Thaddeus Freshwater
   (*note: the word Orphan was scratched out)

Rowe, John   7 January 1822   Bond No. 175
Ward: John Rowe orphan of John Rowe deceased
Guardian: Joshua Pool   Bond amount: 500 pounds
Bondsmen: Joshua Pool, William C. George, Solomon Pool Jr.

Russell, James   4 December 1816   Bond No. 23
Wards: Elizabeth Russel & Malachi Russell orphans of James
       Russell deceased
Guardian: Isaac Overman   Bond amount: 1000 pounds
Bondsmen: Isaac Overman, Charles Grice, William T. Muse

Sawyer, Caleb   2 September 1817   Bond No. 37
Wards: Thomas & Mary Sawyer orphans of Caleb Sawyer deceased
Guardian: Evan Forbes   Bond amount: 500 pounds
Bondsmen: Evan Forbes, Jeremiah Forbes, Joseph Perkins

Sawyer, Thomas   2 June 1818   Bond No. 76
Wards: Mary & William Sawyer orphans of Thomas Sawyer
Guardian: James Gregory   Bond amount: 3000 pounds
Bondsmen: James Gregory, Benoni Cartwright, John N. Barron

Sawyer, Thomas   9 March 1820   Bond No. 133
Wards: Polly Sawyer & William Sawyer orphans of Thomas
       Sawyer deceased
Guardian: Timothy Pendleton   Bond amount: 2000 pounds
Bondsmen: Timothy Pendleton, William Muse, John Ehringhaus

Guardian Bond Book 1816 - 1822

Scott, James　　　　　2 March 1819　　　Bond No. 98
Ward: Margaret Scott orphan of James Scott deceased
Guardian: John C. Ehringhaus　　　Bond amount: 300 pounds
Bondsmen: John C. Ehringhaus, William Martin, John Mullen

Scott, Marmaduke　　　4 December 1816　　Bond No. 22
Wards: Miriam Scott, Nancy Scott & Armon Scott orphans of
　　　　Marmaduke Scott deceased
Guardian: David Pritchard　　　Bond amount: 2000 pounds
Bondsmen: David Pritchard, John Rowe, Lemuel Jackson

Scott, Marmaduke　　　4 December 1816　　Bond No. 25
Wards: Susannah Scott, George Scott & Sophia Scott orphans of
　　　　Marmaduke Scott deceased
Guardian: David Pritchard　　　Bond amount: 2000 pounds
Bondsmen: David Pritchard, John Rowe, Lemual Jackson

Scott, Marmaduke　　　9 September 1818　　Bond No. 86
Wards: Milly & Nancy Scott orphans of Marmaduke Scott
Guardian: Jacob Richardson　　　Bond amount: 1000 pounds
Bondsmen: Jacob Richardson, Joel Sawyer, Daniel McPherson

Scott, Marmaduke　　　9 September 1818　　Bond No. 87
Wards: Armon & Anna Scott orphans of Marmaduke Scott
Guardian: Jacob Richardson　　　Bond amount: 1000 pounds
Bondsmen: Jacob Richardson, Joel Sawyer, Daniel McPherson

Scott, Marmaduke　　　9 September 1818　　Bond No. 88
Wards: Susan, George & Stephen orphans of Marmaduke Scott
Guardian: Jacob Richardson　　　Bond amount: 1500 pounds
Bondsmen: Jacob Richardson, Joel Sawyer, Daniel McPherson

Scott, Thomas　　　　3 March 1819　　　Bond No. 99
Ward: Ruben Scott orphan of Thomas Scott deceased
Guardian: Stephen Scott　　　Bond amount: 300 pounds
Bondsmen: Stephen Scott, Robert Scott, Robert Simpson

Scott, Thomas 3 March 1819 Bond No. 101
Ward: Thomas Scott orphan of Thomas Scott deceased
Guardian: Stephen Scott Bond amount: 300 pounds
Bondsmen: Stephen Scott, Robert Simpson, Robert Scott

Shepherd, Cyprian 7 March 1820 Bond No. 121
Wards: John Shepherd, Ann Shepherd & Margaret Shepherd
    orphans of Cyprian Shepherd deceased
Guardian: John C. Ehringhaus Bond amount: 500 pounds
Bondsmen: John C. Ehringhaus, Ambrose Knox, William T. Muse

Snowden, Thaddeus 5 September 1820 Bond No. 141
Ward: William Snowden orphan of Thaddeus Snowden deceased
Guardian: William Snowden Bond amount: 50 pounds
Bondsmen: William Snowden, Lemuel Snowden, James Turner

Spence, Samuel 4 September 1821 Bond No. 160
Ward: Joseph Spence orphan of Samuel Spence deceased
Guardian: Willis Spence Bond amount: 500 pounds
Bondsmen: Willis Spence, Thomas Temple, James Smith

Stafford, John 2 July 1821 Bond No. 159
Ward: Joseph Stafford orphan of John Stafford deceased
Guardian: James Harris Bond amount: 100 pounds
Bondsmen: James Harris, John C. Ehringhaus

Stott, Thomas 2 September 1817 Bond No. 33
Ward: William Stott orphan of Thomas Stott deceased
Guardian: James Pool Bond amount: 2000 pounds
Bondsmen: James Pool Jr., John Pool Sr., Richard Pool

Temple, Joseph 2 September 1817 Bond No. 34
Ward: Dozier Temple orphan of Joseph Temple deceased
Guardian: Robert Temple Bond amount: 1000 pounds
Bondsmen: Robert Temple, James Temple, Mark Williams

Guardian Bond Book 1816 - 1822

Thompson, Henry 6 June 1820 Bond No. 136
Ward: John Thompson orphan of Henry Thompson deceased
Guardian: Edmund Trueblood Bond amount: 500 pounds
Bondsmen: Edmund Trueblood, Abner Williams, Stephen Stafford

Trueblood, James 9 December 1818 Bond No. 95
Wards: Wilson Trueblood & Malachi Trueblood orphans of James
    Trueblood deceased
Guardian: Isaac Overman Bond amount: 500 pounds
Bondsmen: Isaac Overman, George F. Overman, Joshua Trueblood

Trueblood, John 7 January 1822 Bond No. 176
Wards: Sarah Trueblood, Clarkey Trueblood, Fred B. Trueblood,
    Josiah Trueblood & Stephen Trueblood orphans of John
    Trueblood deceased
Guardian: Joshua A. Pool Bond amount: 750 pounds
Bondsmen: Joshua A. Pool, William C. George, Solomon Pool Jr.

Trueblood, Samuel 3 March 1819 Bond No. 102
Ward: Mary Trueblood orphan of Samuel Trueblood deceased
Guardian: Robert Bailey Bond amount: 1000 pounds
Bondsmen: Robert Bailey, George Bailey, John Bailey

Trueblood, Samuel 5 December 1820 Bond No. 145
Wards: Exum Trueblood & Andrew Trueblood orphans of Samuel
    Trueblood deceased
Guardian: William Trueblood Bond amount: 3000 pounds
Bondsmen: William Trueblood, Nathan Morris, Anderson Morris

Warner, Samuel 7 March 1820 Bond No. 122
Wards: Margaret, Mary, Priscilla, (*Muhuly*) & William Warner
    orphans of Samuel Warner deceased
Guardian: Margaret Warner Bond amount: 5000 pounds
Bondsmen: Margaret Warner, Samuel Warner, J. H. Robertson,
    Anthony R. Markham

Weymouth, Thomas 9 September 1818 Bond No. 89
Ward: Wilson Weymouth orphan of Thomas Weymouth deceased
Guardian: Robert Weymouth   Bond amount: 1000 pounds
Bondsmen: Robert Weymouth, Frederick Whitehurst, Lemuel
    Jennings

White, Benjamin 5 June 1816 Bond No. 2
Ward: Benjamin White orphan of Benjamin White deceased
Guardian: Malachi Jackson   Bond amount: 2000 pounds
Bondsmen: Malachi Jackson, Bailey Davis, Ambrose Knox

White, Benjamin 2 March 1818 Bond No. 51*
Wards: Samuel and Elizabeth White orphans of Benjamin White
Guardian: James Turner   Bond amount: 1000 pounds
Bondsmen: James Turner
    (*Note: the bond number was scratched out)

White, Benjamin 2 June 1818 Bond No. 57
Ward: Benjamin White orphan of Benjamin White deceased
Guardian: William Perry   Bond amount: 500 pounds
Bondsmen: William Perry, Nathan Morgan, Eli White

White, Benjamin 4 March 1818 Bond No. 72
Wards: Samuel & Elizabeth White orphans of Benjamin White
Guardian: Henry P. Overman   Bond amount: 200 pounds
Bondsmen: Henry P. Overman, James Pool, William Wilson

White, Benjamin 2 June 1818 Bond No. 78
Ward: Lydia White orphan of Benjamin White deceased
Guardian: William Perry   Bond amount: 300 pounds
Bondsmen: William Perry, Nathan Morgan, Benjamin Bailey

White, Benjamin 2 June 1818 Bond No. 79
Wards: George & Miley White orphans of Benjamin White
Guardian: Eli White   Bond amount: 700 pounds
Bondsmen: Eli White, Nathan Morgan, Benjamin Bailey

Guardian Bond Book 1816 - 1822

White, Benjamin　　　7 June 1819　　　Bond No. 104
Ward: Benjamin White orphan of Benjamin White deceased
Guardian: Joseph Keaton　　　Bond amount: 1000 pounds
Bondsmen: Joseph Keaton, William T. Muse, Malachi Jackson

White, Benjamin　　　7 January 1822　　　Bond No. 172
Wards: Samuel & Elizabeth White orphans of Benjamin White
Guardian: William W. Freshwater　　　Bond amount: 750 pounds
Bondsmen: Wm. W. Freshwater, Edmund H. Perkins, L. B. Pool

White, James　　　5 June 1821　　　Bond No. 157
Wards: Patsy & Mary White orphans of James White deceased
Guardian: Nancy White　　　Bond amount: 300 pounds
Bondsmen: Nancy White, Henry P. Overman, William C. George

White, Josiah　　　1 September 1817　　　Bond No. 32
Ward: Rebecca White orphan of Josiah White Jr. deceased
Guardian: Joseph Pritchard　　　Bond amount: 100 pounds
Bondsmen: Joseph Pritchard, Benjamin Pritchard Jr., Thomas
　　　　　Jordan Jr.

White, Josiah　　　8 September 1818　　　Bond No. 81
Wards: Jennetta & Anna White orphans of Josiah White deceased
Guardian: David White　　　Bond amount: 1000 pounds
Bondsmen: David White, Nathan Morris, Edmund White

White, Josiah　　　8 September 1818　　　Bond No. 82
Wards: Martha & Jeptha White orphans of Josiah White deceased
Guardian: David White　　　Bond amount: 1000 pounds
Bondsmen: David White, Nathan Morris, Edmund White

White, Stephen　　　8 June 1819　　　Bond No. 108
Ward: Martha White orphan of Stephen White deceased
Guardian: Robert Perry　　　Bond amount: 500 pounds
Bondsmen: Robert Perry, John Winslow, Benjamin Morgan

White, Stephen 6 June 1820 Bond No. 137
Ward: Matthew White orphan of Stephen White deceased
Guardian: Robert Perry Bond amount: 1000 pounds
Bondsmen: Robert Perry, John Winslow, John Weeks

Williams, David L. 4 March 1818 Bond No. 56
Ward: John Thomas Williams orphan of David L. Williams
Guardian: Thomas Commander Bond amount: 2000 pounds
Bondsmen: Thomas Commander, John Lowery, William Barns

Williams, Lodowick 3 June 1817 Bond No. 29
Ward: Evan Williams orphan of Lodowick Williams deceased
Guardian: Smith Jones Bond amount: 500 pounds
Bondsmen: Smith Jones, James Temple, Robert Temple

Williams, Lodowick 5 September 1820 Bond No. 142
Ward: Mary Williams daughter of Lodowick Williams who was
  found to be in a state of lunacy*
Guardian: James Jones Bond amount: 500 pounds
Bondsmen: James Jones, John Richardson, Tully Varden
  (*Note: the word orphan was scratched out)

Wilroy, Nathaniel 3 March 1819 Bond No. 100
Ward: Nathaniel Wilroy orphan of Nathaniel Wilroy deceased
Guardian: William Martin Bond amount: 1000 pounds
Bondsmen: William Martin, Lemuel C. Moore, Samuel Matthews

Wilson, Frances 4 December 1821 Bond No. 167
Ward: Milly Wilson orphan of Francis Wilson deceased
Guardian: Carter Barnard Bond amount: 400 pounds
Bondsmen: Carter Barnard, Jesse Bernard, Nathan O. Morris

Pasquotank County, North Carolina
Guardian Bonds
Book 1822 - 1824

Allen, William 2 March 1824 Bond No. 230
Wards: James P., Thomas, Nancy, Lucy & Mary Allen orphans of
   William Allen deceased
Guardian: Carter Barnard Bond amount: 10,000 pounds
Bondsmen: Carter Barnard, James Pool, Thomas Commander

Bailey, Benjamin 5 March 1822 Bond No. 30
Ward: Joseph Bailey orphan of Benjamin Bailey
Guardian: William H. Davis Bond amount: 500 pounds
Bondsmen: William H. Davis, Ambrose Knox, William T. Muse

Bailey, Benjamin   5 March 1822   Bond No. 31
Ward: Rebecca Bailey orphan of Benjamin Bailey deceased
Guardian: William H. Davis   Bond amount: 500 pounds
Bondsmen: William H. Davis, Ambrose Knox, William T. Muse

Bailey, Benjamin   5 March 1822   Bond No. 32
Ward: John Bailey orphan of Benjamin Bailey deceased
Guardian: William H. Davis   Bond amount: 500 pounds
Bondsmen: William H. Davis, Ambrose Knox, William T. Muse

Bailey, Benjamin   5 March 1822   Bond No. 33
Ward: Mary C. Bailey orphan of Benjamin Bailey deceased
Guardian: William H. Davis   Bond amount: 500 pounds
Bondsmen: William H. Davis, Ambrose Knox, William T. Muse

Bailey, David   5 March 1822   Bond No. 131
Ward: Nancy Bailey orphan of David Bailey deceased
Guardian: Malachi Jackson   Bond amount: 200 pounds
Bondsmen: Malachi Jackson, Ambrose Knox, William H. Davis

Bailey, John   5 May 1823   Bond No. 180
Wards: Polly, Tamer and John Bailey orphans of John Bailey
Guardian: Benjamin Bailey   Bond amount: 500 pounds
Bondsmen: Benjamin Bailey, George Bailey, John Bailey

Bailey, Thomas   5 March 1822   Bond No. 73
Ward: Mary Bailey orphan of Thomas Bailey deceased
Guardian: John Bailey   Bond amount: 1000 pounds
Bondsmen: John Bailey, Robert Bailey, George Bailey

Banks, Jonathan   (*No Date*)   Bond No. 41
Ward: William Banks orphan of Jonathan Banks deceased
Guardian: Thaddeus Freshwater   Bond amount: 700 pounds
Bondsmen: Thaddeus Freshwater, Wm. Hardy, Wm. W. Freshwater

Banks, Jonathan   5 March 1822   Bond No. 42
Ward: Martha Banks orphan of Jonathan Banks deceased
Guardian: Thaddeus Freshwater   Bond amount: 700 pounds
Bondsmen: Thaddeus Freshwater, Wm. Hardy, Wm. W. Freshwater

Guardian Bond Book 1822 - 1824

Banks, Jonathan   5 March 1822   Bond No. 43
Ward: Thaddeus Banks orphan of Jonathan Banks
Guardian: Thaddeus Freshwater   Bond amount: 700 pounds
Bondsmen: Thaddeus Freshwater, Wm. Hardy, William W. Freshwater

Banks, Jonathan   5 March 1822   Bond No. 44
Ward: Jonathan Banks orphan of Jonathan Banks
Guardian: Thaddeus Freshwater   Bond amount: 700 pounds
Bondsmen: Thaddeus Freshwater, Wm. Hardy, William W. Freshwater

Banks, Jonathan   2 December 1823   Bond No. 198
Wards: John, Thaddeus & Patsy Banks orphans of Jonathan Banks
Guardian: William Banks   Bond amount: 8000 dollars *
Bondsmen: Wm. Banks, Thaddeus Freshwater, Lemuel Snowden
*(*Note: the word pounds was scratched out)*

Banks, Thomas   5 March 1822   Bond No. 24
Ward: Jonathan Banks orphan of Thomas Banks deceased
Guardian: William T. Muse   Bond amount: 1000 pounds
Bondsmen: William T. Muse, Ambrose Knox, William H. Davis

Banks, Thomas   5 March 1822   Bond No. 25
Ward: Thomas Banks orphan of Thomas Banks deceased
Guardian: William T. Muse   Bond amount: 1000 pounds
Bondsmen: William T. Muse, Ambrose Knox, William H. Davis

Banks, Thomas   5 March 1822   Bond No. 26
Ward: Reding Banks orphan of Thomas Banks deceased
Guardian: William T. Muse   Bond amount: 1000 pounds
Bondsmen: William T. Muse, Ambrose Knox, William H. Davis

Banks, Thomas   5 May 1823   Bond No. 179
Ward: William Banks orphan of Thomas Banks deceased
Guardian: Benoni Cartwright   Bond amount: 500 pounds
Bondsmen: Benoni Cartwright, James Gregory, Broshir Pool

Banks, Thomas　　　　　　3 September 1823　　Bond No. 191
Ward: Redding Banks orphan of Thomas Banks deceased
Guardian: James Pool　　　　　Bond amount: 5000 pounds
Bondsmen: James Pool Sr., Thaddeus Freshwater, Richard Pool

Banks, Thomas　　　　　　2 December 1823　　Bond No. 196
Ward: Thomas Banks orphan of Thomas Banks deceased
Guardian: Jonathan Banks　　　Bond amount: 5000 dollars *
Bondsmen: Jonathan Banks, James Pool, Solomon Pool
　　　　(*Note: the word pounds was scratched out)

Banks, Thomas　　　　　　2 February 1824　　Bond No. 223
Ward: William Banks orphan of Thomas Banks deceased
Guardian: Jonathan Banks　　　Bond amount: 4000 dollars*
Bondsmen: Jonathan Banks, James Pool, George Gaskins
　　　　(*Note: the word pounds was scratched out)

Benton, James　　　　　　4 June 1822　　Bond No. 147
Wards: Margaret, James & Lemuel Benton orphans of James Benton
Guardian: William Gregory　　　Bond amount: 100 pounds
Bondsmen: William Gregory, John C. Ehringhaus

Boushall, Thomas　　　　　3 December 1823　　Bond No. 207
Ward: Penelope Boushall orphan of Thomas Boushall deceased
Guardian: William Wilson　　　Bond amount: 1000 dollars*
Bondsmen: William Wilson, Ambrose Knox
　　　　(*Note: the word pounds was scratched out)

Brite, Jabez　　　　　　　3 September 1822　　Bond No. 152
Wards: Charles, Jesse, Jabez & Mary Bright orphans of Jabez Brite*
Guardian: Benjamin Pritchard　　Bond amount: 1000 pounds
Bondsmen: Benjamin Pritchard, Thomas Pool Jr.
　　　(*Note: Both spellings for the surname were used as shown)

Broshir, John L.　　　　　5 March 1822　　Bond No. 45
Ward: William Broshir orphan of John L. Broshir deceased
Guardian: Thaddeus Freshwater　Bond amount: 4000 pounds
Bondsmen: Thaddeus Freshwater, Wm. Hardy, William W.
　　　　Freshwater

Guardian Bond Book 1822 - 1824

Broshir, Joseph *(No Date)* Bond No. 46
Ward: Benjamin Broshir orphan of Joseph Broshir deceased
Guardian: Thaddeus Freshwater   Bond amount: 250 pounds
Bondsmen: Thaddeus Freshwater, Wm. Hardy, William W. Freshwater

Broshir, Joseph 5 March 1822 Bond No. 47
Ward: Ann Broshir orphan of Joseph Broshir deceased
Guardian: Thaddeus Freshwater   Bond amount: 250 pounds
Bondsmen: Thaddeus Freshwater, Wm. Hardy, William W. Freshwater

Brothers, Richard 4 June 1823 Bond No. 184
Wards: Clark, Elizabeth, James & Nancy Brothers orphans of Richard Brothers deceased
Guardian: William Fletcher   Bond amount: 1000 pounds
Bondsmen: William Fletcher, Aaron Fletcher

Bundy, Benjamin 6 January 1823 Bond No. 162
Ward: Jesse Bundy orphan of Benjamin Bundy deceased
Guardian: Caleb Morris   Bond amount: 100 pounds
Bondsmen: Caleb Morris, Joshua Morris

Bundy, Benjamin 6 January 1823 Bond No. 163
Ward: Ricks Bundy orphan of Benjamin Bundy deceased
Guardian: Caleb Morris   Bond amount: 100 pounds
Bondsmen: Caleb Morris, Joshua Morris

Bundy, James 4 March 1822 Bond No. 7
Ward: William Bundy orphan of James Bundy deceased
Guardian: Jacob Symons   Bond amount: 300 pounds
Bondsmen: Jacob Symons, Simon Delon, Benjamin Bundy

Bundy, Joseph 4 March 1822 Bond No. 5
Ward: Ricks Bundy orphan of Joseph Bundy deceased
Guardian: Jacob Symons   Bond amount: 300 pounds
Bondsmen: Jacob Symons, Simon Delon, Benjamin Bundy

Pasquotank County, North Carolina

Bundy, Joseph   4 March 1822   Bond No. 6
Ward: Nancy Bundy orphan of Joseph Bundy deceased
Guardian: Jacob Symons   Bond amount: 300 pounds
Bondsmen: Jacob Symons, Simon Delon, Benjamin Bundy

Burnham, Thomas   3 February 1823   Bond No. 167
Ward: Nancy Burnham orphan of Thomas Burnham deceased
Guardian: Thomas Temple   Bond amount: 200 pounds
Bondsmen: Thomas Temple, Abel Sawyer, Seth Williams

Cartwright, McKeel   5 March 1822   Bond No. 83
Ward: John Cartwright orphan of McKeel Cartwright deceased
Guardian: Lemuel Snowden   Bond amount: 500 pounds
Bondsmen: Lemuel Snowden, Benjamin M. Jackson, William W. Freshwater

Cartwright, Thomas   5 March 1822   Bond No. 64
Ward: Malachi Cartwright orphan of Thomas Cartwright deceased
Guardian: Abner Williams   Bond amount: 300 pounds
Bondsmen: Abner Williams, Edmund Trueblood, David Sharber

Cartwright, Thomas   5 March 1822   Bond No. 74
Ward: Susannah Cartwright orphan of Thomas Cartwright deceased
Guardian: James Cartwright   Bond amount: 200 pounds
Bondsmen: James Cartwright, Daniel McPherson, James Cartwright

Cartwright, Thomas   5 March 1822   Bond No. 75
Ward: Nancy Cartwright orphan of Thomas Cartwright deceased
Guardian: James Cartwright   Bond amount: 200 pounds
Bondsmen: James Cartwright, Daniel McPherson, James Cartwright

Carver, ____   3 February 1823   Bond No. 168
Ward: Olia Carver orphan of _____ * deceased
Guardian: Abel Sawyer   Bond amount: 600 pounds
Bondsmen: Abel Sawyer, Thomas Temple, James Williams
     (*Note: the names of Polly & Elizabeth are listed as the orphans at a different place on the guardian bond)

Guardian Bond Book 1822 - 1824

Carver, Alfred 4 March 1822 Bond No. 8
Ward: Elias Carver orphan of Alfred Carver deceased
Guardian: John McDonell Bond amount: 1000 pounds
Bondsmen: John MacDonell, Samuel Brothers, William C. George

Carver, Alfred 4 March 1822 Bond No. 9
Ward: Mary Carver orphan of Alfred Carver deceased
Guardian: John McDonell Bond amount: 1000 pounds
Bondsmen: John MacDonell, Samuel Brothers, William C. George

Carver, James 2 September 1822 Bond No. 148
Ward: James Carver orphan of James Carver deceased
Guardian: George Ferebee Bond amount: 1000 pounds
Bondsmen: George Ferebee, Samuel Proctor

Carver, James 2 September 1822 Bond No. 149
Ward: Elias Carver orphan of James Carver deceased
Guardian: George Ferebee Bond amount: 1000 pounds
Bondsmen: George Ferebee, Samuel Proctor

Carver, James 2 September 1822 Bond No. 150
Ward: Nancy Carver orphan of James Carver deceased
Guardian: George Ferebee Bond amount: 1000 pounds
Bondsmen: George Ferebee, Samuel Proctor

Carver, James 2 September 1822 Bond No. 151
Ward: (*Lucky or Sucky?*) Carver orphan of James Carver deceased
Guardian: George Ferebee Bond amount: 1000 pounds
Bondsmen: George Ferebee, Samuel Proctor

Chamberlain, James 5 March 1822 Bond No. 34
Ward: Margaret Chamberlain orphan of James Chamberlain
Guardian: Ambrose Knox Bond amount: 500 pounds
Bondsmen: Ambrose Knox, William T. Muse, William H. Davis

Chamberlain, James 5 March 1822 Bond No. 35
Ward: Mary Chamberlain orphan of James Chamberlain deceased
Guardian: Ambrose Knox Bond amount: 500 pounds
Bondsmen: Ambrose Knox, William T. Muse, William H. Davis

Pasquotank County, North Carolina

Commander, Joseph   5 May 1823   Bond No. 182
Wards: James Commander and Carter Commander orphans of
   Joseph Commander deceased
Guardian: Thomas Barnard   Bond amount: 4000 pounds
Bondsmen: Thomas Barnard, Carter Barnard, William Barns

Commander, Joseph   7 October 1823   Bond No. 192
Ward: Joseph Commander orphan of Joseph Commander deceased
Guardian: Thomas Barnard   Bond amount: 5000 pounds
Bondsmen: Thomas Barnard, Carter Barnard, Thomas Commander

Commander, Joseph   2 December 1823   Bond No. 202
Ward: Joseph Commander orphan of Joseph Commander deceased
Guardian: Parthenia Commander   Bond amount: 10,000 dollars*
Bondsmen: Parthenia Commander, William Barnes, Edmund Blount
   (*Note: the word pounds was scratched out)

Cotter, Timothy   5 March 1822   Bond No. 77
Ward: Timothy Cotter orphan of Timothy Cotter deceased
Guardian: John Caman   Bond amount: 500 pounds
Bondsmen: John Caman, John Winslow, William T. Muse

Cotter, Timothy   5 March 1822   Bond No. 78
Ward: Wilson Cotter orphan of Timothy Cotter deceased
Guardian: John Caman   Bond amount: 500 pounds
Bondsmen: John Caman, John Winslow, William T. Muse

Cotter, Timothy   4 March 1823   Bond No. 174
Wards: Timothy & Wilson Cotter orphans of Timothy Cotter
Guardian: John L. Bailey   Bond amount: 1000 pounds
Bondsmen: John L. Bailey, John Winslow, John Pool, Thomas
   Elliott

Cox, Jacob   3 September 1822   Bond No. 156
Ward: William Cox orphan of Jacob Cox
Guardian: Solomon Pool   Bond amount: 500 pounds
Bondsmen: Solomon Pool, James Pool, John Pool Jr.

Guardian Bond Book 1822 - 1824

Davis, Shadrach 5 March 1822 Bond No. 107
Ward: Elizabeth Davis orphan of Shadrach Davis deceased
Guardian: Daniel McPherson Bond amount: 500 pounds
Bondsmen: Daniel McPherson, John Case, James Cartwright

Delon, William 5 March 1822 Bond No. 50
Ward: Miriam Delon orphan of William Delon deceased
Guardian: Simon Delon Bond amount: 100 pounds
Bondsmen: Simon Delon, Frederick Pendleton, Jesse Delon

Delon, William 5 March 1822 Bond No. 51
Ward: Francis Delon orphan of William Delon deceased
Guardian: Simon Delon Bond amount: 100 pounds
Bondsmen: Simon Delon, Frederick Pendleton, Jesse Delon

Delon, William 5 March 1822 Bond No. 52
Ward: Nancy Delon orphan of William Delon deceased
Guardian: Simon Delon Bond amount: 100 pounds
Bondsmen: Simon Delon, Frederick Pendleton, Jesse Delon

Etherage, James 5 March 1822 Bond No. 119
Ward: Matthias Etherage orphan of James Etherage deceased
Guardian: Robert Bailey Bond amount: 250 pounds
Bondsmen: Robert Bailey, Noah Hollowell, Benjamin Bailey

Etherage, Richard 5 March 1822 Bond No. 79
Ward: Seth Etherage orphan of Richard Etherage deceased
Guardian: Thomas Markham Bond amount: 200 pounds
Bondsmen: Thomas Markham, Thaddeus Freshwater, Frances
   Fletcher

Etherage, Richard 5 March 1822 Bond No. 80
Ward: Morris Etherage orphan of Richard Etherage deceased
Guardian: Thomas Markham Bond amount: 200 pounds
Bondsmen: Thomas Markham, Thaddeus Freshwater, Frances
   Fletcher

Pasquotank County, North Carolina

Etherage, Richard   5 March 1822   Bond No. 81
Ward: William Etherage orphan of Richard Etherage deceased
Guardian: Thomas Markham   Bond amount: 200 pounds
Bondsmen: Thomas Markham, Thaddeus Freshwater, Frances
          Fletcher

Evans, Benjamin   5 March 1822   Bond No. 58
Ward: Ann Evans orphan of Benjamin Evans deceased
Guardian: James Palmer   Bond amount: 200 pounds
Bondsmen: James Palmer, Thomas Commander, Ambrose Knox

Ferebee, James   6 January 1823   Bond No. 161
Ward: Alfred Ferebee child of James Ferebee*
Guardian: James Ferebee   Bond amount: 50 pounds
Bondsmen: James Ferebee, Arthur Heath, David Davis
          (*Note: the word orphan was scratched out)

Gambling, Jesse   5 January 1824   Bond No. 209
Ward: John Gambling orphan of Jesse Gambling deceased
Guardian: David Sharber   Bond amount: 500 dollars*
Bondsmen: David Sharber, Abner Williams, Barney Clark
          (*Note: the word pounds was scratched out)

Gaskins, Thomas   5 March 1822   Bond No. 39
Ward: Nancy Gaskins orphan of Thomas Gaskins deceased
Guardian: William W. Freshwater   Bond amount: 1000 pounds
Bondsmen: William W. Freshwater, Wm. Hardy

Gaskins, William   _ September 1822   Bond No. 157
Ward: Fanny Gaskins orphan of William Gaskins deceased
Guardian: Solomon Pool   Bond amount: 1500 pounds
Bondsmen: Solomon Pool, James Pool, John Pool Jr.

Gaskins, William   3 September 1822   Bond No. 158
Ward: Thomas Gaskins orphan of William Gaskins deceased
Guardian: Solomon Pool   Bond amount: 1500 pounds
Bondsmen: Solomon Pool, James Pool, John Pool Jr.

Guardian Bond Book 1822 - 1824

Gaskins, William 3 September 1822 Bond No. 159
Ward: William Gaskins orphan of William Gaskins deceased
Guardian: Solomon Pool Bond amount: 1500 pounds
Bondsmen: Solomon Pool, James Pool, John Pool Jr.

Gilbert, John 5 March 1822 Bond No. 89
Ward: William Gilbert child of John Gilbert *
Guardian: John Gilbert Bond amount: 200 pounds
Bondsmen: John Gilbert, Hamilton Cotter, John Richardson
  (*Note: The word orphan was scratched out)

Gordon, William 4 March 1822 Bond No. 15
Ward: John D. Gordon orphan of William Gordon deceased
Guardian: William Crutch Bond amount: 250 pounds
Bondsmen: William Crutch, William C. George

Gordon, William 4 March 1822 Bond No. 16
Ward: William Gordon orphan of William Gordon deceased
Guardian: William Crutch Bond amount: 250 pounds
Bondsmen: William Crutch, William C. George

Gordon, William 4 March 1822 Bond No. 17
Ward: Joseph Gordon orphan of William Gordon deceased
Guardian: William Crutch Bond amount: 250 pounds
Bondsmen: William Crutch, William C. George

Greaves, John 3 March 1823 Bond No. 170
Ward: John William Greaves orphan of John Greaves deceased
Guardian: William S. Bagley Bond amount: 250 pounds
Bondsmen: William S. Bagley, Samuel R. Warner, Anthony A.
  Markham

Griffin, Thomas 4 March 1822 Bond No. 19
Ward: Moses Griffin orphan of Thomas Griffin deceased
Guardian: James Morgan Bond amount: 250 pounds
Bondsmen: James Morgan, Nathan Morgan, Eli White

Harris, Isaac 7 September 1824 Bond No. 241
Ward: Grandy Harris orphan of Isaac Harris deceased
Guardian: David Jennings Bond amount: 800 dollars*
Bondsmen: David Jennings, Ruben T. Harris, Barney Clark
(*Note: the word pounds was scratched out)

Harris, John 3 February 1823 Bond No. 169
Ward: Susan Harris orphan of John Harris deceased
Guardian: Lemuel Jennings Bond amount: 200 pounds
Bondsmen: Lemuel Jennings, Reuben Harris, Jeremiah Sawyer

Harris, Thomas 2 February 1824 Bond No. 225
Wards: Davis & Martha Harris orphans of Thomas Harris deceased
Guardian: Barney Clark Bond amount: 500 dollars*
Bondsmen: Barney Clark, James Harris, Josiah Pritchard
(*Note: the word pounds was scratched out)

Harvey, Benjamin 5 March 1823 Bond No. 176
Wards: Julian & Thomas Harvey orphans of Benjamin Harvey
Guardian: Ambrose Knox Bond amount: 250 pounds
Bondsmen: Ambrose Knox, John C. Ehringhaus

(Hos?), George 3 February 1823 Bond No. 166
Wards: Mary & William Hos orphans of George *(Hos?)* deceased
Guardian: Joseph Hos Bond amount: 100 pounds
Bondsmen: Joseph Hos, Ambrose Knox, Lemuel Snowden

Humphries, Jonathan 2 December 1823 Bond No. 205
Ward: Mourning Humphries orphan of Jonathan Humphries
Guardian: John Bray Bond amount: 2000 dollars*
Bondsmen: John Bray, William Bray, Jacob Richardson
(*Note: the word pounds was scratched out)

Humphries, Jonathan 2 December 1823 Bond No. 206
Ward: Richardson R. Humphries orphan of Jonathan Humphries
Guardian: John Bray Bond amount: 2000 dollars*
Bondsmen: John Bray, William Bray, Jacob Richardson
(*Note: the word pounds was scratched out)

Guardian Bond Book 1822 - 1824

Jackson, Arthur 5 March 1822 Bond No. 110
Ward: Maximillian Jackson orphan of Arthur Jackson deceased
Guardian: Jacob Richardson Bond amount: 500 pounds
Bondsmen: Jacob Richardson, Joel Sawyer, John Bray

Jackson, Arthur 5 March 1822 Bond No. 111
Ward: Polly Jackson orphan of Arthur Jackson deceased
Guardian: Jacob Richardson Bond amount: 500 pounds
Bondsmen: Jacob Richardson, Joel Sawyer, John Bray

Jackson, Arthur 5 March 1822 Bond No. 112
Ward: Milly Jackson orphan of Arthur Jackson deceased
Guardian: Jacob Richardson Bond amount: 500 pounds
Bondsmen: Jacob Richardson, Joel Sawyer, John Bray

Jackson, Arthur 5 March 1822 Bond No. 113
Ward: Louisa Jackson orphan of Arthur Jackson deceased
Guardian: Jacob Richardson Bond amount: 500 pounds
Bondsmen: Jacob Richardson, Joel Sawyer, John Bray

Jackson, Arthur 5 March 1822 Bond No. 117
Ward: Sophia Jackson orphan of Arthur Jackson deceased
Guardian: Jacob Richardson Bond amount: 1000 pounds
Bondsmen: Jacob Richardson, Joel Sawyer, John Bray

Jackson, Malachi 2 December 1823 Bond No. 203
Ward: Palin Jackson orphan of Malachi Jackson deceased
Guardian: Barnes B. Jackson Bond amount: 5000 dollars*
Bondsmen: Barnes Jackson, William T. Relfe, William H. Davis
*(*Note: the word pounds was scratched out)*

Jackson, Malachi 2 December 1823 Bond No. 204
Ward: Stephen Jackson orphan of Malachi Jackson deceased
Guardian: Barnes B. Jackson Bond amount: 5000 dollars*
Bondsmen: Barnes B. Jackson, William Relfe, William H. Davis
*(*Note: the word pounds was scratched out)*

Jackson, Mala. (Malachi?) 3 March 1824 Bond No. 233
Ward: Palin Jackson orphan of Mala. Jackson deceased
Guardian: Ambrose Knox Bond amount: 10,000 pounds
Bondsmen: Ambrose Knox, William Wilson, William H. Davis

Jackson, Ma. (Malachi?) 3 March 1824 Bond No. 234
Ward: Stephen Jackson orphan of Ma. Jackson deceased
Guardian: Ambrose Knox Bond amount: 10,000 pounds
Bondsmen: Ambrose Knox, William Wilson, William H. Davis

James, Benjamin 5 March 1822 Bond No. 108
Ward: William James orphan of Benjamin James deceased
Guardian: Lemuel Snowden Bond amount: 1000 pounds
Bondsmen: Lemuel Snowden, William W. Freshwater, Thomas Markham

Jennings, James (Blank) Bond No. 53
Ward: Mary Jennings orphan of James Jennings deceased
Guardian: James Whidbee Bond amount: 2000 pounds
Bondsmen: James Whidbee, Joseph Pritchard, Benjamin Pritchard

Jordan, Thomas L. 2 March 1824 Bond No. 232
Wards: Thomas L. Jordan deceased orphans - *(Jordan heirs)*
Guardian: John White Bond amount: 2000 pounds
Bondsmen: John White, Thomas Jordan, John Tooley

Knox, __le 4 March 1823 Bond No. 175
Ward: Thomas A. Knox orphan of __le Knox deceased
Guardian: William C. Brooks Bond amount: 1500 pounds
Bondsmen: William C. Brooks, Richard Pool, Benjamin Bailey

Lawrence, ___ 2 December 1823 Bond No. 197
Ward: James Lawrence orphan of ___ Lawrence deceased
Guardian: William Barnes Bond amount: 500 dollars *
Bondsmen: William Barnes, Edmund Blount, William Trueblood
   (*Note: the word pounds was scratched out)

Guardian Bond Book 1822 - 1824

Lowry, Benjamin 3 September 1823 Bond No. 189
Wards: William Lowry, John Lowry & Robert Lowry orphans of Benjamin Lowry deceased
Guardian: Robert H. Burcher Bond amount: 2000 pounds
Bondsmen: Robert H. Burcher, Thaddeus Freshwater Jr., John Tooley

Lowery, John 2 February 1824 Bond No. 218
Wards: Benjamin Lowry, William Lowry & John Lowery orphans of John Lowery deceased
Guardian: William Trueblood Bond amount: 10 shillings*
Bondsmen: Wm. Trueblood, Anderson Morris, Mordecai Morris Jr.
(*Note: the word pounds was scratched out)

Luton, Constantine 3 June 1822 Bond No. 143
Ward: Susannah Luton orphan of Constantine Luton deceased
Guardian: William Freshwater Bond amount: 100 pounds
Bondsmen: William Freshwater, Thaddeus Freshwater, Constantine Luton

Luton, Constantine 3 June 1822 Bond No. 144
Ward: *(Maryh?)* Luton orphan of Constantine Luton deceased
Guardian: William Freshwater Bond amount: 100 pounds
Bondsmen: William Freshwater, Thaddeus Freshwater, Constantine Luton

Luton, Harvey 5 March 1822 Bond No. 40
Ward: Thaddeus Luton orphan of Harvey Luton deceased
Guardian: Thaddeus Freshwater Bond amount: 3000 pounds
Bondsmen: Thaddeus Freshwater, Wm. Hardy, William W. Freshwater

Madison, Matthias 5 March 1822 Bond No. 70
Ward: Matthias Madison orphan of Matthias Madison deceased
Guardian: Edmund Trueblood Bond amount: 300 pounds
Bondsmen: Edmund Trueblood, Abner Williams, David Sharber

Madison, Matthias　　　8 June 1824　　　Bond No. 236
Ward: Matthias Madison orphan of Matthias ____ deceased
Guardian: Edmund Trueblood　　Bond amount: 1000 dollars*
Bondsmen: Edmund Trueblood, Robert Weymouth, Adam Stafford
*(*Note: the word pounds was scratched out)*

Markham, Anthony　　　4 September 1822　　Bond No. 153
Ward: Demarcus Markham orphan of Anthony Markham
Guardian: Anthony R. Markham　　Bond amount: 2000 pounds
Bondsmen: Anthony Markham, Wm. Barns, Thomas Commander

Markham, Anthony　　　4 September 1822　　Bond No. 154
Ward: Martha Markham orphan of Anthony Markham deceased
Guardian: Anthony R. Markham　　Bond amount: 2000 pounds
Bondsmen: Anthony Markham, Wm. Barns, Thomas Commander

Markham, Anthony　　　4 September 1822　　Bond No. 155
Ward: Nancy Markham orphan of Anthony Markham deceased
Guardian: Anthony R. Markham　　Bond amount: 2000 pounds
Bondsmen: Anthony Markham, Wm. Barns, Thomas Commander

Markham, Charles　　　1 April 1822　　　Bond No. 141
Ward: Margaret Markham orphan of Charles Markham deceased
Guardian: William Rose　　　Bond amount: 100 pounds
Bondsmen: William Rose, John Tooley

Markham, Charles　　　1 April 1822　　　Bond No. 142
Ward: Benjamin Markham orphan of Charles Markham deceased
Guardian: William Rose　　　Bond amount: 100 pounds
Bondsmen: William Rose, John Tooley

Markham, Charles　　　2 March 1824　　　Bond No. 226
Ward: Benjamin Markham orphan of Charles Markham deceased
Guardian: Richard Etheridge　　Bond amount: 100 pounds
Bondsmen: Richard Etheridge, Frances Fletcher, Thomas Markham

Guardian Bond Book 1822 - 1824

Markham, Thomas 5 March 1822   Bond No. 84
Ward: William Markham orphan of Thomas Markham deceased
Guardian: John Tooley   Bond amount: 1000 pounds
Bondsmen: John Tooley, Robert Stone, John Thomas

Markham, Thomas 5 March 1822   Bond No. 85
Ward: Penny Markham orphan of Thomas Markham deceased
Guardian: John Tooley   Bond amount: 1000 pounds
Bondsmen: John Tooley, Robert Stone, John Thomas

Markham, Thomas 5 March 1822   Bond No. 86
Ward: Anthony Markham orphan of Thomas Markham deceased
Guardian: John Tooley   Bond amount: 200 pounds
Bondsmen: John Tooley, Robert Stone, John Thomas

Markham, Thomas 5 March 1822   Bond No. 87
Ward: Thomas Markham orphan of Thomas Markham deceased
Guardian: John Tooley   Bond amount: 200 pounds
Bondsmen: John Tooley, Robert Stone, John Shannon

Markham, Thomas 5 March 1822   Bond No. 88
Ward: John Markham orphan of Thomas Markham deceased
Guardian: John Tooley   Bond amount: 200 pounds
Bondsmen: John Tooley, Robert Stone, John Shannon

Miller, William   8 June 1824   Bond No. 238
Wards: William Miller Heirs *
Guardian: Daniel McPherson   Bond amount: 1000 dollars*
Bondsmen: Daniel McPherson, John Carey*, Edmund Trueblood
   (*Note: the words orphan of and pounds were scratched out;
    the signature shows the name to be John Case)

Morgan, Benjamin   3 February 1823   Bond No. 165
Wards: the heirs of Benjamin Morgan*
Guardian: Cader Munden   Bond amount: 200 pounds
Bondsmen: Cader Munden, Nathan Morgan, William Wood
   (*Note: the word orphan was scratched out)

Pasquotank County, North Carolina

Morgan, Isaac   2 February 1824   Bond No. 222
Wards: Nathan, Jonathan, David & Beoni orphans of Isaac Morgan
Guardian: Nancy Morgan   Bond amount: 250 dollars*
Bondsmen: Nancy Morgan, Thomas White, James Morgan
     *(*Note: the word pounds was scratched out)*

Morris, John B.   2 December 1823   Bond No. 195
Ward: Beoni Morris - - - *
Guardian: John B. Morris   Bond amount: 500 dollars *
Bondsmen: John B. Morris, Edmund Blount, John Tooley
     *(*Note: the words orphan of and pounds were scratched out)*

Morris, Joshua   5 March 1822   Bond No. 55
Ward: Mordecai Morris orphan of Joshua Morris deceased
Guardian: Anderson Morris   Bond amount: 2000 pounds
Bondsmen: Anderson Morris, Mordecai Morris Jr., Joseph Pritchard

Morris, Joshua   5 March 1822   Bond No. 56
Ward: Hannah Morris orphan of Joshua Morris deceased
Guardian: Anderson Morris   Bond amount: 2000 pounds
Bondsmen: Anderson Morris, Mordecai Morris Jr., Joseph Pritchard

Morris, Joshua   5 March 1822   Bond No. 57
Ward: Joseph H. Morris orphan of Joshua Morris deceased
Guardian: Anderson Morris   Bond amount: 2000 pounds
Bondsmen: Anderson Morris, Mordecai Morris Jr., Joseph Pritchard

Morris, Mark   9 June 1824   Bond No. 239
Wards: Sarah & Mark Morris orphans of Mark Morris deceased
Guardian: Hannah Morris   Bond amount: 500 dollars*
Bondsmen: Hannah Morris, Caleb White, Samuel Knight
     *(*Note: the word pounds was scratched out)*

Morris, Mark   5 March 1822   Bond No. 60
Ward: Sarah Morris orphan of Mark Morris deceased
Guardian: Matthew Overman   Bond amount: 200 pounds
Bondsmen: Matthew Overman, Samuel Morgan, Samuel Knight

Morris, Mark 5 March 1822 Bond No. 61
Ward: Mark Morris orphan of Mark Morris deceased
Guardian: Matthew Overman Bond amount: 200 pounds
Bondsmen: Matthew Overman, Samuel Morgan, Samuel Knight

Morris, Mark 5 March 1822 Bond No. 62
Ward: James Morris orphan of Mark Morris deceased
Guardian: Matthew Overman Bond amount: 50 pounds
Bondsmen: Matthew Overman, Samuel Morgan, Samuel Knight

Morris, Thomas 5 March 1822 Bond No. 48
Ward: Margaret Morris orphan of Thomas Morris deceased
Guardian: Thomas Pritchard Bond amount: 300 pounds
Bondsmen: Thos. Pritchard, Joseph Pritchard, Benjamin Pritchard

Morris, Thomas 2 February 1824 Bond No. 212
Ward: Margaret Morris orphan of Thomas Morris deceased
Guardian: Anderson Morris Bond amount: 2000 dollars*
Bondsmen: Anderson Morris, Mordecai Morris Jr., Wm. Trueblood
(*Note: the word pounds was scratched out)

Morris, Thomas 2 February 1824 Bond No. 213
Ward: Joshua Morris orphan of Thomas Morris deceased
Guardian: Anderson Morris Bond amount: 2000 dollars*
Bondsmen: Anderson Morris, Mordecai Morris Jr., Wm. Trueblood
(*Note: the word pounds was scratched out)

Morris, Thomas 2 February 1824 Bond No. 214
Ward: Sarah Ann Morris orphan of Thomas Morris deceased
Guardian: Anderson Morris Bond amount: 2000 dollars*
Bondsmen: Anderson Morris, Mordecai Morris Jr., Wm. Trueblood
(*Note: the word pounds was scratched out)

Morris, Thomas 5 March 1822 Bond No. 63
Ward: Margaret Morris orphan of Thomas Morris deceased
Guardian: Matthew Overman Bond amount: 50 pounds
Bondsmen: Matthew Overman, Samuel Morgan, Samuel Knight

Morris, Thomas 4 March 1823 Bond No. 172
Wards: Margaret, Joshua, Sarah Ann orphans of Thomas Morris
Guardian: Anderson Morris Bond amount: 2000 pounds
Bondsmen: Anderson Morris, William Trueblood, Mordecai Morris

Nixon, James 4 March 1822 Bond No. 3
Ward: Samuel Nixon orphan of James Nixon deceased
Guardian: Sarah Perry Bond amount: 1000 pounds
Bondsmen: Sarah Perry, John Winslow, Richard Pool

Nixon, James 4 March 1822 Bond No. 4
Ward: Margaret Nixon orphan of James Nixon deceased
Guardian: Sarah Perry Bond amount: 1000 pounds
Bondsmen: Sarah Perry, John Winslow, Richard Pool

Overman, Charles 5 March 1822 Bond No. 101
Ward: Susannah Overman orphan of Charles Overman deceased
Guardian: Joseph Parker Bond amount: 400 pounds
Bondsmen: Joseph Parker, Stephen White, William T. Muse

Overman, Charles 5 March 1822 Bond No. 102
Ward: Elizabeth Overman orphan of Charles Overman deceased
Guardian: Joseph Parker Bond amount: 400 pounds
Bondsmen: Joseph Parker, Stephen White, William T. Muse

Overman, Charles 5 March 1822 Bond No. 103
Ward: Ann Overman orphan of Charles Overman deceased
Guardian: Joseph Parker Bond amount: 400 pounds
Bondsmen: Joseph Parker, Stephen White, William T. Muse

Overman, Henry P. 2 March 1824 Bond No. 231
Ward: Henry Overman orphan of Henry P. Overman deceased
Guardian: George Pendleton Bond amount: 2000 pounds
Bondsmen: George Pendleton, John White, James W. Turner

Overman, Mordecai 4 August 1823 Bond No. 186
Ward: George Overman orphan of Mordecai Overman deceased
Guardian: William I. Hardy Bond amount: 1000 pounds
Bondsmen: Wm. I. Hardy, William Freshwater, William C. George

Guardian Bond Book 1822 - 1824

Overman, Nathan 3 September 1823 Bond No. 190
Wards: Thomas Overman, Mary Overman & Henry Overman
  orphans of Nathan Overman deceased
Guardian: William W. Freshwater Bond amount: 1000 pounds
Bondsmen: William W. Freshwater, Thaddeus Freshwater,
  Lemuel Snowden

Overman, Nathan 2 February 1824 Bond No. 221
Wards: Mary, Martha & Elizabeth orphans of Nathan Overman
Guardian: Charles Overman Bond amount: 250 dollars*
Bondsmen: Charles Overman, Benjamin Bailey, Robinson White
  *(*Note: the word pounds was scratched out)*

Overman, Robert 6 March 1822 Bond No. 126
Ward: Robert Overman orphan of Robert Overman deceased
Guardian: William Wilson Bond amount: 300 pounds
Bondsmen: William Wilson, Ambrose Knox, William T. Muse

Overman, Thomas 1 April 1822 Bond No. 139
Ward: Charles Overman orphan of Thomas Overman deceased
Guardian: Isaac Overman Bond amount: 150 pounds
Bondsmen: Isaac Overman, Joseph Pritchard

Overman, Thomas 1 April 1822 Bond No. 140
Ward: Grandy Overman orphan of Thomas Overman deceased
Guardian: Isaac Overman Bond amount: 150 pounds
Bondsmen: Isaac Overman, Joseph Pritchard

Overton, ___ 9 June 1824 Bond No. 240
Ward: Archibald Overton orphan of _____ deceased
Guardian: Samuel Brothers Bond amount: 200 dollars*
Bondsmen: Samuel Brothers, Thomas Barnard, David Davis
  *(*Note: the word pounds was scratched out)*

Palin, Thomas 5 March 1822 Bond No. 65
Ward: Joseph Palin orphan of Thomas Palin deceased
Guardian: Abner Pendleton Bond amount: 100 pounds
Bondsmen: Abner Pendleton, Frederick Pendleton, Timothy
  Pendleton

Palin, Thomas 5 March 1822 Bond No. 66
Ward: Sarah Palin orphan of Thomas Palin deceased
Guardian: Abner Pendleton Bond amount: 100 pounds
Bondsmen: Abner Pendleton, Fred. Pendleton, Timothy Pendleton

Palin, Thomas 5 March 1822 Bond No. 67
Ward: Henry Palin orphan of Thomas Palin deceased
Guardian: Abner Pendleton Bond amount: 100 pounds
Bondsmen: Abner Pendleton, Fred. Pendleton, Timothy Pendleton

Palin, Thomas 5 March 1822 Bond No. 68
Ward: John Palin orphan of Thomas Palin deceased
Guardian: Abner Pendleton Bond amount: 100 pounds
Bondsmen: Abner Pendleton, Fred. Pendleton, Timothy Pendleton

Palin, Thomas 5 March 1822 Bond No. 69
Ward: Nancy Palin orphan of Thomas Palin deceased
Guardian: Abner Pendleton Bond amount: 100 pounds
Bondsmen: Abner Pendleton, Fred. Pendleton, Timothy Pendleton

Pendleton, George W. 5 March 1823 Bond No. 177
Ward: Angelica Pendleton orphan of George W. Pendleton
Guardian: William C. George Bond amount: 1000 pounds
Bondsmen: William C. George, Ambrose Knox, Hugh B. Knox

Pendleton, George W. 2 December 1823 Bond No. 199
Ward: Charles S. Pendleton orphan of George W. Pendleton
Guardian: Edmund H. Perkins Bond amount: 5000 dollars *
Bondsmen: Edm. Perkins, Thaddeus Freshwater, John McDonald
  (*Note: the word pounds was scratched out)

Pool, Isaac 5 March 1822 Bond No. 72
Ward: Patrick Pool orphan of Isaac Pool deceased
Guardian: Thomas Pool Jr. Bond amount: 500 pounds
Bondsmen: Thomas Poole Jr., Benjamin Pritchard, Rich. Pool

Pool, Isaac 2 February 1824 Bond No. 220
Ward: Patrick Pool orphan of Isaac Pool deceased

Guardian Bond Book 1822 - 1824

Guardian: Thomas Pool   Bond amount: 2000 dollars*
Bondsmen: Thomas Pool, Solomon Pool, James Pool
*(*Note: the word pounds was scratched out)*

Pool, John   5 March 1822   Bond No. 92
Ward: Robert Pool orphan of John Pool deceased
Guardian: Caleb Raper   Bond amount: 1000 pounds
Bondsmen: Caleb Raper, Richard Pool, Mary Jackson

Pool, John Jr.   3 May 1824   Bond No. 235
Wards: Eliza, Maria, Robert & Emaline orphans of John Pool Jr.
Guardian: Robert Pool   Bond amount: 1500 dollars*
Bondsmen: Robert Pool, Solomon Pool, James A. Pool
*(*Note: the word pounds was scratched out)*

Pritchard, Caleb   2 February 1824   Bond No. 219
Ward: Benjamin Pritchard orphan of Caleb Pritchard deceased
Guardian: Benjamin Pritchard   Bond amount: 600 dollars*
Bondsmen: Benj. Pritchard, Mordecai Morris Jr., Anderson Morris
*(*Note: the word pounds was scratched out)*

Pritchard, James   5 March 1822   Bond No. 132
Ward: William Pritchard orphan of James Pritchard deceased
Guardian: John Pool   Bond amount: 1000 pounds
Bondsmen: John Pool, Richard Pool, William T. Muse

Pritchard, ____   5 March 1822   Bond No. 133
Ward: Mary Pritchard orphan of ___ Pritchard deceased
Guardian: John Pool   Bond amount: 1000 pounds
Bondsmen: John Pool, Richard Pool, William T. Muse

Pritchard, ____   5 March 1822   Bond No. 134
Ward: Margaret Pritchard orphan of ___ Pritchard deceased
Guardian: John Pool   Bond amount: 1000 pounds
Bondsmen: John Pool, Richard Pool, William T. Muse

Pritchard, ____   5 March 1822   Bond No. 135
Ward: Ann Pritchard orphan of ___ Pritchard deceased

Guardian: John Pool   Bond amount: 1000 pounds
Bondsmen: John Pool, Richard Pool, William T. Muse

Pritchard, ____   5 March 1822   Bond No. 136
Ward: Sarah Pritchard orphan of ___ Pritchard deceased
Guardian: John Pool   Bond amount: 1000 pounds
Bondsmen: John Pool, Richard Pool, William T. Muse

Proby, Paul S.   5 March 1822   Bond No. 49
Ward: Sarah Proby orphan of Paul S. Proby deceased
Guardian: Thomas Pritchard   Bond amount: 100 pounds
Bondsmen: Thos. Pritchard, Joseph Pritchard, Benjamin Pritchard

Raper, Cornelius   3 February 1823   Bond No. 164
Wards: Fanny & Samuel & Robert orphans of Cornelius Raper
Guardian: Benjamin Bailey   Bond amount: 100 pounds
Bondsmen: Benjamin Bailey, Nathan Bundy, Nathan Morgan

Raper, Henry   5 March 1822   Bond No. 93
Ward: John Raper orphan of Henry Raper deceased
Guardian: Richard Pool   Bond amount: 200 pounds
Bondsmen: Richard Pool, John Pool Jr., James Pool

Raper, John   5 March 1822   Bond No. 90
Ward: John Raper orphan of John Raper deceased
Guardian: Caleb Raper   Bond amount: 1000 pounds
Bondsmen: Caleb Raper, Richard Pool, Mary Jackson

Raper, John   5 March 1822   Bond No. 91
Ward: Patsy Raper orphan of John Raper deceased
Guardian: Caleb Raper   Bond amount: 1000 pounds
Bondsmen: Caleb Raper, Richard Pool, Mary Jackson

Relfe, ___   5 March 1822   Bond No. 127
Ward: Stephen Relfe orphan of _____ deceased
Guardian: William Wilson   Bond amount: 50 pounds
Bondsmen: William Wilson, Ambrose Knox, William T. Muse

Guardian Bond Book 1822 - 1824

Relfe, ___   5 March 1822   Bond No. 128
Ward: Joseph Relfe orphan of _____ deceased
Guardian: William Wilson   Bond amount: 50 pounds
Bondsmen: William Wilson, Ambrose Knox, William T. Muse

Relfe, ___   5 March 1822   Bond No. 129
Ward: Malachi Relfe orphan of _____ deceased
Guardian: William Wilson   Bond amount: 50 pounds
Bondsmen: William Wilson, Ambrose Knox, William T. Muse

Relfe, ___   5 March 1822   Bond No. 130
Ward: Josiah Relfe orphan of _____ deceased
Guardian: William Wilson   Bond amount: 50 pounds
Bondsmen: William Wilson, Ambrose Knox, William T. Muse

Relfe, Enoch   4 August 1823   Bond No. 187
Wards: Mary Ann Relfe & Margaret Relfe orphans of Enoch Relfe
Guardian: Arthur Heath   Bond amount: 100 pounds
Bondsmen: Arthur Heath, David Davis, Arthur Davis

Rhodes, Linkham   4 December 1822   Bond No. 160
Ward: George Rhodes orphan of Linkham *(Lincoln?)* Rhodes
Guardian: Joshua A. Pool   Bond amount: 1000 pounds
Bondsmen: Joshua A. Pool, Isaac Overman, Abner Williams

Rhodes, Linkham   5 January 1824   Bond No. 208
Ward: George Rhodes orphan of Linkham *(Lincoln?)* Rhodes
Guardian: Abner Williams   Bond amount: 3000 dollars*
Bondsmen: Abner Williams, David Sharber, Edmund Trueblood
    (*Note: the word pounds was scratched out)

Richardson, Miles   5 March 1822   Bond No. 27
Ward: Sally Richardson orphan of Miles Richardson deceased
Guardian: George Ferebee   Bond amount: 500 pounds
Bondsmen: George Ferebee, F. Whitehurst, William Wilson

Richardson, Miles   5 March 1822   Bond No. 28
Ward: Miles Richardson orphan of Miles Richardson deceased

Guardian: George Ferebee   Bond amount: 500 pounds
Bondsmen: George Ferebee, F. Whitehurst, William Wilson

Richardson, Miles   5 March 1822   Bond No. 29
Ward: Benjamin Richardson orphan of Miles Richardson deceased
Guardian: George Ferebee   Bond amount: 500 pounds
Bondsmen: George Ferebee, F. Whitehurst, William Wilson

Russell, James   4 March 1822   Bond No. 1
Ward: Elizabeth Russell orphan of James Russell deceased
Guardian: Isaac Overman   Bond amount: 1000 pounds
Bondsmen: Isaac Overman, Thomas Trueblood, Josiah Overman

Russell, James   4 March 1822   Bond No. 2
Ward: Malachi Russell orphan of James Russell deceased
Guardian: Isaac Overman   Bond amount: 1000 pounds
Bondsmen: Isaac Overman, Thomas Trueblood, Josiah Overman

Sanderlin, Asa   2 December 1823   Bond No. 200
Ward: William Sanderlin orphan of Asa Sanderlin deceased
Guardian: Bridget Sanderlin   Bond amount: 1000 pounds
Bondsmen: Bridget Sanderlin, Maximilian Sanderlin, Wm. Wilson

Sanderlin, Asa   2 December 1823   Bond No. 201
Wards: Patsy, Elizabeth & Asa Sanderlin orphans of Asa Sanderlin
Guardian: Bridget Sanderlin   Bond amount: 1000 pounds
Bondsmen: Bridget Sanderlin, Maximilian Sanderlin, Wm. Wilson

(Sapell?), Benjamin   5 May 1823   Bond No. 181
Wards: Margaret & Mary Sapell orphans of Benjamin *(Sapell?)*
Guardian: Wilson Sanderlin   Bond amount: 500 pounds
Bondsmen: Wilson Sanderlin, Abner Williams, David Sharber

Sawyer, Hollowell   5 March 1822   Bond No. 82
Ward: Ira Sawyer orphan of Hollowell Sawyer deceased
Guardian: Jonathan Brite   Bond amount: 200 pounds
Bondsmen: Jonathan Brite, Harvey Williams, John Richardson Sr.

Guardian Bond Book 1822 - 1824

Scott, Marmaduke   5 March 1822   Bond No. 114
Ward: Armon Scott orphan of Marmaduke Scott deceased
Guardian: Jacob Richardson   Bond amount: 1000 pounds
Bondsmen: Jacob Richardson, Joel Sawyer, John Bray

Scott, Marmaduke   5 March 1822   Bond No. 115
Ward: Anna Scott orphan of Marmaduke Scott deceased
Guardian: Jacob Richardson   Bond amount: 1000 pounds
Bondsmen: Jacob Richardson, Joel Sawyer, John Bray

Scott, Marmaduke   5 March 1822   Bond No. 116
Ward: George W. Scott orphan of Marmaduke Scott deceased
Guardian: Jacob Richardson   Bond amount: 1000 pounds
Bondsmen: Jacob Richardson, Joel Sawyer, John Bray

Scott, Marmaduke   5 March 1822   Bond No. 118
Ward: Jeremiah Scott orphan of Marmaduke Scott deceased
Guardian: Jeremiah Sawyer   Bond amount: 1000 pounds
Bondsmen: Jeremiah Sawyer, Lemuel Jennings, William Thomas

Scott, Marmaduke   2 March 1824   Bond No. 228
Ward: George Scott orphan of Marmaduke Scott deceased
Guardian: Allen B. Jones   Bond amount: 2000 pounds
Bondsmen: Allen B. Jones, Miles Early, Jeremiah Sawyer

Scott, Marmaduke   2 March 1824   Bond No. 229
Ward: Sophia Scott orphan of Marmaduke Scott deceased
Guardian: Allen B. Jones   Bond amount: 2000 pounds
Bondsmen: Allen B. Jones, Miles Early, Jeremiah Sawyer

Scott, Samuel   _ March 1822   Bond No. 100
Ward: James Scott orphan of Samuel Scott deceased
Guardian: John Casse   Bond amount: 100 pounds
Bondsmen: John Casse, Abner Williams

Shannonhouse, James L.   4 August 1823   Bond No. 188
Ward: Eleanor L. Shannonhouse orphan of James L. Shannonhouse

Guardian: John McMorrine   Bond amount: 5000 pounds
Bondsmen: John McMorrine, Thomas L. Shannonhouse,
           Benjamin Sutton

Shirley, Daniel   4 March 1822   Bond No. 10
Ward: John Shirley orphan of Daniel Shirley deceased
Guardian: Thomas Jordan   Bond amount: 200 pounds
Bondsmen: Thomas Jordan, William C. George, William T. Muse

Shirley, Daniel   4 March 1822   Bond No. 11
Ward: Nancy Shirley orphan of Daniel Shirley deceased
Guardian: Thomas Jordan   Bond amount: 200 pounds
Bondsmen: Thomas Jordan, William C. George, William T. Muse

Simpson, John   5 March 1822   Bond No. 120
Ward: Harriet Simpson orphan of John Simpson deceased
Guardian: Robert Simpson   Bond amount: 300 pounds
Bondsmen: Robert Simpson, Daniel McPherson, James Nash

Simpson, John   5 March 1822   Bond No. 121
Ward: Sarah Simpson orphan of John Simpson deceased
Guardian: Robert Simpson   Bond amount: 300 pounds
Bondsmen: Robert Simpson, Daniel McPherson, James Nash

Simpson, John   5 March 1822   Bond No. 122
Ward: George Simpson orphan of John Simpson deceased
Guardian: Robert Simpson   Bond amount: 300 pounds
Bondsmen: Robert Simpson, Daniel McPherson, James Nash

Simpson, John   5 March 1822   Bond No. 123
Ward: John Simpson orphan of John Simpson deceased
Guardian: Robert Simpson   Bond amount: 300 pounds
Bondsmen: Robert Simpson, Daniel McPherson, James Nash

Small, Joseph   4 March 1822   Bond No. 18
Ward: Joseph Small orphan of Joseph Small deceased
Guardian: Robert Stone   Bond amount: 300 pounds
Bondsmen: Robert Stone, S. Warner, Thomas Lister

Guardian Bond Book 1822 - 1824

Smith, Robert 5 March 1822 Bond No. 104
Ward: Joseph Smith orphan of Robert Smith deceased
Guardian: David Scaff Bond amount: 150 pounds
Bondsmen: David Scaff, James Scaff, James Richardson

Smith, Robert 5 March 1822 Bond No. 105
Ward: Lydia Smith orphan of Robert Smith deceased
Guardian: David Scaff Bond amount: 150 pounds
Bondsmen: David Scaff, James Scaff, James Richardson

Smith, Robert 5 March 1822 Bond No. 106
Ward: Sally Smith orphan of Robert Smith deceased
Guardian: David Scaff Bond amount: 150 pounds
Bondsmen: David Scaff, James Scaff, James Richardson

Smithson, Elisha 3 June 1823 Bond No. 183
Wards: Polly & Charity Smithson children of Elisha Smithson*
Guardian: William Scott Bond amount: 1000 pounds
Bondsmen: William Scott, James Nash, Daniel McPherson
*(*Note: the word orphans was scratched out)*

Spence, Mark 5 March 1822 Bond No. 94
Ward: Elizabeth Spence orphan of Mark Spence deceased
Guardian: Parthenia Spence Bond amount: 150 pounds
Bondsmen: Parthenia Spence, Joel Sawyer, Elisha Draper

Spence, Mark 5 March 1822 Bond No. 95
Ward: Martha Spence orphan of Mark Spence deceased
Guardian: Parthenia Spence Bond amount: 150 pounds
Bondsmen: Parthenia Spence, Joel Sawyer, Elisha Draper

Spence, Mark 5 March 1822 Bond No. 96
Ward: William Spence orphan of Mark Spence deceased
Guardian: Parthenia Spence Bond amount: 150 pounds
Bondsmen: Parthenia Spence, Joel Sawyer, Elisha Draper

Spence, Mark 5 March 1822 Bond No. 97
Ward: Nancy Spence orphan of Mark Spence deceased

Guardian: Parthenia Spence Bond amount: 150 pounds
Bondsmen: Parthenia Spence, Joel Sawyer, Elisha Draper

Stott, Thomas 5 March 1822 Bond No. 98
Ward: Elizabeth Stott orphan of Thomas Stott
Guardian: James Pool Bond amount: 2000 pounds
Bondsmen: James Pool, Richard Pool, John Pool

Stott, Thomas 5 March 1822 Bond No. 99
Ward: William Stott orphan of Thomas Stott
Guardian: James Pool Bond amount: 2000 pounds
Bondsmen: James Pool, Richard Pool, John Pool Jr.

Stott, Thomas 2 February 1824 Bond No. 224
Wards: Elizabeth & William Stott orphans of Thomas Stott
Guardian: James Pool Bond amount: 4000 dollars*
Bondsmen: James Pool, Thomas Poole Jr., Jonathan Banks
 (*Note: the word pounds was scratched out)

Temple, Joseph 4 June 1822 Bond No. 146
Ward: David Temple orphan of Joseph Temple
Guardian: Robert Temple Bond amount: 500 pounds
Bondsmen: Robert Temple, Thomas Humpris, D. Davis

Thompson, Henry 5 March 1822 Bond No. 71
Ward: John Thompson orphan of Henry Thompson
Guardian: Edmund Trueblood Bond amount: 200 pounds
Bondsmen: Edmund Trueblood, Abner Williams, David Sharber

Trueblood, Aaron 2 March 1824 Bond No. 227
Wards: Millicent, Sarah, Isaac orphans of Aaron Trueblood
Guardian: Thomas Trueblood Bond amount: 200 pounds
Bondsmen: Thos. Trueblood, Joshua Trueblood, Ephraim Trueblood

Trueblood, James 1 April 1822 Bond No. 137
Ward: Malachi Trueblood orphan of James Trueblood deceased
Guardian: Isaac Overman Bond amount: 200 pounds
Bondsmen: Isaac Overman, Joseph Pritchard

Guardian Bond Book 1822 - 1824

Trueblood, James 1 April 1822 Bond No. 138
Ward: Wilson Trueblood orphan of James Trueblood deceased
Guardian: Isaac Overman Bond amount: 200 pounds
Bondsmen: Isaac Overman, Joseph Pritchard

Trueblood, Joshua 6 March 1822 Bond No. 125
Ward: Millicent Trueblood orphan of Joshua Trueblood deceased
Guardian: William Wilson Bond amount: 3000 pounds
Bondsmen: William Wilson, Ambrose Knox, William T. Muse

Trueblood, Samuel 5 March 1822 Bond No. 76
Ward: Mary Trueblood orphan of Samuel Trueblood deceased
Guardian: Robert Bailey Bond amount: 1000 pounds
Bondsmen: Robert Bailey, George Bailey, John Bailey

Trueblood, Samuel 2 February 1824 Bond No. 216
Ward: Ansalem Trueblood orphan of Samuel Trueblood deceased
Guardian: William Trueblood Bond amount: 700 dollars*
Bondsmen: Wm. Trueblood, Anderson Morris, Mordecai Morris Jr.
(*Note: the word pounds was scratched out)

Trueblood, Samuel 2 February 1824 Bond No. 217
Ward: Exum Trueblood orphan of Samuel Trueblood deceased
Guardian: William Trueblood Bond amount: 500 dollars
Bondsmen: Wm. Trueblood, Anderson Morris, Mordecai Morris Jr.

Trueblood, Timothy 5 March 1822 Bond No. 109
Ward: Margaret Trueblood orphan of Timothy Trueblood deceased
Guardian: William Allen Bond amount: 100 pounds
Bondsmen: William Allen, Henry White, Asa Jackson

Trueblood, Timothy 8 June 1824 Bond No. 237
Ward: Peggy Trueblood orphan of Timothy Trueblood
Guardian: Benjamin Bailey Bond amount: 500 dollars*
Bondsmen: Benjamin Bailey, John Pool, John L. Bailey
(*Note: the word pounds was scratched out)

Turner, James W. 7 April 1823 Bond No. 178
Wards: William & Fanny Turner children of James W. Turner*

Guardian: James W. Turner   Bond amount: 300 pounds
Bondsmen: James W. Turner, John Tooley, William Rose
*(*Note: the word orphan was scratched out)*

Warner, Samuel   4 March 1823   Bond No. 171
Wards: Margaret, Mary, Priscilla, Nicholas & William Warner
    orphans of Samuel Warner deceased
Guardian: _____   Bond amount: 3000 pounds
Bondsmen: Margaret Warner, Samuel Warner, A. R. Markham

White, ___   4 June 1822   Bond No. 145
Ward: Benjamin White orphan of ____ deceased
Guardian: Joseph Keaton   Bond amount: 1000 pounds
Bondsmen: Joseph Keaton, William T. Muse, Malachi Jackson

White, Benjamin   4 March 1822   Bond No. 20
Ward: Lydia White orphan of Benjamin White deceased
Guardian: Eli White   Bond amount: 250 pounds
Bondsmen: Eli White, Nathan Morgan, James Morgan

White, Benjamin   4 March 1822   Bond No. 21
Ward: George White orphan of Benjamin White deceased
Guardian: Eli White   Bond amount: 250 pounds
Bondsmen: Eli White, Nathan Morgan, James Morgan

White, Benjamin   4 March 1822   Bond No. 22
Ward: Milly White orphan of Benjamin White deceased
Guardian: Eli White   Bond amount: 250 pounds
Bondsmen: Eli White, Nathan Morgan, James Morgan

White, Benjamin   2 December 1823   Bond No. 193
Ward: Benjamin _ White orphan of Benjamin White deceased
Guardian: James Leigh   Bond amount: 4000 pounds
Bondsmen: James Leigh, Edmund Blount, John M. Skinner

White, Edmund   4 August 1823   Bond No. 185
Wards: Alfred & Elizabeth White orphans of Edmund White
Guardian: Aaron White   Bond amount: 6000 pounds
Bondsmen: Aaron White, Joseph Pritchard, Joshua Morris

Guardian Bond Book 1822 - 1824

White, Edmund 2 December 1823 Bond No. 194
Ward: Margarett S. White orphan of Edmund White deceased
Guardian: Aaron White Bond amount: 12,000 dollars
Bondsmen: Aaron White, Caleb Morris, Joseph Pritchard

White, James 2 February 1824 Bond No. 215
Ward: Mary White orphan of James White deceased
Guardian: Ann White Bond amount: 200 dollars
Bondsmen: Ann White, William W. Freshwater, William C. George

White, Josiah 5 March 1822 Bond No. 36
Ward: Anne White orphan of Josiah White deceased
Guardian: David White Bond amount: 500 pounds
Bondsmen: David White, Joseph Pritchard, Thomas Elliott

White, Josiah 5 March 1822 Bond No. 37
Ward: Martha White orphan of Josiah White deceased
Guardian: David White Bond amount: 500 pounds
Bondsmen: David White, Joseph Pritchard, Thomas Elliott

White, Josiah 5 March 1822 Bond No. 38
Ward: Jepethih White orphan of Josiah White deceased
Guardian: David White Bond amount: 500 pounds
Bondsmen: David White, Joseph Pritchard, Thomas Elliott

White, Josiah 5 March 1822 Bond No. 54
Ward: Rebecca White orphan of Josiah White deceased
Guardian: Joseph Pritchard Bond amount: 50 pounds
Bondsmen: Joseph Pritchard, Benjamin Pritchard, Anderson Morris

White, Stephen 4 March 1822 Bond No. 23
Ward: Matthew White orphan of Stephen White deceased
Guardian: Josiah Perry Bond amount: 1000 pounds
Bondsmen: Josiah Perry, Eli White, Nathan Morgan

Williams, David L. 5 March 1822 Bond No. 59
Ward: John Thomas Williams orphan of David L. Williams
Guardian: Thomas Commander Bond amount: 2000 pounds
Bondsmen: Thos. Commander, Wm. Trueblood, Miles Commander

Williams, Elisha 4 March 1822 Bond No. 12
Ward: Mary Williams orphan of Elisha Williams deceased
Guardian: Seth Williams Bond amount: 200 pounds
Bondsmen: Seth Williams, James Smith, James Gray

Williams, Elisha 4 March 1822 Bond No. 13
Ward: Owen Williams orphan of Elisha Williams deceased
Guardian: Seth Williams Bond amount: 200 pounds
Bondsmen: Seth Williams, James Smith, James Gray

Williams, Elisha 4 March 1822 Bond No. 14
Ward: Lurancey Williams orphan of Elisha Williams deceased
Guardian: Seth Williams Bond amount: 200 pounds
Bondsmen: Seth Williams, James Smith, James Gray

Williams, Elisha 5 January 1824 Bond No. 210
Ward: Owen Williams orphan of Elisha Williams deceased
Guardian: Maxey Williams Bond amount: 200 dollars*
Bondsmen: Maxey Williams, Daniel McPherson, Jesse Davis
*(*Note: the word pounds was scratched out)*

Williams, Elisha 5 January 1824 Bond No. 211
Ward: Susanna Williams orphan of Elisha Williams deceased
Guardian: Maxey Williams Bond amount: 200 dollars*
Bondsmen: Maxey Williams, Daniel McPherson, Jesse Davis
*(*Note: the word pounds was scratched out)*

Wilson, ___ 5 March 1822 Bond No. 124
Wards: Nathaniel Wilson orphan of _____ deceased
Guardian: William Martin Bond amount: 500 pounds
Bondsmen: William Martin, William T. Muse, John C. Ehringhaus

Wood, Joseph 4 March 1823 Bond No. 173
Wards: John, Spence, William, Polly, Sally & Gray Wood orphans
    of Joseph Wood deceased
Guardian: Sarah Wood Bond amount: 1000 pounds
Bondsmen: Sarah Wood, *(Fruterin?)* Whitehurst, Elliott
    Whitehurst

Pasquotank County, North Carolina
Guardian Bonds
Book 1824 - 1827

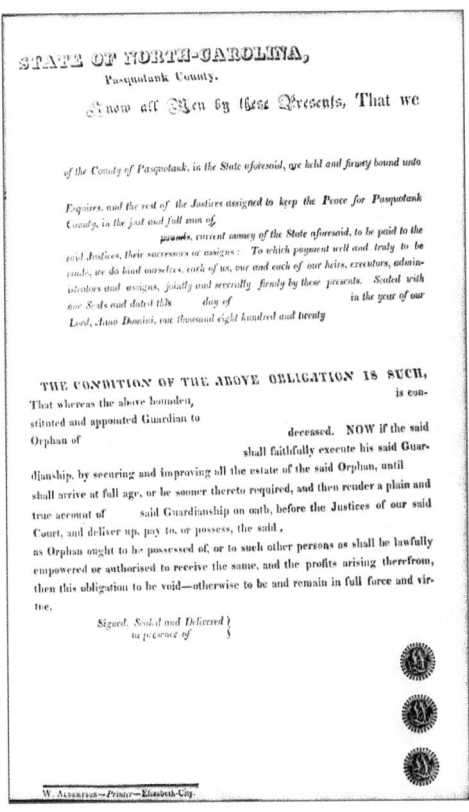

This was the first guardian bond book where the standard currency for Pasquotank County, N. C. was the American dollar. The forms, which were printed by W. Albertson – Printer – Elizabeth City, still had the word "pounds" for the accepted form of payment. This word was marked through on most of these forms and the word dollar was written in by hand.

I have omitted writing out the word dollar in these abstracts and have chosen instead to use a dollar sign ($) when writing the amounts on these bonds.

Ackiss, Thomas　　　　　1 March 1825　　　Bond No. 47
Ward: Francis Ackiss orphan of Thomas Ackiss deceased
Guardian: Stephen White　　　　　Bond amount: $6,000
Bondsmen: Stephen White, John Bailey, William Newbold

Bailey, Benjamin　　　　　8 June 1825　Bond No. 87
Wards: Rebecca Bailey, John Bailey & Mary Bailey orphans of
　　　Benjamin Bailey deceased
Guardian: William H. Davis　　　　　Bond amount: $300
Bondsmen: William H. Davis, Ambrose Knox, William Wilson

Bailey, Thomas　　　　　6 February 1826　　Bond No. 117
Wards: Thomas Bailey heirs deceased
Guardian: Benjamin Bailey　　　　　Bond amount: $100
Bondsmen: Benjamin Bailey, John Bailey, John Brothers

Banks, Jonathan　　　　　5 February 1827　　Bond No. 160
Ward: Thaddeus Banks orphan of Jonathan Banks deceased
Guardian: William F. Banks　　　　　Bond amount: $2000
Bondsmen: Wm. F. Banks, Wm. Freshwater, Thaddeus Freshwater

Banks, Jonathan　　　　　5 February 1827　　Bond No. 161
Ward: Jonathan Banks orphan of Jonathan Banks deceased
Guardian: William F. Banks　　　　　Bond amount: $2,000
Bondsmen: Wm. F. Banks, Wm. Freshwater, Thaddeus Freshwater

Banks, Thomas　　　　　7 December 1825　　Bond No. 108
Ward: Reding Banks orphan of Thomas Banks deceased
Guardian: Jonathan Banks　　　　　Bond amount: $3,000
Bondsmen: Jonathan Banks, Thaddeus Freshwater, Richard Pool

Banks, William C.　　　　7 March 1826　　Bond No. 121
Wards: Sarah Banks, William Banks, Rebecca Banks & Benjamin
　　　Banks orphans of William C. Banks deceased
Guardian: Benjamin B. Lowry　　　　　Bond amount: $10,000
Bondsmen: Benjamin B. Lowry, William Hardy, William W.
　　　Freshwater

Guardian Bond Book 1824 - 1827

Barclift, Rowan 5 June 1827 Bond No. 186
Wards: Juliet & Cassandra Barclift orphans of Rowan Barclift
Guardian: William Pritchard Bond amount: $500
Bondsmen: William Pritchard, John L. Bailey, John Bailey

Bell, John 5 June 1827 Bond No. 188
Wards: Southey, *(Majae?)* & Bailey Bell orphans of John Bell
Guardian: William Bartlett Bond amount: $5,000
Bondsmen: William Bartlett, Caleb Perkins, James Nash

Brite, Jabez 6 February 1826 Bond No. 113
Wards: Jabez Brite, Jesse Brite & Mary Brite orphans of Jabez
 Brite deceased
Guardian: Benjamin Pritchard Bond amount: $100
Bondsmen: Benjamin Pritchard, Caleb White, Samuel Pritchard

Brite, Jabez 5 February 1827 Bond No. 167
Wards: Jabez & Mary Brite orphans of Jabez Brite deceased
Guardian: Wilson Pike Bond amount: $100
Bondsmen: Wilson Pike, Benjamin Pike, Jonathan Pike

Broshir, Simon L. 7 February 1825 Bond No. 32
Ward: Elizabeth Broshir orphan of Simon L. Broshir deceased
Guardian: Simon B. Pool Bond amount: $2,000
Bondsmen: Simon B. Pool, Edmund H. Perkins, Thaddeus
 Freshwater

Broshir, Simon L. 7 February 1825 Bond No. 33
Ward: Joseph P. Broshir orphan of Simon L. Broshir deceased
Guardian: Simon B. Pool Bond amount: $2,000
Bondsmen: Simon B. Pool, Edmund H. Perkins, Thaddeus
 Freshwater

Broshur, John L. 8 March 1825 Bond No. 49
Ward: William Broshur orphan of John L. Broshur deceased
Guardian: Thaddeus Freshwater Bond amount: $500
Bondsmen: Thaddeus Freshwater, Thomas Markham, Lemuel
 Snowden

Broshur, Joseph 8 March 1825 Bond No. 50
Wards: Benjamin & Ann Broshur orphan of Joseph Broshur
Guardian: Thaddeus Freshwater Bond amount: $500
Bondsmen: Thaddeus Freshwater, Thomas Markham, Lemuel Snowden

Brothers, Richard 6 March 1827 Bond No. 183
Wards: Richard Brothers heirs deceased
Guardian: William Fletcher Bond amount: $1,000
Bondsmen: William Fletcher, Aaron Fletcher

Bundy, Benjamin 7 March 1826 Bond No. 126
Ward: Rix Bundy orphan of Benjamin Bundy deceased
Guardian: Caleb Morris Bond amount: $100
Bondsmen: Caleb Morris, Aaron White

Bundy, John 7 February 1825 Bond No. 12
Wards: Mary & Martha Bundy orphans of John Bundy deceased
Guardian: Nathan Bundy Bond amount: $100
Bondsmen: Nathan Bundy, Nathan Morgan, Jacob Symons

Bundy, Joseph 7 February 1825 Bond No. 20
Wards: Nancy & William Bundy orphans of Joseph Bundy deceased
Guardian: Jacob Symons Bond amount: $1,000
Bondsmen: Jacob Symons, Nathan Bundy, Anderson Morris

Cartwright, Benoni 9 March 1825 Bond No. 66
Ward: Elizabeth Cartwright orphan of Benoni Cartwright deceased
Guardian: William Wilson Bond amount: $500
Bondsmen: William Wilson, Ambrose Knox, L. B. Pool

Cartwright, Benoni 9 March 1825 Bond No. 67
Ward: William Cartwright orphan of Benoni Cartwright deceased
Guardian: William Wilson Bond amount: $500
Bondsmen: William Wilson, Ambrose Knox, L. B. Pool

Cartwright, Benoni 9 March 1825 Bond No. 68
Ward: Sarah Cartwright orphan of Benoni Cartwright deceased

Guardian Bond Book 1824 - 1827

Guardian: William Wilson   Bond amount: $500
Bondsmen: William Wilson, Ambrose Knox, L. B. Pool

Cartwright, Benoni   9 March 1825   Bond No. 69
Ward: Benoni Cartwright orphan of Benoni Cartwright deceased
Guardian: William Wilson   Bond amount: $500
Bondsmen: William Wilson, Ambrose Knox, L. B. Pool

Carver, Alfred   1 March 1825   Bond No. 46
Wards: Eliza & Mary Carver orphans of Alfred Carver deceased
Guardian: John McDonnell   Bond amount: $3,000
Bondsmen: John McDonnell, Edmund Perkins, William C. George

Carver, Elias   6 December 1825   Bond No. 105
Ward: Elias A. Carver orphan of Elias Carver deceased
Guardian: Joel Sawyer   Bond amount: $1,000
Bondsmen: Joel Sawyer, Job Carver, Abel Sawyer

Carver, Elias   6 December 1826   Bond No. 152
Ward: Mary Carver orphan of Elias Carver deceased
Guardian: Job Carver   Bond amount: $5,000
Bondsmen: Job Carver, Thornton Spence, Joel Sawyer

Carver, Elias   6 December 1826   Bond No. 153
Ward: Elizabeth Carver orphan of Elias Carver deceased
Guardian: Job Carver   Bond amount: $5,000
Bondsmen: Job Carver, Thornton Spence, Joel Sawyer

Casey, John   7 March 1826   Bond No. 123
Ward: John Casey orphan of John Casey deceased
Guardian: Stephen Scott   Bond amount: $2,000
Bondsmen: Stephen Scott, Abner Williams, Hollowell Scott

Casey, John   5 February 1827   Bond No. 166
Ward: John Casey orphan of John Casey deceased
Guardian: Robert Chancey*   Bond amount: $2,000
Bondsmen: Robert Casey, William Scott, James Scott
   (*Note: Robert Chancey was recorded as Guardian but the signature
   of the bondsman shows the name to be Robert Casey)

Casey, John   4 September 1827   Bond No. 190
Ward: Charity Casey orphan of John Casey deceased
Guardian: Sarah Casey   Bond amount: $200
Bondsmen: Sarah Casey Thomas Trueblood, William A. Pritchard

Chamberlain, James   8 June 1825   Bond No. 86
Wards: Margaret Chamberlain & Mary Chamberlain orphans of
        James Chamberlain deceased
Guardian: Ambrose Knox   Bond amount: $1500
Bondsmen: Ambrose Knox, William Wilson, William H. Davis

Commander, Thomas   4 September 1827   Bond No. 192
Ward: Mary Elizabeth Commander orphan of Thos. Commander
Guardian: Parthenia Commander   Bond amount: $4,000
Bondsmen: Parthenia Commander, Thos. Barnard, Carter Barnard

Coppersmith, John   5 February 1827   Bond No. 158
Wards: the heirs of John Coppersmith deceased
Guardian: Jacob Lister   Bond amount: $100
Bondsmen: Jacob Lister, Thomas Lister, Israel Lister

Crutch, William   7 December 1824   Bond No. 4
Wards: George & William Crutch orphans of William Crutch
Guardian: Demsey B. Pendleton   Bond amount: $2,000
Bondsmen: Demsey B. Pendleton, William W. Freshwater,
        Frederick Pendleton

Davis, Durant   9 March 1825   Bond No. 73
Wards: the orphans of Durant Davis deceased
Guardian: Carter Barnard   Bond amount: $200
Bondsmen: Carter Barnard, Thomas Barnard, William Barns

Davis, Edmund   7 June 1825   Bond No. 89
Wards: Edmund Davis's orphans; __ Davis, Devotion Davis,
        Josephine Davis, Edmund Davis & Elizabeth Davis
Guardian: John Bailey   Bond amount: $500
Bondsmen: John Bailey, Robert Bailey, Nathan Small

Guardian Bond Book 1824 - 1827   131

Etheridge, James   4 April 1825 Bond No. 76
Ward: Matthias Etheridge orphan of James Etheridge deceased
Guardian: Robert Bailey   Bond amount: $500
Bondsmen: Robert Bailey, John Bailey, John Overman

Etheridge, Richard   8 March 1825   Bond No. 52
Ward: Seth Etheridge orphan of Richard Etheridge deceased
Guardian: Thomas Markham   Bond amount: $1,000
Bondsmen: Thomas Markham, Lemuel Snowden, Thaddeus
 Freshwater

Etheridge, Richard   8 March 1825   Bond No. 53
Ward: William Etheridge orphan of Richard Etheridge deceased
Guardian: Thomas Markham   Bond amount: 1,000 pounds
Bondsmen: Thomas Markham, Lemuel Snowden, Thaddeus
 Freshwater

Etheridge, Richard   8 March 1825   Bond No. 54
Ward: Morris Etheridge orphan of Richard Etheridge deceased
Guardian: Thomas Markham   Bond amount: 1,000 pounds
Bondsmen: Thomas Markham, Lemuel Snowden, Thaddeus
 Freshwater

Evans, Benjamin   7 June 1825 Bond No. 83
Ward: Ann Evans orphan of Benjamin Evans deceased
Guardian: James Palmer   Bond amount: $400
Bondsmen: James Palmer, Wm. W. Freshwater, Benjamin Jackson

Ferebee, James   7 September 1826   Bond No. 141
Ward: Alfred Ferebee orphan of James Ferebee deceased
Guardian: Thomas R. Cobb   Bond amount: $500
Bondsmen: Thomas R. Cobb, John C. Ehringhaus, Lemuel C. Moore

Gambling, Jesse   6 March 1827   Bond No. 174
Ward: John Gambling orphan of Jesse Gambling deceased
Guardian: David Sharborough   Bond amount: $500
Bondsmen: David Sharborough, Robert Simpson, Cader Biddle

Gaskins, Thomas   7 December 1824   Bond No. 7
Ward: Nancy Gaskins orphan of Thomas Gaskins deceased
Guardian: Demsey B. Pendleton   Bond amount: $2,000
Bondsmen: Demsey B. Pendleton, William W. Freshwater,
        Frederick Pendleton

Gaskins, William   7 June 1826 Bond No. 133
Ward: William Gaskins orphan of William Gaskins deceased
Guardian: Solomon Pool Jr.   Bond amount: $2,000
Bondsmen: Solomon Pool Jr., John Winslow, John Pool

Gaskins, William   7 June 1826 Bond No. 134
Ward: Fanny Gaskins orphan of William Gaskins deceased
Guardian: Solomon Pool Jr.   Bond amount: $2,000
Bondsmen: Solomon Pool Jr., John Winslow, John Pool

Gaskins, William   7 June 1826 Bond No. 135
Ward: Thomas Gaskins orphan of William Gaskins deceased
Guardian: Solomon Pool Jr.   Bond amount: $2,000
Bondsmen: Solomon Pool Jr., John Winslow, John Pool

George, William C.   2 January 1826   Bond No. 111
Wards: Ann George & David George orphans of William C. George
Guardian: George W. Bailey   Bond amount: $500
Bondsmen: George W. Bailey, Carter Barnard, Thomas Jordan

Gilbert, John   7 June 1825 Bond No. 85
Wards: William Gilbert, Rhoda Gilbert & Susan Gilbert orphans
        of John Gilbert deceased
Guardian: Abel Sawyer   Bond amount: $700
Bondsmen: Abel Sawyer, Daniel Spence, Thomas Temple

Gilbert, John   5 September 1826   Bond No. 140
Wards: William Gilbert, Rhoda Gilbert & Susan Gilbert orphans
        of John Gilbert deceased
Guardian: Job Carver   Bond amount: $1500
Bondsmen: Job Carver, Mark Spence, Thomas Temple Jr.

Guardian Bond Book 1824 - 1827

Godfrey, Jacob 9 March 1825 Bond No. 70
Wards: Clarkey & Nancy Godfrey orphans of Jacob Godfrey
Guardian: Edmund Godfrey Bond amount: $3,000
Bondsmen: Edmund Godfrey, William Wilson, Solomon P. Pool

Godfrey, Jacob 8 June 1825 Bond No. 88
Wards: Clarkey & Nancy Godfrey orphans of Jacob Godfrey
Guardian: George W. Godfrey Bond amount: $1500
Bondsmen: George W. Godfrey, Edward E. Wilson, Nathan Small

Gray, Joseph 7 December 1824 Bond No. 5
Ward: Joseph Gray orphan of Joseph Gray deceased
Guardian: Griffin Gray Bond amount: $600
Bondsmen: Griffin Gray, Alson Spence, Harvey Williams

Gray, Joseph 7 December 1824 Bond No. 6
Ward: Elizabeth Gray orphan of Joseph Gray deceased
Guardian: Griffin Gray Bond amount: $600
Bondsmen: Griffin Gray, Alson Spence, Harvey Williams

Gray, Thornton 8 March 1825 Bond No. 59
Ward: _aney* Gray orphan of Thornton Gray deceased
Guardian: Harvey Williams Bond amount: $300
Bondsmen: Harvey Williams, Edward Williams, James Gray
   (*Note: possibly Thaney or Haney; identified as female)

Gray, Thornton 8 March 1825 Bond No. 60
Ward: Fanny Gray orphan of Thornton Gray deceased
Guardian: Harvey Williams Bond amount: $300
Bondsmen: Harvey Williams, Edward Williams, James Gray

Gray, Thornton 8 March 1825 Bond No. 61
Ward: Nancy Gray orphan of Thornton Gray deceased
Guardian: Harvey Williams Bond amount: $300
Bondsmen: Harvey Williams, Edward Williams, James Gray

Gray, Thornton 8 March 1825 Bond No. 62
Ward: Julin Gray orphan of Thornton Gray deceased

Guardian: Harvey Williams   Bond amount: $300
Bondsmen: Harvey Williams, Edward Williams, James Gray

Gregory, James   5 December 1826   Bond No. 143
Wards: Morris & Lemuel Gregory orphans of James Gregory
Guardian: Thaddeus Freshwater   Bond amount: $3,000
Bondsmen: Thaddeus Freshwater, William I. Hardy

Griffin, Thomas   8 February 1825   Bond No. 42
Ward: Moses H. Griffin orphan of Thomas Griffin deceased
Guardian: James Morgan   Bond amount: $300
Bondsmen: James Morgan, Caleb Raper, Charles Overman

Harris, John   7 March 1826   Bond No. 127
Ward: Susannah Harris orphan of John Harris deceased
Guardian: Lemuel Jennings   Bond amount: $500
Bondsmen: Lemuel Jennings, Jeremiah Sawyer

Harris, John   6 March 1827   Bond No. 175
Ward: Susannah Harris orphan of John Harris deceased
Guardian: Lemuel Jennings   Bond amount: $200
Bondsmen: Lemuel Jennings, Fred. Whitehurst, Jeremiah Sawyer

Hollowell, John   7 March 1826   Bond No. 125
Wards: Edmund, Zachariah, Margaret & Mary Hollowell orphans
    of John Hollowell deceased
Guardian: John White   Bond amount: $200
Bondsmen: John White, John Winslow, Aaron Lowe

Hollowell, Samuel   8 March 1825   Bond No. 55
Wards: Samuel Hollowell Heirs*
Guardian: Samuel Brothers   Bond amount: $300
Bondsmen: Samuel Brothers, Thomas Jordan, John MacDonall
          (*Note: the word orphan was scratched out)

Hollowell, Samuel   6 March 1827   Bond No. 173
Wards: John & Ambrose Hollowell orphans of Samuel Hollowell
Guardian: John McDonnell   Bond amount: $600
Bondsmen: John McDonnell, Edmund Perkins, Edward B. Godfrey

Guardian Bond Book 1824 - 1827

Humphries, Jonathan   5 February 1827   Bond No. 164
Ward: Mourning Humphries orphan of Jonathan Humphries
Guardian: John Bray   Bond amount: $1,000
Bondsmen: John Bray, Jesse Davis, James Bray

Humphries, Jonathan   5 February 1827   Bond No. 165
Ward: Richardson R. Humphries orphan of Jonathan Humphries
Guardian: John Bray   Bond amount: $1,000
Bondsmen: John Bray, Jesse Davis, James Bray

Jackson, Miles   6 December 1826   Bond No. 144
Ward: Mary Jackson daughter of Miles Jackson*
Guardian: Benjamin Bailey   Bond amount: $1,000
Bondsmen: Benjamin Bailey, John Bailey, John L. Bailey
(*Note: the word orphan was scratched out)

Jackson, William   8 December 1824   Bond No. 8
Ward: Lowry Jackson orphan of William Jackson deceased
Guardian: Thomas Jennings   Bond amount: $150
Bondsmen: Thomas Jennings, Lemuel Jennings, Samuel Jennings

James, Benjamin   8 March 1825   Bond No. 51
Ward: William James orphan of Benjamin James deceased
Guardian: Lemuel Snowden   Bond amount: $2,000
Bondsmen: Lemuel Snowden, Thaddeus Freshwater, Thomas Markham

Jennings, James   7 June 1825   Bond No. 80
Ward: Mary Jennings orphan of James Jennings deceased
Guardian: James Whidbee   Bond amount: $1,000
Bondsmen: James Whidbee, Joseph Pritchard, Joseph Albertson

Jones, Samuel   7 February 1825   Bond No. 25
Wards: Joseph E. Jones, John R. Jones & James I. Jones orphans
   of Samuel Jones deceased
Guardian: Anthony Davis   Bond amount: 1,000 pounds
Bondsmen: Anthony Davis, Joseph Davis, Joel Sawyer

Knox, Hugh 8 March 1826 Bond No. 128
Ward: Thomas D. Knox orphan of Hugh Knox deceased
Guardian: William C. Brooks Bond amount: $2,000
Bondsmen: William C. Brooks, John M. Skinner, John Pool

Lister, Jacob 9 March 1825 Bond No. 63
Ward: Sarah Lister orphan of Jacob Lister deceased
Guardian: William Wilson Bond amount: $500
Bondsmen: William Wilson, Ambrose Knox, L. B. Pool

Lister, Jacob 9 March 1825 Bond No. 64
Ward: Thomas Lister orphan of Jacob Lister deceased
Guardian: William Wilson Bond amount: $500
Bondsmen: William Wilson, Ambrose Knox, L. B. Pool

Lister, Jacob 9 March 1825 Bond No. 65
Ward: Susannah Lister orphan of Jacob Lister deceased
Guardian: William Wilson Bond amount: $500
Bondsmen: William Wilson, Ambrose Knox, L. B. Pool

Long, Jesse 6 September 1825 Bond No. 92
Wards: Daniel & Lowry Long orphans of Jesse Long deceased
Guardian: Daniel Long Bond amount: $100
Bondsmen: Daniel Long, Thomas Barnard, Thomas Bell

Madison, Matthias 7 February 1825 Bond No. 18
Ward: Matthias Madison orphan of Matthias Madison deceased
Guardian: Edmund Trueblood Bond amount: $1,000
Bondsmen: Edmund Trueblood, Abner Williams, David Sharber

Markham,* Thomas 7 June 1825 Bond No. 84
Wards: William Markham, Penelope Markham & Anthony S.
       Markham, Thos. R. Markham & John Markham orphans
       of Thomas __* deceased
Guardian: John Tooley Bond amount: $5,000
Bondsmen: John Tooley, Jonathan Banks, Anthony R. Markham
  *(*Note: only his given name was written on the bond)*

Guardian Bond Book 1824 - 1827

McDonell, John 6 September 1825 Bond No. 96
Wards: Grizell, Elizabeth & Johanna orphans of John McDonell
Guardian: George W. Bailey Bond amount: $5,000
Bondsmen: George Bailey, Thomas Commander, Carter Barnard

McDonnell, John 6 December 1826 Bond No. 145
Ward: Grizzle McDonnell orphan of John W. McDonnell deceased
Guardian: John MacDonell Bond amount: $8,000
Bondsmen: John MacDonell, Thad. Freshwater, Edmund Perkins

McDonnell, John 6 December 1826 Bond No. 146
Ward: Elizabeth McDonnell orphan of John W. McDonnell
Guardian: John MacDonell Bond amount: $8,000
Bondsmen: John MacDonell, Thad. Freshwater, Edmund Perkins

McDonnell, John 6 December 1826 Bond No. 147
Ward: John McDonnell orphan of John W. McDonnell deceased
Guardian: John MacDonell Bond amount: $8,000
Bondsmen: John MacDonell, Thad. Freshwater, Edmund Perkins

Meeds, Benjamin 6 December 1826 Bond No. 151
Ward: Stanton Meeds orphan of Benjamin Meeds deceased
Guardian: Elijah Meeds Bond amount: $ 100
Bondsmen: Elijah Meeds, Thaddeus Freshwater, John James

Morgan, Benjamin 6 February 1826 Bond No. 116
Wards: Benjamin Morgan heirs
Guardian: Cader Munden Bond amount: $1,000
Bondsmen: Cader Munden, Nathan Morgan, Nathan Bundy

Morgan, Charles 7 February 1825 Bond No. 11
Ward: Uria Morgan orphan of Charles Morgan deceased
Guardian: Nathan Morgan Bond amount: $250
Bondsmen: Nathan Morgan, Nathan Bundy, Cader Munden

Morris, Christopher 7 February 1825 Bond No. 22
Ward: Margaret Morris orphan of Christopher Morris deceased
Guardian: Thomas Pritchard Bond amount: $1,000
Bondsmen: Thomas Pritchard, Joseph Pritchard, Nathan Bundy

Morris, Joshua   7 February 1825   Bond No. 26
Ward: Hannah Morris orphan of Joshua Morris deceased
Guardian: Anderson Morris   Bond amount: 2,000 pounds
Bondsmen: Anderson Morris, Benjamin Pritchard, Wm. Trueblood

Morris, Joshua   7 February 1825   Bond No. 27
Ward: Joseph H. Morris orphan of Joshua Morris deceased
Guardian: Anderson Morris   Bond amount: 2,000 pounds
Bondsmen: Anderson Morris, Benjamin Pritchard, Wm. Trueblood

Morris, Joshua   6 February 1826   Bond No. 118
Ward: Hannah Elliott orphan of Joshua Morris deceased
Guardian: Anderson Morris   Bond amount: $2,000
Bondsmen: Anderson Morris, Mordecai Morris

Morris, Joshua   6 February 1826   Bond No. 119
Ward: Joseph H. Morris orphan of Joshua Morris deceased
Guardian: Anderson Morris   Bond amount: $2,000
Bondsmen: Anderson Morris, Mordecai Morris Jr.

Morris, Mark   7 December 1826   Bond No. 154
Ward: Sarah Morris orphan of Mark Morris deceased
Guardian: Caleb White   Bond amount: $500
Bondsmen: Caleb White, Anderson Morris, Stephen White

Morris, Mark   7 December 1826   Bond No. 155
Ward: Mark Morris orphan of Mark Morris deceased
Guardian: Caleb White   Bond amount: $500
Bondsmen: Caleb White, Anderson Morris, Stephen White

Morris, Mordecai   6 February 1826   Bond No. 115
Wards: Susanna & John W. Morris children of Mordecai Morris*
Guardian: Mordecai Morris Jr.   Bond amount: $3,000
Bondsmen: Mordecai Morris Jr., Anderson Morris, Nathan Morris
      (*Note: the word orphan was scratched out)

Morris, Thomas   5 February 1827   Bond No. 156
Ward: Joshua Morris orphan of Thomas Morris deceased

Guardian Bond Book 1824 - 1827

Guardian: Anderson Morris   Bond amount: $2,000
Bondsmen: Anderson Morris, Mordecai Morris, Caleb White

Morris, Thomas   5 February 1827   Bond No. 157
Ward: Sarah Ann Morris orphan of Thomas Morris deceased
Guardian: Anderson Morris   Bond amount: $2,000
Bondsmen: Anderson Morris, Mordecai Morris, Caleb White

Mullin, John   5 June 1826   Bond No. 130
Wards: Margaret Ann Mullin & Louise Francis Mullin orphan of
    John Mullin deceased
Guardian: Catherine Mullen   Bond amount: $20,000
Bondsmen: Catherine Mullin, Joseph Mullin, Thomas Harvey

Mullin, Stephen   7 September 1824   Bond No. 2
Wards: Elizabeth & Ambrose Mullin orphans of Stephen Mullin
Guardian: Addison Whidbee   Bond amount: $3,000
Bondsmen: Addison Whidbee, Ambrose Knox, William H. Davis

Newbold, Thomas   8 December 1824   Bond No. 9
Ward: William Newbold orphan of Thomas Newbold deceased
Guardian: James Palmer   Bond amount: $500
Bondsmen: James Palmer, William W. Freshwater, Nathan Small

Nixon, James   7 February 1825   Bond No. 13
Ward: Mary Ann Nixon orphan of James Nixon deceased
Guardian: Sarah Perry   Bond amount: $200
Bondsmen: Sarah Perry, Rix Perry, Nathan Morgan

Overman, Charles   7 February 1825   Bond No. 28
Ward: Elizabeth Overman orphan of Charles Overman deceased
Guardian: Joseph Parker   Bond amount: $500
Bondsmen: Joseph Parker, Stephen White, Edmund H. Perkins

Overman, Henry P.   6 December 1825   Bond No. 107
Ward: Nathan Overman orphan of Henry P. Overman deceased
Guardian: George Pendleton   Bond amount: $1,000
Bondsmen: George Pendleton, Edmund B. Godfrey, Nehemiah
    Pendleton

Overman, Mordecai   5 September 1826   Bond No. 139
Ward: George W. Overman orphan of Mordecai Overman deceased
Guardian: William I. Hardy   Bond amount: $1500
Bondsmen: William I. Hardy, Thaddeus Freshwater, William
   Freshwater

Overman, Nathan   5 February 1827   Bond No. 163
Wards: Mary Overman, Martha Overman & Elizabeth Overman
   orphans of Nathan Overman deceased
Guardian: Charles Overman   Bond amount: $1,000
Bondsmen: Charles Overman, Nathan Morgan, Eli White

Overman, Nathan   6 March 1827   Bond No. 176
Ward: Mary Overman orphan of Nathan Overman deceased
Guardian: Will. W. Freshwater   Bond amount: $1,000
Bondsmen: Will. W. Freshwater, W. I. Hardy, Bray B. Long

Overman, Nathan   6 March 1827   Bond No. 177
Ward: Henry Overman orphan of Nathan Overman deceased
Guardian: Will. W. Freshwater   Bond amount: $1,000
Bondsmen: Will. W. Freshwater, W. I. Hardy, Bray B. Long

Overman, Thomas   7 February 1825   Bond No. 36
Wards: Thomas Overman Heirs*
Guardian: Benjamin Bailey   Bond amount: 1,000 pounds
Bondsmen: Benjamin Bailey, Eli White, Nathan Morgan
   (*Note: the word orphan was scratched out)

Palin, Thomas   6 December 1825   Bond No. 103
Wards: John, Henry & Nancy Palin orphans of Thomas Palin
Guardian: Frederick Pendleton   Bond amount: $2,000
Bondsmen: Frederick Pendleton, Abner Pendleton, Demsey B.
   Pendleton

Pendleton, George W.   7 February 1825   Bond No. 29
Ward: Nancy Pendleton orphan of George W. Pendleton deceased
Guardian: Edmund H. Perkins   Bond amount: $800
Bondsmen: Edmund H. Perkins, Joseph Parker, John McDonnell

Guardian Bond Book 1824 - 1827

Pendleton, George W.　　7 February 1825　　Bond No. 30
Ward: Maranda Pendleton orphan of George W. Pendleton
Guardian: Edmund H. Perkins　　　Bond amount: $800
Bondsmen: Edmund H. Perkins, Joseph Parker, John McDonnell

Pendleton, Timothy　　6 December 1826　　Bond No. 148
Ward: Timothy Pendleton orphan of Timothy Pendleton deceased
Guardian: William Weaver　　　Bond amount: $1,000
Bondsmen: William Weaver, Solomon Pool, Ambrose Sewell

Perry, Cader　　7 February 1825　　Bond No. 21
Ward: Sarah Perry orphan of Cader Perry deceased
Guardian: Sarah Perry　　　Bond amount: $1,000
Bondsmen: Sarah Perry, Rix Perry, Nathan Morgan

Perry, Hardy　　7 December 1824　　Bond No. 3
Wards: Polly, Sally, Hardy & John Perry orphans of Hardy Perry
Guardian: Rix Perry　　　Bond amount: $1,000
Bondsmen: Rix Perry, John Winslow, William _ Bagley

Perry, Jacob　　5 June 1827　　Bond No. 185
Wards: the heirs of Jacob Perry deceased
Guardian: Aaron Low　　　Bond amount: $500
Bondsmen: Aaron Low, John Winslow, Ruben Overman

Perry, William　　8 March 1825　　Bond No. 56
Ward: Sab_na Perry orphan of William Perry deceased
Guardian: Sarah Perry　　　Bond amount: $500
Bondsmen: Sarah Perry, Robinson White, Benjamin White

Perry, William　　8 March 1825　　Bond No. 57
Ward: Davis W. Perry orphan of William Perry deceased
Guardian: Sarah Perry　　　Bond amount: $500
Bondsmen: Sarah Perry, Robinson White, Benjamin White

Perry, William　　8 March 1825　　Bond No. 58
Ward: Sarah E. Perry orphan of William Perry deceased
Guardian: Sarah Perry　　　Bond amount: $500
Bondsmen: Sarah Perry, Robinson White, Benjamin White

Perry, William & Sarah 7 June 1826 Bond No. 137
Wards: Alexis A., Matthew, William, Nelson, Davis & Elizabeth
    Perry orphans of William & Sarah Perry deceased
Guardian: Jacob Winslow Sanders Bond amount: $20,000
Bondsmen: Jacob Winslow Sanders, Joseph White Sr., William R.
    Nixon

Pike, Jesse 7 February 1825 Bond No. 14
Ward: Wilson Pike orphan of Jesse Pike deceased
Guardian: Abner Williams Bond amount: $200
Bondsmen: Abner Williams, David Sharber, Edmund Trueblood

Pike, Jesse 7 February 1825 Bond No. 15
Ward: Jesse Pike orphan of Jesse Pike deceased
Guardian: Abner Williams Bond amount: $200
Bondsmen: Abner Williams, David Sharber, Edmund Trueblood

Pike, Jesse 7 February 1825 Bond No. 16
Ward: Ferebee Pike orphan of Jesse Pike deceased
Guardian: Abner Williams Bond amount: $400
Bondsmen: Abner Williams, David Sharber, Edmund Trueblood

Pool, James 6 December 1825 Bond No. 101
Wards: Alfred Pool, Elizabeth Pool, Mary Pool, Ann Pool &
    Patrick Pool orphans of James Pool deceased
Guardian: Thomas Pool Bond amount: $20,000
Bondsmen: Thomas Pool, Solomon Pool, Stephen Charles

Pool, Jno. Jr. 5 February 1827 Bond No. 162
Wards: Jno. Pool Jr.'s orphans
Guardian: Robert Pool Bond amount: $1500
Bondsmen: Robert Pool, Solomon Pool Jr., Carter Barnard

Pritchard, Caleb 6 March 1827 Bond No. 178
Ward: Benjamin Pritchard orphan of Caleb Pritchard deceased
Guardian: Caleb White Bond amount: $1,000
Bondsmen: Caleb White, Miles White, Anderson Morris

Guardian Bond Book 1824 - 1827

Pritchard, Hugh   9 December 1825   Bond No. 110
Wards: Joseph & Jane Pritchard orphans of Hugh Pritchard deceased
Guardian: Elisha Draper   Bond amount: $4,000
Bondsmen: Elisha Draper, Joel Sawyer, Job Carver

Pritchard, Hugh   6 March 1827   Bond No. 168
Ward: Joseph Pritchard orphan of Hugh Pritchard deceased
Guardian: Jonathan Brite   Bond amount: $2,000
Bondsmen: Jonathan Brite, Elisha Draper, Lodwick Williams

Pritchard, Hugh   6 March 1827   Bond No. 169
Ward: Jane Pritchard orphan of Hugh Pritchard deceased
Guardian: Jonathan Brite   Bond amount: $2,000
Bondsmen: Jonathan Brite, Elisha Draper, Lodwick Williams

Pritchard, James   6 September 1825   Bond No. 93
Ward: Margaret Pritchard orphan of James Pritchard deceased
Guardian: William A. Pritchard   Bond amount: $3,000
Bondsmen: William A. Pritchard, John Bailey, Nathan Small

Pritchard, James   6 September 1825   Bond No. 94
Ward: Ann Pritchard orphan of James Pritchard deceased
Guardian: William A. Pritchard   Bond amount: $3,000
Bondsmen: William A. Pritchard, John Bailey, Nathan Small

Pritchard, James   6 September 1825   Bond No. 95
Ward: Sally Pritchard orphan of James Pritchard deceased
Guardian: William A. Pritchard   Bond amount: $3,000
Bondsmen: William A. Pritchard, John Bailey, Nathan Small

Pritchard, John   5 December 1825   Bond No. 100
Ward: Lacy Pritchard orphan of John Pritchard deceased
Guardian: Samuel Brothers   Bond amount: $500
Bondsmen: Samuel Brothers, Robert Simpson, John Brothers

Pritchard, Richard   6 September 1825   Bond No. 97
Ward: Peter Pritchard orphan of Richard Pritchard deceased

Pasquotank County, North Carolina

Guardian: Lemuel Jennings   Bond amount: $600
Bondsmen: Lemuel Jennings Fredrick Whitehurst, Jeremiah
      Sawyer

Pritchard, Richard   6 September 1825   Bond No. 98
Ward: Philip Pritchard orphan of Richard Pritchard deceased
Guardian: Lemuel Jennings   Bond amount: $600
Bondsmen: Lemuel Jennings Frederick Whitehurst, Jeremiah
      Sawyer

Pritchard, Thomas   6 March 1826   Bond No. 120
Ward: Thomas Pritchard orphan of Thomas Pritchard deceased
Guardian: Sarah Pritchard   Bond amount: $100
Bondsmen: Sarah Pritchard, Rubin T. Harris, Maxey Harris

Proby, Paul   7 February 1825   Bond No. 23
Ward: Sarah Proby orphan of Paul Proby deceased
Guardian: Thomas Pritchard   Bond amount: $100
Bondsmen: Thomas Pritchard, Joseph Pritchard, Nathan Bundy

Raper, Cornelius   6 February 1826   Bond No. 114
Wards: Samuel Raper & Robert Raper orphans of Cornelius Raper
Guardian: Benjamin Bailey   Bond amount: $300
Bondsmen: Benjamin Bailey, John Bailey, John Brothers

Raper, Henry   8 March 1825   Bond No. 48
Ward: Joshua Raper orphan of Henry Raper deceased
Guardian: Richard Pool   Bond amount: $500
Bondsmen: Richard Pool, James Pool, John Pool

Raper, John   8 February 1825   Bond No. 43
Ward: John Raper orphan of John Raper deceased
Guardian: Caleb Raper   Bond amount: $600
Bondsmen: Caleb Raper, Richard Pool, James Morgan

Raper, John   8 February 1825   Bond No. 44
Ward: Patsy Raper orphan of John Raper deceased

Guardian Bond Book 1824 - 1827　　　145

Guardian: Caleb Raper　　　　　　　Bond amount: $1,000
Bondsmen: Caleb Raper, Richard Pool, James Morgan

Raper, John　　　　8 February 1825　　　Bond No. 45
Ward: Robert Raper orphan of John Raper deceased
Guardian: Caleb Raper　　　　　　　Bond amount: $2,000
Bondsmen: Caleb Raper, Richard Pool, James Morgan

Relfe, Joseph　　　　4 April 1825　　　Bond No. 74
Wards: the orphans of Joseph Relfe deceased
Guardian: William Wilson　　　　　Bond amount: $1,000
Bondsmen: William Wilson, Ambrose Knox

Richardson, Daniel　　6 December 1825　　　Bond No. 104
Wards: William Richardson & John Richardson orphans of Daniel
　　　Richardson deceased
Guardian: Demsey Richardson　　　Bond amount: $3,000
Bondsmen: Demsey Richardson, Thomas Temple, Levi Richardson

Richardson, Daniel　　7 December 1825　　　Bond No. 109
Wards: William Richardson & John Richardson orphans of Daniel
　　　Richardson deceased
Guardian: Daniel Spence　　　　　Bond amount: $1,000
Bondsmen: Daniel Spence, Mark Spence, Elisha Draper
　　*(Note: at the bottom of the bond the following was written; "In this
　　Case, Demsey Richardson has been appointed, this Court"*

Richardson, Miles　　8 February 1825　　　Bond No. 41
Wards: Gabby Richardson, Miles Richardson & Benjamin
　　　Richardson orphans of Miles Richardson deceased
Guardian: George Ferebee　　　　Bond amount: $1,000
Bondsmen: George Ferebee, Thomas Temple

Richardson, Richard　　6 March 1827　　　Bond No. 172
Ward: Fanny Richardson orphan of Richard Richardson deceased
Guardian: Malachi W. Jones　　　Bond amount: $500
Bondsmen: Malachi W. Jones, Fredrick Jones, David Nichols

Saltenstall, Dudley   5 September 1826   Bond No. 138
Ward: Louisa Saltenstall orphan of Dudley Saltenstall deceased
Guardian: Chaprin Saltenstall   Bond amount: $ 2,000
Bondsmen: Chaprin Saltenstall, Robert Bailey, William Davis

Sawyer, Abel   5 June 1827   Bond No. 187
Wards: Daniel Sawyer, Mark Sawyer, Spence Sawyer & Margaret
      Sawyer orphans of Abel Sawyer deceased
Guardian: Job Carver   Bond amount: $6,000
Bondsmen: Job Carver, Jordan Gray, David Nichols

Sawyer, Enoch   6 March 1827   Bond No. 182
Wards: Clarkey & William Sawyer orphans of Enoch Sawyer
Guardian: Joseph Stokely   Bond amount: $100
Bondsmen: Joseph Stokely, James Williams, Edward Williams

Sawyer, Enoch   4 September 1827   Bond No. 189
Ward: Ann Elizabeth Sawyer orphan of Enoch Sawyer deceased
Guardian: Daniel Spence   Bond amount: $1,000
Bondsmen: Daniel Spence, Lodwick Williams, David Nichols

Sawyer, Hollowell   6 December 1825   Bond No. 102
Ward: Ira Sawyer orphan of Hollowell Sawyer deceased
Guardian: Jonathan Brite   Bond amount: $300
Bondsmen: Jonathan Brite, Harvey Williams, Alson Spence

Sawyer, John   7 September 1824   Bond No. 1
Wards: Thomas Sawyer & Charity Sawyer orphans of John Sawyer
Guardian: John Whaley   Bond amount: $500
Bondsmen: John Whaley, Miles Gregory, A. Williams

Sawyer, Thomas   6 June 1826   Bond No. 131
Ward: William Sawyer orphan of Thomas Sawyer deceased
Guardian: Ambrose Sewell   Bond amount: $2,000
Bondsmen: Ambrose Sewell, John White, Thomas Palin

Sawyer, Wilson   7 June 1826   Bond No. 136
Wards: Julian, Enoch, William Templeman & Fanny Sawyer
      orphans of Wilson Sawyer deceased

Guardian Bond Book 1824 - 1827   147

Guardian: William B. Shepard   Bond amount: $20,000
Bondsmen: William B. Shepard, Ambrose Knox, Enoch Sawyer

Scott, Marmaduke   7 February 1825   Bond No. 34
Ward: Susannah Scott orphan of Marmaduke Scott deceased
Guardian: Jeremiah Sawyer   Bond amount: $2,000
Bondsmen: Jeremiah Sawyer, Lemuel Jennings, Allen B. Jones

Scott, Marmaduke   6 March 1827   Bond No. 170
Ward: Sophia Scott orphan of Marmaduke Scott deceased
Guardian: Allen B. Jones   Bond amount: $1,000
Bondsmen: Alan B. Jones, James Bray, Jeremiah Sawyer

Scott, Marmaduke   6 March 1827   Bond No. 171
Ward: George W. Scott orphan of Marmaduke Scott deceased
Guardian: Allen B. Jones   Bond amount: $1,000
Bondsmen: Alan B. Jones, James Bray, Jeremiah Sawyer

Scott, Stephen   6 February 1826   Bond No. 112
Wards: Ruth Scott, Joseph Scott, Benoni Scott & Elizabeth Scott
         orphans of Stephen Scott deceased
Guardian: William Scott   Bond amount: $3,000
Bondsmen: William Scott, James Scott, Robert Casey

Scott, Stephen   6 December 1826   Bond No. 149
Wards: Sally Scott & *(Samuel or Lemuel?)* Scott orphan of
         Stephen Scott deceased
Guardian: William I. Hardy   Bond amount: $500
Bondsmen: William I. Hardy, Thaddeus Freshwater, Lemuel
         Snowden

Sexton, Samuel   8 June 1825   Bond No. 90
Wards: Olly Sexton, William Sexton, Mary Sexton & Elizabeth
         Sexton orphans of Samuel Sexton deceased
Guardian: Maxey Williams   Bond amount: $2,000
Bondsmen: Maxey Williams, Daniel McPherson, Jesse Davis

Simpson, Hezekiah 7 February 1825 Bond No. 10
Wards: Mairus Simpson, Catherine Simpson & (unreadable)
    Simpson orphans of Hezekiah Simpson deceased
Guardian: Asa Rogerson Bond amount: $2,000
Bondsmen: Asa Rogerson, Lemuel C. Morris, ___ Charles

Simpson, Joab 7 February 1825 Bond No. 37
Wards: _lly Simpson & Robert Simpson orphans of Joab Simpson
Guardian: Zachariah Brothers Bond amount: 500 pounds
Bondsmen: Zachariah Brothers, Caleb Brothers, John White

Simpson, John 7 February 1825 Bond No. 17
Wards: Harriett Simpson & George Simpson orphans of John
    Simpson deceased
Guardian: Abner Williams Bond amount: $1,000
Bondsmen: Abner Williams, David Sharber, Edmund Trueblood

Small, Joseph 6 June 1826 Bond No. 132
Ward: Joseph Small orphan of Joseph Small deceased
Guardian: Thomas Lister Bond amount: $750
Bondsmen: Thomas Lister, Jacob Lister, Elisha Lister

Smith, Robert 7 February 1825 Bond No. 39
Ward: Sally Smith orphan of Robert Smith deceased
Guardian: David Scaff Bond amount: $300
Bondsmen: David Scaff, James Scaff, John Scaff

Smith, Robert 7 February 1825 Bond No. 40
Ward: Joseph Smith orphan of Robert Smith deceased
Guardian: David Scaff Bond amount: $300
Bondsmen: David Scaff, James Scaff, John Scaff

Smith, Robert 5 September 1827 Bond No. 193
Ward: Sally Smith orphan of Robert Smith deceased
Guardian: Asa McCoy Bond amount: $200
Bondsmen: Asa McCoy, Abner Williams, Spencer Sawyer

Smith, Robert 5 September 1827 Bond No. 194
Ward: Joseph Smith orphan of Robert Smith deceased
Guardian: Asa McCoy Bond amount: $200
Bondsmen: Asa McCoy, Abner Williams, Spencer Sawyer

Smithson, Elisha 7 February 1825 Bond No. 38
Wards: Polly Smithson & Charity Smithson orphans of Elisha
       Smithson deceased
Guardian: James Scott Bond amount: 1,000 pounds
Bondsmen: James Scott, William Scott, Jesse Simpson

Spence, Mark 7 February 1825 Bond No. 31
Wards: Elizabeth Spence, Martha Spence, William Spence &
       Nancy Spence orphans of Mark Spence deceased
Guardian: Parthenia Spence Bond amount: $500
Bondsmen: Parthenia Spence, Joel Sawyer, Elisha _ Delon

Stott, Thomas 1 August 1825 Bond No. 91
Ward: William Stott orphan of Thomas Stott deceased
Guardian: Francis Fletcher Bond amount: $1500
Bondsmen: Francis Fletcher, Solomon Pool, Thaddeus Freshwater

Stott, Thomas 6 December 1825 Bond No. 106
Wards: William Scott & Elizabeth Stott orphans of Thomas Stott
Guardian: Jonathan Banks Bond amount: $3,000
Bondsmen: Jonathan Banks, William F. Lowry, John Tooley

Thomson, Henry 7 February 1825 Bond No. 19
Ward: John Thomson orphan of Henry Thomson deceased
Guardian: Edmund Trueblood Bond amount: $500
Bondsmen: Edmund Trueblood, Abner Williams, David Sharber

Trueblood, Samuel 4 April 1825 Bond No. 75
Ward: Mary Trueblood orphan of Samuel Trueblood deceased
Guardian: Robert Bailey Bond amount: $1500
Bondsmen: Robert Bailey, John Bailey, John Overman

Tubbs, William   7 March 1826   Bond No. 122
Ward: William D. Tubbs orphan of William Tubbs deceased
Guardian: Horatio N. Williams   Bond amount: $12,000
Bondsmen: Horatio N. Williams, John McMorine, Isaiah Fearing

White, Benjamin   7 February 1825   Bond No. 24
Ward: Samuel White orphan of Benjamin White deceased
Guardian: William W. Freshwater   Bond amount: $500
Bondsmen: William W. Freshwater, James Palmer, Thaddeus
     Freshwater

White, Benjamin   7 February 1825   Bond No. 35
Ward: George White orphan of Benjamin White deceased
Guardian: Eli White   Bond amount: 2,000 pounds
Bondsmen: Eli White, Benjamin Bailey, Nathan Morgan

White, Benjamin   5 February 1827   Bond No. 159
Ward: George White orphan of Benjamin White deceased
Guardian: Eli White   Bond amount: $2,000
Bondsmen: Eli White, Nathan Morgan, Charles Overman

White, Benjamin   4 September 1827   Bond No. 191
Ward: George White orphan of Benjamin White deceased
Guardian: Charles Overman   Bond amount: $1,000
Bondsmen: Charles Overman, Nathan Morgan, Benjamin White

White, Edmund   5 December 1826   Bond No. 142
Ward: Margaret S. White orphan of Edmund White deceased
Guardian: Aaron White   Bond amount: $14,000
Bondsmen: Aaron White, Alfred White, Benjamin Pritchard

White, James   7 March 1826   Bond No. 124
Ward: Mary White orphan of James White deceased
Guardian: William W. Freshwater   Bond amount: $200
Bondsmen: William W. Freshwater, Thaddeus Freshwater,
     William Hardy

Guardian Bond Book 1824 - 1827 151

White, Josiah 4 April 1825 Bond No. 77
Ward: Ruben White orphan of Josiah White deceased
Guardian: Joseph Pritchard Bond amount: $500
Bondsmen: Joseph Pritchard, Benjamin Pritchard

White, Josiah 7 June 1825 Bond No. 81
Ward: Martha White orphan of Josiah White Esq. deceased
Guardian: David White Bond amount: $1500
Bondsmen: David White, Joseph Pritchard, James Whidbee

White, Josiah 7 June 1825 Bond No. 82
Ward: Jeptha White orphan of Josiah White Esq. deceased
Guardian: David White Bond amount: $1500
Bondsmen: David White, Joseph Pritchard, James Whidbee

White, Nathan 5 June 1826 Bond No. 129
Ward: Miriam White orphan of Nathan White deceased
Guardian: Thomas White Bond amount: $200
Bondsmen: Thomas White, William Nixon, John Overman

White, Stephen 6 June 1825 Bond No. 79
Ward: Matthew White orphan of Stephen White deceased
Guardian: Josiah Perry Bond amount: $1200
Bondsmen: Josiah Perry, Benjamin Bailey, William Newbold

Whitney, Abner 5 June 1827 Bond No. 184
Ward: Franklin Whitney orphan of Abner Whitney deceased
Guardian: William D. Whitney Bond amount: $1,000
Bondsmen: William D. Whitney, Joseph Stokely, Harvey
        Williams

Wilcocks, Jeremiah 6 September 1825 Bond No. 99
Wards: Eliz, James, Susannah, Jesse, Stephen & __ orphans of
        Jeremiah Wilcocks deceased
Guardian: Elliott Whitehurst Bond amount: $ 2,000
Bondsmen: Elliott Whitehurst, Fredrick Whitehurst, Shadrach
        Davis

Williams, Demcy 9 March 1825 Bond No. 71
Ward: John T. Williams orphan of Demcy Williams deceased
Guardian: Thomas Jordan Bond amount: $2,000
Bondsmen: Thos. Jordan, Thomas Commander, William C. George

Williams, Owen 6 March 1827 Bond No. 179
Ward: Elizabeth Williams orphan of Owen Williams deceased
Guardian: Joseph Stokely Bond amount: $2,000
Bondsmen: Joseph Stokely, James Williams, Noah Sawyer

Williams, Owen 6 March 1827 Bond No. 180
Ward: Sarah Williams orphan of Owen Williams deceased
Guardian: Joseph Stokely Bond amount: $2,000
Bondsmen: Joseph Stokely, James Williams, Noah Sawyer

Williams, Owen 6 March 1827 Bond No. 181
Ward: Mejiah Williams orphan of Owen Williams deceased
Guardian: Joseph Stokely Bond amount: $1,000
Bondsmen: Joseph Stokely, James Williams, Noah Sawyer

Wilroy, Nathaniel 4 April 1825 Bond No. 78
Ward: Nathaniel Wilroy orphan of Nathaniel Wilroy deceased
Guardian: William Martin Bond amount: $1,000
Bondsmen: William Martin, John C. Ehringhaus, Lemuel Moore

Wilson, Frances 9 March 1825 Bond No. 72
Ward: Wilson Wilson orphan of Francis Wilson deceased
Guardian: Carter Barnard Bond amount: $200
Bondsmen: Carter Barnard, Thomas Barnard, William Barns

Pasquotank County, North Carolina
Guardian Bonds
Book 1827 - 1831

STATE OF NORTH-CAROLINA,
Pasquotank County.

KNOW ALL MEN BY THESE PRESENTS, That we

of the County of Pasquotank, in the State aforesaid, are held and firmly bound unto his Excellency   Esquire, Governor and Commander in Chief in and over the State of North Carolina, in the just and full sum of   Dollars, current money of the State aforesaid, to be paid to the said Governor or his successor in office: To which payment well and truly to be made, we do bind ourselves, each of us, our and each of our heirs, executors, administrators, and assigns, jointly and severally, firmly by these presents. Sealed with our Seals, and dated this   day of   in the year of our Lord, Anno. Dom. one thousand eight hundred and twenty

THE CONDITION OF THE ABOVE OBLIGATION IS SUCH, That whereas the above bounden   is constituted and appointed Guardian to   Orphan of   deceased. NOW if the said,   shall faithfully execute his said Guardianship, by securing and improving all the estate of the said Orphan, until   shall arrive at full age, or be sooner thereto required, and then render a plain and true account of   said Guardianship on oath, before the Justices of the Court of the County aforesaid, and deliver up, pay to, or possess, the said   as Orphan ought to be possessed of, or to such other persons as shall be lawfully empowered or authorized to receive the same, and the profits arising therefrom, then this obligation to be void, otherwise, to be and remain in full force and virtue.

Signed, Sealed and delivered
in the presence of

Ackiss, Thomas   3 March 1828   Bond No. 34
Ward: Francis Ackiss orphan of Thomas Ackiss deceased
Guardian: Stephen White   Bond amount: $3,000
Bondsmen: Stephen White, John Bailey, Thomas Wilson

Bailey, George   4 February 1828   Bond No. 26
Wards: Cassandra, Ann & Penelope orphans of George Bailey
Guardian: John S. Brothers   Bond amount: $2,000
Bondsmen: John S. Brothers, Benjamin Bailey, Nathan Small

Bailey, George 8 March 1831 Bond No. 170
Wards: Cassandra Bailey, Ann Bailey & Penelope Bailey orphans
  of George Bailey deceased
Guardian: John S. Brothers Bond amount: $2,000
Bondsmen: John S. Brothers, John L. Bailey, Benjamin Bailey

Bailey, Robert 8 March 1831 Bond No. 169
Wards: Mary Bailey & Salina Bailey orphans of Robert Bailey
Guardian: Benjamin Bailey Bond amount: $3,000
Bondsmen: Benjamin Bailey, John L. Bailey, John Brothers

Banks, Frederick S. 3 March 1829 Bond No. 89
Ward: Margaret Banks orphan of Frederick S. Banks deceased
Guardian: William Wilson Bond amount: $600
Bondsmen: William Wilson, Simon B. Pool, Edward E. Wilson

Banks, Jonathan 8 December 1829 Bond No. 109
Ward: Thomas Banks orphan of Jonathan Banks deceased
Guardian: Benjamin Powers Bond amount: $1,000
Bondsmen: Benjamin Powers, John Tooley, William Markham

Banks, Jonathan 7 December 1830 Bond No. 150
Ward: John Banks orphan of Jonathan Banks deceased
Guardian: William F. Banks Bond amount: $1,000
Bondsmen: William F. Banks, Thaddeus Freshwater, Thomas L.
  Broshir

Banks, Thomas 4 December 1827 Bond No. 5
Ward: William Banks orphan of Thomas Banks deceased
Guardian: William Charles Bond amount: $2,000
Bondsmen: William Charles, Stephen Charles, Robert Pool

Barclift, Rowan 3 December 1827 Bond No. 3
Ward: Juliet Ann orphan of Rowan Barclift deceased
Guardian: William Pritchard Bond amount: $1,000
Bondsmen: William Pritchard, Abner Williams, Lemuel Jackson

Guardian Bond Book 1827 - 1831

Barclift, Rowan 3 December 1827 Bond No. 4
Ward: Cassandra Barclift orphan of Rowan Barclift deceased
Guardian: William Pritchard Bond amount: $1,000
Bondsmen: William Pritchard, Abner Williams, Lemuel Jackson

Barclift, Rowan 8 March 1831 Bond No. 175
Wards: Julian & Cassandra Barclift orphans of Rowan Barclift
Guardian: William A. Pritchard Bond amount: $1,000
Bondsmen: William A. Pritchard, Nathan Small, Frances Ackiss

Brite, Charles L. 8 September 1830 Bond No. 146
Wards: Susan Brite & Louisa Brite orphans of Charles L. Brite
Guardian: John Jennings Bond amount: $500
Bondsmen: John Jennings, Wilson Davis, William Scott

Brooks, William C. 4 March 1829 Bond No. 92
Ward: George A. W. Brooks son of said William C. Brooks*
Guardian: William C. Brooks Bond amount: $1,000
Bondsmen: William C. Brooks, John Pool, John M. Skinner
  (*Note: the words *orphan* and *deceased* were scratched out)

Broshir, Joseph L. 3 February 1829 Bond No. 81
Wards: Benjamin & Ann Broshir orphans of Joseph L. Broshir
Guardian: William Broshir Bond amount: $800
Bondsmen: William Broshir, Thaddeus Freshwater, William F.
  Banks

Broshir, Simon L. 4 March 1828 Bond No. 35
Ward: Elizabeth Broshir orphan of Simon L. Broshir deceased
Guardian: Simon B. Pool Bond amount: $2,000
Bondsmen: Simon B. Pool, Edmund H. Perkins, William Wilson

Broshir, Simon L. 4 March 1828 Bond No. 36
Ward: Joseph P. Broshir orphan of Simon L. Broshir deceased
Guardian: Simon B. Pool Bond amount: $2,000
Bondsmen: Simon B. Pool, Edmund H. Perkins, William Wilson

Broshir, Simon L.   7 December 1830   Bond No. 148
Ward: Joseph P. Broshir orphan of Simon L. Broshir deceased
Guardian: Thomas L. Broshir   Bond amount: $2,000
Bondsmen: Thomas L. Broshir, Simon B. Pool, William Banks

Broshir, William   7 December 1830   Bond No. 152
Wards: Benjamin & Ann Broshir orphans of William Broshir
Guardian: Rubin M. Davis   Bond amount: $500
Bondsmen: Ruben M. Davis, William Griffin, John Bailey

Bundy, John   4 February 1828   Bond No. 16
Ward: Mary Bundy orphan of John Bundy deceased
Guardian: Nathan Bundy   Bond amount: $100
Bondsmen: Nathan Bundy, Mordecai Morris, Anderson Morris

Bundy, John   4 February 1828   Bond No. 17
Ward: Martha Bundy orphan of John Bundy deceased
Guardian: Nathan Bundy   Bond amount: $100
Bondsmen: Nathan Bundy, Mordecai Morris, Anderson Morris

Bundy, John   7 February 1831   Bond No. 161
Ward: Mary Bundy orphan of John Bundy deceased
Guardian: Nathan Bundy   Bond amount: $500
Bondsmen: Nathan Bundy, Caleb White, Cader Munden

Bundy, John   7 February 1831   Bond No. 162
Ward: Martha Bundy orphan of John Bundy deceased
Guardian: Nathan Bundy   Bond amount: $500
Bondsmen: Nathan Bundy, Caleb White, Cader Munden

Bundy, Joseph   4 February 1828   Bond No. 21
Ward: William Bundy orphan of Joseph Bundy deceased
Guardian: Jacob Symons   Bond amount: $1,000
Bondsmen: Jacob Symons, Mordecai Morris, Anderson Morris

Butler, William C.   2 June 1828   Bond No. 45
Wards: William C., Elizabeth, Mary, Penelope & Rebecca Butler
    orphans of William C. Butler deceased

Guardian Bond Book 1827 - 1831

Guardian: John Williams   Bond amount: $4,000
Bondsmen: John Williams, Horatio N. Williams, Charles R. Kinney

Cartwright, Benoni   8 December 1829   Bond No. 116
Wards: Sally Cartwriight & Benoni Cartwright orphans of Benoni
   Cartwright deceased
Guardian: Edmund B. Godfrey   Bond amount: $10,000
Bondsmen: Edmund B. Godfrey, Edmund H. Perkins, John
   McDonnell

Cartwright, Job   9 December 1830   Bond No. 157
Wards: Sally Cartwright & Pendleton Cartwright orphans of Job
   Cartwright deceased
Guardian: Benjamin Bailey   Bond amount: $1500
Bondsmen: Benjamin Bailey, Grandy Cartwright, John L. Bailey

Cartwright, John   4 March 1828   Bond No. 38
Wards: Lancaster, Lodwick, Matilda, William & Thomas
   Cartwright orphans of John Cartwright [of John] deceased
Guardian: James Cartwright   Bond amount: $200
Bondsmen: James Cartwright, William Scott, James Nash

Cartwright, John   9 March 1831   Bond No. 180
Wards: Lancaster, Lodwick, Matilda, William & Thomas
   Cartwright orphans of John Cartwright deceased
Guardian: James Cartwright   Bond amount: $500
Bondsmen: James Cartwright, William Scott, Peter Cartwright

Carver, Alfred   2 December 1828   Bond No. 61
Wards: Eliza & Mary Carver orphans of Alfred Carver deceased
Guardian: John McDonnell   Bond amount: $4,000
Bondsmen: John McDonnell, Edmund H. Perkins, G.W. Godfrey

Casey, Enoch   9 December 1830   Bond No. 155
Wards: Bathia &Maria Casey orphans of Enoch Casey deceased
Guardian: Frederick Casey   Bond amount: $500
Bondsmen: Frederick Casey, Thomas Casey, Isaac Casey

Casey: John 7 February 1831   Bond No. 166
Ward: John Casey orphan of John Casey deceased
Guardian: Sarah Casey   Bond amount: $500
Bondsmen: Sarah Casey, William A. Pritchard, __hen Scott

Clark, William 9 March 1831   Bond No. 179
Wards: Sally Clark & Timothy Clark orphans of William Clark
Guardian: Ephraim Harris   Bond amount: $500
Bondsmen: Ephraim Harris, John Harris Sr., John Harris Jr.

Collins, William 9 December 1830   Bond No. 158
Ward: Janetta Collins orphan of William Collins deceased
Guardian: John Weeks   Bond amount: $500
Bondsmen: John Weeks, John L. Bailey, Benjamin Bailey

Commander, Joseph 4 March 1829   Bond No. 95
Ward: Joseph Commander orphan of Joseph Commander deceased
Guardian: Parthenia Commander   Bond amount: $6,000
Bondsmen: Parthenia Commander, Carter Barnard, Thos. Barnard

Commander, Joseph 7 September 1830   Bond No. 140
Ward: Joseph Commander orphan of Joseph Commander deceased
Guardian: James H. Williams   Bond amount: $7,000
Bondsmen: James H. Williams, John M. Skinner, Hamilton W. Cotter

Commander, Thomas 7 September 1830   Bond No. 141
Ward: Mary Elizabeth Commander orphan of Thomas Commander
Guardian: James H. Williams   Bond amount: $7,000
Bondsmen: James H. Williams, John M. Skinner, Hamilton W. Cotter

Copper, John 8 June 1830   Bond No. 138
Ward: John Coppers Heirs & orphans
Guardian: Thomas Lister   Bond amount: $1,000
Bondsmen: Thomas Lister, Israel Lister, Jacob Lister

Guardian Bond Book 1827 - 1831

Cotter, Timothy   2 June 1829   Bond No. 101
Ward: Wilson Cotter orphan of Timothy Cotter deceased
Guardian: Frederick Davis   Bond amount: $500
Bondsmen: Frederick Davis, David Davis

Crutch, William   4 December 1827   Bond No. 10
Ward: William Crutch orphan of William Crutch deceased
Guardian: David H. Kenyon   Bond amount: $2,000
Bondsmen: David Kenyon, Demsey Pendleton, Solomon Pool Jr.

Crutch, William   4 December 1827   Bond No. 11
Ward: George Crutch orphan of William Crutch deceased
Guardian: David H. Kenyon   Bond amount: $2,000
Bondsmen: David Kenyon, Demsey Pendleton, Solomon Pool Jr.

Crutch, William   2 March 1830   Bond No. 131
Ward: John Crutch orphan of William Crutch deceased
Guardian: Demsey B. Pendleton   Bond amount: $500
Bondsmen: Demsey B. Pendleton, Frederick Pendleton, Jesse Delon

Davis, Arthur   8 December 1829   Bond No. 110
Wards: Wilson & Mary Elizabeth Davis orphans of Arthur Davis
Guardian: Isaac Sawyer   Bond amount: $600
Bondsmen: Isaac Sawyer, David Sawyer, Peter Ferebee

Davis, David   9 December 1830   Bond No. 156
Wards: Ann Davis, Evergen Davis, James Davis & Mary Davis
    orphans of David Davis deceased
Guardian: Alfred C. Davis   Bond amount: $500
Bondsmen: Alfred C. Davis, William Weaver, Robert Chancey

Davis, Edmund   2 December 1828   Bond No. 68
Wards: Edmund Davis's heirs; _ay* Davis, Devotion Davis,
    Josephine Davis, Edmund Davis & Elizabeth Davis
Guardian: John Bailey   Bond amount: $500
Bondsmen: John Bailey, Robert Bailey & Will. Newbold
    (*Note: the first letter of the name could be L, S or T)

Delon, Henry   2 February 1829   Bond No. 80
Wards: Nancy Delon, Mary Delon, Josiah Delon, Samuel Delon &
      Jonathan Delon orphans of Henry Delon deceased
Guardian: Nathan Delon   Bond amount: $1,000
Bondsmen: Nathan Delon, Caleb Brothers, Mark Anthony Delon

Elliott, John A.   8 September 1830   Bond No. 145*
Wards: Mordecai & Abigail orphans of John A. Elliott deceased
Guardian: Joseph H. Pool   Bond amount: $3,000
Bondsmen: Joseph H. Pool, John Pool
      *(*Note: this was the second bond with the same number)*

Etheridge, Richard   2 December 1828   Bond No. 69
Ward: Morris Etheridge orphan of Richard Etheridge deceased
Guardian: Richard Etheridge   Bond amount: $700
Bondsmen: Richard Etheridge, Seth Etheridge, Thad. Freshwater

Gilbert, John   8 December 1829   Bond No. 114
Wards: Joseph & John Gilbert orphans of John Gilbert deceased
Guardian: Joseph Stokely   Bond amount: $1,000
Bondsmen: Joseph Stokely, John Carver, Elisha Draper

Godfrey, Jacob   2 December 1828   Bond No. 66
Wards: the heirs of Jacob Godfrey*
Guardian: George W. Godfrey   Bond amount: $5,000
Bondsmen: George Godfrey, John McDonnell, Edmund B. Godfrey
      *(*Note: the word orphan was scratched out)*

Gray, Joseph   4 February 1828   Bond No. 28
Wards: Elizabeth & Joseph Gray orphans of Joseph Gray deceased
Guardian: Griffin Gray   Bond amount: $1,000
Bondsmen: Griffin Gray, Jordan Gray, Alson Spence

Gray, Thornton   4 March 1829   Bond No. 96
Ward: Fanny Gray orphan of Thornton Gray deceased
Guardian: Joseph Stokely   Bond amount: $100
Bondsmen: Joseph Stokely, Joseph Harrell, Dennis Dozier

Guardian Bond Book 1827 - 1831

Gray, Thornton   4 March 1829   Bond No. 97
Ward: Nancy Gray orphan of Thornton Gray deceased
Guardian: Joseph Stokely   Bond amount: $100
Bondsmen: Joseph Stokely, Joseph Harrell, Dennis Dozier

Gray, Thornton   4 March 1829   Bond No. 98
Ward: Julian Gray orphan of Thornton Gray deceased
Guardian: Joseph Stokely   Bond amount: $100
Bondsmen: Joseph Stokely, Joseph Harrell, Dennis Dozier

Grice, Charles   3 March 1830   Bond No. 133
Wards: Elizabeth M. Grice, Warren D. Grice, Sarah Ann Grice &
    Mary S. Grice children of said Charles Grice*
Guardian: Charles Grice   Bond amount: $2,000
Bondsmen: Charles Grice, William Rogerson, James M. Grice
    (*Note: the word orphan was scratched out)

Griffin, Isaac   7 December 1830   Bond No. 153
Wards: Thomas W. Griffin & Sophie Griffin orphans of Isaac
    Griffin deceased
Guardian: Sarah Griffin   Bond amount: $20,000
Bondsmen: Sarah Griffin, Fredrick Whitehurst, Asa McCoy

Griffin, James   4 December 1827   Bond No. 6
Wards: James & Mary Griffin orphan of James Griffin deceased
Guardian: Joseph Palin   Bond amount: $300
Bondsmen: Joseph Palin, Solomon Pool Jr., Frederick Pendleton

Griffin, James   9 March 1831   Bond No. 181
Wards: Robert & Mary Griffin orphans of James Griffin deceased
Guardian: Joseph Palin   Bond amount: $300
Bondsmen: Joseph Palin, Frederick Pendleton, Abner Pendleton

Harris, Isaac   4 February 1828   Bond No. 29
Ward: Grandy Harris orphan of Isaac Harris deceased
Guardian: Lemuel Jennings   Bond amount: $2,000
Bondsmen: Lemuel Jennings, John Bray, Elliott Whitehurst

Harris, Isaac 7 June 1831 Bond No. 186
Ward: Grandy Harris orphan of Isaac Harris deceased
Guardian: Lemuel Jennings Bond amount: $3,000
Bondsmen: Lemuel Jennings, Fredrick Whitehurst, Elliott Whitehurst

Harris, John 7 June 1831 Bond No. 187
Ward: Susannah Harris orphan of John Harris deceased
Guardian: Lemuel Jennings Bond amount: $20
Bondsmen: Lemuel Jennings, Fredrick Whitehurst, Elliott Whitehurst

Holloway, Jesse 2 March 1829 Bond No. 84
Wards: Jesse Holloway's heirs*
Guardian: John White Bond amount: $500
Bondsmen: John White, John Winslow, Rix Perry
(*Note: the word orphan was scratched out)

Humphries, Jonathan 7 June 1830 Bond No. 134
Ward: Richardson R. Humphries orphan of Jonathan Humphries
Guardian: John Bray Bond amount: $1,000
Bondsmen: John Bray, Shadrack Davis, James Bray

Humphries, Thomas 4 March 1828 Bond No. 39
Ward: William Humphries orphan of Thomas Humphries deceased
Guardian: Job Carver Bond amount: $200
Bondsmen: Job Carver, Joseph Harrell, Alson Spence

Humphries, Thomas 3 June 1828 Bond No. 47
Wards: Nancy Humphries & Betsy Humphries orphans of Thomas Humphries deceased
Guardian: Joseph Stokely Bond amount: $500
Bondsmen: Joseph Stokely, Job Carver, William Whitney

Jackson, Benjamin M. 4 December 1827 Bond No. 9
Ward: Benjamin F. Jackson orphan of Benjamin M. Jackson
Guardian: John M. Jackson Bond amount: $3,000
Bondsmen: John M. Jackson, Dempsey B. Pendleton, Lemuel Jackson

Guardian Bond Book 1827 - 1831

Jackson, Benjamin M.   3 February 1829   Bond No. 82
Ward: Benjamin F. Jackson orphan of Benjamin M. Jackson
Guardian: John M. Skinner   Bond amount: $2,000
Bondsmen: John M. Skinner, Edmund Blount, Joseph C. Blount

Jackson, Lemuel   7 December 1830   Bond No. 151
Ward: William L. Quincey Jackson orphan of Lemuel Jackson
Guardian: Francis Ackiss   Bond amount: $500
Bondsmen: Francis Ackiss, Simon Overman, William A. Pritchard

Jackson, Miles   6 June 1831   Bond No. 182
Ward: Mary Jackson orphan of Miles Jackson deceased
Guardian: Benjamin Bailey   Bond amount: $500
Bondsmen: Benjamin Bailey, John L. Bailey, John S. Brothers

Jackson, William   5 December 1827   Bond No. 14
Ward: Lowry Jackson orphan of William Jackson deceased
Guardian: Thomas Jennings   Bond amount: $100
Bondsmen: Thomas Jennings, Lemuel Jennings, James Casey

Jackson, Zacharias   2 December 1828   Bond No. 64
Wards: the heirs of Zacharias Jackson*
Guardian: William Scott   Bond amount: $3,000
Bondsmen: William Scott, James Nash, James Cartwright
  (*Note: the word orphan was scratched out)

Jennings, James   2 December 1828   Bond No. 59
Ward: Mary Jennings orphan of James Jennings deceased
Guardian: James Whidbee Esq.   Bond amount: $2,000
Bondsmen: James Whidbee, James Whidbee Jr.

Jennings, John   9 December 1829   Bond No. 117
Wards: Miles Jennings & Frederick Jennings orphans of John
        Jennings Sr. deceased
Guardian: Fredrick Whitehurst   Bond amount: $3,000
Bondsmen: Fredrick Whitehurst, Lemuel Jennings

Jones, Samuel   2 December 1828   Bond No. 57
Wards: Samuel Jones heirs*
Guardian: Anthony Davis   Bond amount: $600
Bondsmen: Anthony Davis, Joseph Davis, Joel Sawyer
   (*Note: the words orphan of and deceased were scratched out)

Keaton, Joseph L.   7 September 1830   Bond No. 142
Wards: Rebecca Keaton, Fanny Keaton, Benjamin F. Keaton &
   William Keaton orphans of Joseph L. Keaton deceased
Guardian: Thaddeus Freshwater   Bond amount: $1,000
Bondsmen: Thaddeus Freshwater, William W. Freshwater,
   William Broshir

Knox, Hugh   4 March 1829   Bond No. 91
Ward: Thomas D. Knox orphan of Hugh Knox deceased
Guardian: William C. Brooks   Bond amount: $2,000
Bondsmen: William C. Brooks, John Pool, John M. Skinner

Koen, Murden   4 March 1828   Bond No. 41
Wards: the heirs of Murden Koen deceased
Guardian: Joseph Stokely   Bond amount: $1,000
Bondsmen: Joseph Stokely, Job Carver, William R. Coen

Lister, Jacob   8 December 1829   Bond No. 112
Ward: Thomas Lister orphan of Jacob Lister deceased
Guardian: William Sanderlin   Bond amount: $5,000
Bondsmen: William Sanderlin, Henry Pendleton, Robert
   Pendleton

Lister, Jacob   8 December 1829   Bond No. 113
Ward: Susanna Lister orphan of Jacob Lister deceased
Guardian: William Sanderlin   Bond amount: $2,000
Bondsmen: William Sanderlin, Henry Pendleton, Robert Pendleton

Low, Aron   7 June 1831   Bond No. 191
Wards: Christian Low, Sarah Low, Alfred Low, Ann Low &
   Elizabeth Low orphans of Aron Low deceased
Guardian: Nathan Morgan   Bond amount: $400
Bondsmen: Nathan Morgan, Thomas White, John Weeks

Guardian Bond Book 1827 - 1831

Markham, Thomas   1 February 1830   Bond No. 122
Wards: Anthony, Thomas & John Markham orphans of Thomas
    Markham deceased
Guardian: John M. Skinner   Bond amount: $1,000
Bondsmen: John M. Skinner, Joseph C. Blount, Benjamin B. Lowry

McDonell, John   8 June 1830   Bond No. 135
Ward: Grizell McDonnell orphan of John McDonell deceased
Guardian: John McDonnell   Bond amount: $4,000
Bondsmen: John McDonnell, Edmund H. Perkins, Edmund Godfrey

McDonell, John   8 June 1830   Bond No. 136
Ward: Elizabeth McDonnell orphan of John McDonell deceased
Guardian: John McDonnell   Bond amount: $4,000
Bondsmen: John McDonnell, Edmund Perkins, Edmund B. Godfrey

McDonell, John   8 June 1830   Bond No. 137
Ward: Joanna McDonnell orphan of John McDonell deceased
Guardian: John McDonnell   Bond amount: $4,000
Bondsmen: John McDonnell, Edmund H. Perkins, Edmund Godfrey

Miller, *(Willi?)*   7 December 1829   Bond No. 106
Ward: Jamy Miller orphan of *(Willi?)* Miller deceased
Guardian: Shadrack Davis   Bond amount: $1,000
Bondsmen: Shadrack Davis, James Bray, Noah Sawyer

Mitchell, Frances   5 December 1827   Bond No. 15
Wards: Carrey Mitchell, Tillmon Mitchell, Doretta Mitchell &
    Mary orphans of Francis Mitchell deceased
Guardian: Cealah Mitchell   Bond amount: $500
Bondsmen: Cealah Mitchell, John M. Skinner, James Palmer

Mitchell, Frances   3 June 1829   Bond No. 102
Wards: Doretta Mitchell & Mary Mitchell orphans of Francis
    Mitchell deceased
Guardian: James Palmer   Bond amount: $1,000
Bondsmen: James Palmer, John M. Skinner, John B. Manyard

Morgan, Benjamin 3 February 1829 Bond No. 83
Wards: Benjamin Morgan heirs*
Guardian: Cader Munden Bond amount: $2,000
Bondsmen: Cader Munden, Josiah Perry, Thomas White
   (*Note: the word orphan was scratched out)

Morris, Joshua 3 March 1829 Bond No. 86
Ward: Joseph H. Morris orphan of Joshua Morris deceased
Guardian: Anderson Morris Bond amount: $4,000
Bondsmen: Anderson Morris, Mordecai Morris

Morris, Mordecai 1 February 1830 Bond No. 120
Ward: John W. Morris orphan of Mordecai Morris deceased
Guardian: Mordecai Morris Jr. Bond amount: $1200
Bondsmen: Mordecai Morris Jr., Anderson Morris

Morris, Thomas 1 February 1830 Bond No. 118
Ward: Joshua Morris orphan of Thomas Morris deceased
Guardian: Anderson Morris Bond amount: $2400
Bondsmen: Anderson Morris, Mordecai Morris Jr.

Morris, Thomas 1 February 1830 Bond No. 119
Ward: Sarah Ann Morris orphan of Thomas Morris deceased
Guardian: Anderson Morris Bond amount: $2400
Bondsmen: Anderson Morris, Mordecai Morris Jr.

(Newbold*), Thomas 2 December 1828 Bond No. 67
Ward: William Newbold orphan of Thomas ____* deceased
Guardian: William Newbold Bond amount: $500
Bondsmen: William Newbold, John Bailey
   (*Note: the father's surname was not recorded on the bond)

Nixon, Samuel 1 February 1830 Bond No. 121
Ward: Emily K. Nixon orphan of Samuel Nixon deceased
Guardian: Lavinia S. Nixon Bond amount: $5,000
Bondsmen: Lavinia S. Nixon, Soliman Pool, William T. Relfe

Guardian Bond Book 1827 - 1831

Overman, ___   4 March 1829   Bond No. 94
Ward: Thomas Overman orphan of _____ deceased
Guardian: Benjamin Bailey   Bond amount: $500
Bondsmen: Benjamin Bailey, John Bailey, John S. Brothers

Overman, Benjamin S.   4 December 1827   Bond No. 12
Ward: James Overman orphan of Benjamin S. Overman deceased
Guardian: Solomon Pool Jr.   Bond amount: $100
Bondsmen: Solomon Pool Jr., Joseph H. Pool, David A. Kenyan

Overman, Henry P.   4 March 1829   Bond No. 93
Wards: Mekale Overman & Pet. O. orphans of Henry P. Overman
Guardian: Benjamin Pendleton   Bond amount: $1,000
Bondsmen: Benjamin Pendleton, George W. Pendleton, Meke__ Pendleton

Palin, Thomas   3 March 1829   Bond No. 87
Ward: Nancy Palin orphan of Thomas Palin deceased
Guardian: Frederick Pendleton   Bond amount: $400
Bondsmen: Frederick Pendleton, Abner Pendleton, Demsey B. Pendleton

Pendleton, George W.   2 December 1828   Bond No. 62
Ward: Miranda Pendleton orphan of George W. Pendleton deceased
Guardian: Edmund H. Perkins   Bond amount: $4,000
Bondsmen: Edmund H. Perkins, John McDonnell, Edmund Godfrey

Perry, Cader   7 June 1831   Bond No. 184
Ward: Sarah Perry orphan of Cader Perry deceased
Guardian: Sarah Perry   Bond amount: $200
Bondsmen: Sarah Perry, William Davis, Nathan Small

Perry, Hardy   4 February 1828   Bond No. 18
Ward: Mary Perry orphan of Hardy Perry deceased
Guardian: Rix Perry   Bond amount: $500
Bondsmen: Rix Perry, Jacob Saunders, John Symons

Perry, Hardy   4 February 1828   Bond No. 19
Ward: Sarah Perry orphan of Hardy Perry deceased
Guardian: Rix Perry   Bond amount: $500
Bondsmen: Rix Perry, Jacob Saunders, John Symons

Perry, Hardy   4 February 1828   Bond No. 20
Ward: John Perry orphan of Hardy Perry deceased
Guardian: Rix Perry   Bond amount: $500
Bondsmen: Rix Perry, Jacob Saunders, John Symons

Perry, Jacob   7 December 1830   Bond No. 154
Wards: Mill_*, Druzilla & Abner Perry orphans of Jacob Perry
Guardian: Joshua M. Perry   Bond amount: $250
Bondsmen: Joshua M. Perry, John White, Jonah Perry
    (*Note: the name may be Milles, Millie or Miller)

Perry, Kader   2 June 1828   Bond No. 44
Ward: Sarah Perry orphan of Kader Perry deceased
Guardian: Sarah Perry   Bond amount: $200
Bondsmen: Sarah Perry, John Winslow, Stephen White

Perry, William   7 September 1830   Bond No. 143
Wards: Alexis Perry, Matthew Perry, William, Josiah W. & __
    (Deacel?) Elizabeth Perry orphans of William Perry
Guardian: John B. Perry   Bond amount: $2,000
Bondsmen: John B. Perry, Jacob H. Perry, Israel Perry

Pike, Jesse   2 December 1828   Bond No. 51
Ward: Jesse Pike orphan of Jesse Pike deceased
Guardian: Abner Williams   Bond amount: 1,000 pounds*
Bondsmen: Abner Williams, Asa Rogerson, Asa McCoy
    (*Note: the word pounds was written on the bond)

Pike, Jesse   2 December 1828   Bond No. 55
Ward: Ferebee Pike orphan of Jesse Pike deceased
Guardian: Abner Williams   Bond amount: $500
Bondsmen: Abner Williams, Asa Rogerson, Asa McCoy

Guardian Bond Book 1827 - 1831   169

Pike, Jesse   2 December 1828   Bond No. 56
Ward: Wilson Pike orphan of Jesse Pike deceased
Guardian: Abner Williams   Bond amount: $100
Bondsmen: Abner Williams, Asa Rogerson, Asa McCoy

Pool, Richard   3 March 1829   Bond No. 90
Wards: the heirs of Richard Pool*
Guardian: Robert Pool   Bond amount: $200
Bondsmen: Robert Pool, William Charles, David H. Kinyan
         (*Note: the word orphan was scratched out)

Pool, Solomon   2 June 1828   Bond No. 46
Ward: Jesse Pool son of said Solomon Pool*
Guardian: Solomon Pool Jr.   Bond amount: $2,000
Bondsmen: Solomon Pool Jr., Thomas Pool, John Winslow
         (*Note: the word orphan was scratched out)

Pritchard, Caleb   7 February 1831   Bond No. 163
Ward: Benjamin Pritchard orphan of Caleb Pritchard deceased
Guardian: Caleb White   Bond amount: $1,000
Bondsmen: Caleb White, Anderson Morris, Nathan Bundy

Pritchard, Hugh   2 March 1830   Bond No. 129
Ward: Joseph Pritchard orphan of Hugh Pritchard deceased
Guardian: Jonathan Brite   Bond amount: $3,000
Bondsmen: Jonathan Brite, Daniel Spence, Thomas Temple

Pritchard, Hugh   2 March 1830   Bond No. 130
Ward: Jane Pritchard orphan of Hugh Pritchard deceased
Guardian: Jonathan Brite   Bond amount: $1,000
Bondsmen: Jonathan Brite, Daniel Spence, Thomas Temple

Pritchard, James   3 December 1827   Bond No. 1
Ward: Ann Pritchard orphan of James Pritchard deceased
Guardian: William Pritchard   Bond amount: $2,000
Bondsmen: William Pritchard, Abner Williams, Lemuel Jackson

Pritchard, James   3 December 1827   Bond No. 2
Ward: Sally Pritchard orphan of James Pritchard deceased
Guardian: William Pritchard   Bond amount: $1,000
Bondsmen: William Pritchard, Abner Williams, Lemuel Jackson

Pritchard, Joseph   4 December 1827   Bond No. 7
Wards: Abigail Pritchard, Penina Pritchard, Susanna Pritchard,
    Aseneth Pritchard & Mary Ann Pritchard orphans of
    Joseph Pritchard deceased
Guardian: William Wilson   Bond amount: $10,000
Bondsmen: William Wilson, Stephen White, Thomas Wilson

Pritchard, Joseph   7 March 1831   Bond No. 167
Wards: Pennia Pritchard, Susannah Pritchard, Aseneth Pritchard &
    Mary Ann Pritchard orphans of Joseph Pritchard deceased
Guardian: William Wilson   Bond amount: $7,000
Bondsmen: William Wilson, Jesse Wilson, Joseph Elliott

Proby, Paul   4 December 1827   Bond No. 8
Ward: Sally Proby orphan of Paul Proby deceased
Guardian: David Taylor   Bond amount: $500
Bondsmen: David Taylor, Robert Simpson, William Scott

Raper, John   4 February 1828   Bond No. 23
Ward: Robert Raper orphan of John Raper deceased
Guardian: Caleb Raper   Bond amount: $2,000
Bondsmen: Caleb Raper, Benjamin Bailey, John Bailey

Raper, Thomas   4 February 1828   Bond No. 31
Wards: Davis Raper & Mary Raper orphans of Thomas Raper
Guardian: Lemuel Jackson   Bond amount: $2,000
Bondsmen: Lemuel Jackson, John Jackson, William A. Pritchard

Raper, Thomas   3 June 1828   Bond No. 48
Wards: Davis D. Raper & Mary Raper orphans of Thomas Raper
Guardian: Thomas Trueblood   Bond amount: $1,000
Bondsmen: Thomas Trueblood, Joshua Trueblood, Josiah Overman

Guardian Bond Book 1827 - 1831

Raper, Thomas   *(1828)**   Bond No. none*
Wards: Davis Raper & Mary Raper orphans of Thomas Raper
Guardian: Thomas Avery   Bond amount: none*
Bondsmen: Thomas Avery Will. Bedgood, L. Joseph Jackson
Details: Ordered that Thomas Avery have guardianship of Davis
    Raper & Mary Raper orphans of Thomas Raper deceased*
    *(*Note: No date was recorded but the information was in the group of
    bonds recorded for 2 December 1828, between bond numbers 69
    and 70. This was a handwritten note in the records and not a
    printed Guardian Bond)*

Raper, Thomas   8 September 1830   Bond No. 147
Wards: Davis Raper & Mary Raper orphans of Thomas Raper
Guardian: Nathan M. Raper   Bond amount: $5,000
Bondsmen: Nathan M. Raper, Robert Pool, David H. Kenyon,
    Jesse L. Pool

Relfe, Josiah   4 March 1828   Bond No. 40
Ward: William Relfe orphan of Josiah Relfe deceased
Guardian: James Casey   Bond amount: $50
Bondsmen: James Casey, Edmund Trueblood, John Davis

Relfe, Joseph   2 December 1828   Bond No. 58
Wards: Malachi & Josiah orphans of Joseph Relfe deceased
Guardian: Joseph Relfe   Bond amount: $2,000
Bondsmen: Joseph Relfe, Stephen Relfe, Rix Perry

Relfe, William T.   8 December 1829   Bond No. 115
Wards: Montgomery Relfe, Decatur Relfe, Blakely Relfe &
    Margaret Relfe orphans of William T. Relfe deceased
Guardian:William T. Relfe   Bond amount: $10,000
Bondsmen: William T. Relfe, Solomon Pool, Robert Pool

Richardson, Daniel   2 February 1830   Bond No. 124
Ward: William Richardson orphan of Daniel Richardson deceased
Guardian: Demsey Richardson   Bond amount: $1,000
Bondsmen: Demsey Richardson, Thomas Temple, Joseph Stokely

Pasquotank County, North Carolina

Richardson, Daniel   2 February 1830   Bond No. 125
Ward: John Richardson orphan of Daniel Richardson deceased
Guardian: Demsey Richardson   Bond amount: $1,000
Bondsmen: Demsey Richardson, Thomas Temple, Joseph Stokely

Richardson, Jacob   7 December 1829   Bond No. 107
Wards: James Richardson, Ivy Richardson & Samuel Richardson
    orphans of Jacob Richardson deceased
Guardian: Fredrick Whitehurst   Bond amount: $___
Bondsmen: Fredrick Whitehurst, Lemuel Jennings

Richardson, Levi   2 December 1828   Bond No. 70
Ward: Joseph Richardson orphan of Levi Richardson deceased
Guardian: David Nichols   Bond amount: $1,000
Bondsmen: David Nichols, Daniel Spence, Job Carver

Richardson, Levi   2 December 1828   Bond No. 71
Ward: Sally Richardson orphan of Levi Richardson deceased
Guardian: David Nichols   Bond amount: $1,000
Bondsmen: David Nichols, Daniel Spence, Job Carver

Richardson, Levi   2 December 1828   Bond No. 72
Ward: Olly Richardson orphan of Levi Richardson deceased
Guardian: David Nichols   Bond amount: $1,000
Bondsmen: David Nichols, Daniel Spence, Job Carver

Richardson, Levi   2 December 1828   Bond No. 73
Ward: Daniel Richardson orphan of Levi Richardson deceased
Guardian: David Nichols   Bond amount: $1,000
Bondsmen: David Nichols, Daniel Spence, Job Carver

Richardson, Miles   2 December 1828   Bond No. 65
Ward: Benjamin Richardson orphan of Miles Richardson deceased
Guardian: George Ferebee   Bond amount: $1,000
Bondsmen: George Ferebee, Dennis Dozier, Noah Sawyer

Richardson, Rite   3 March 1830   Bond No. 132
Ward: Fanny Richardson orphan of Rite Richardson deceased

Guardian: Malachi W. Jones Bond amount: $600
Bondsmen: Malachi W. Jones, John Pool, Mark Spence

Riggs, Samuel 4 February 1828 Bond No. 30
Wards: Riddick Riggs & James Riggs orphans of Samuel Riggs
Guardian: Lemuel Jennings Bond amount: $100
Bondsmen: Lemuel Jennings, John Bray, Elliott Whitehurst

Riggs, Samuel 7 June 1831 Bond No. 188
Ward: Riddick Riggs orphan of Samuel Riggs deceased
Guardian: Lemuel Jennings Bond amount: $50
Bondsmen: Lemuel Jennings, Fredrick Whitehurst, Elliott Whitehurst

Riggs, Samuel 7 June 1831 Bond No. 189
Ward: James Riggs orphan of Samuel Riggs deceased
Guardian: Lemuel Jennings Bond amount: $50
Bondsmen: Lemuel Jennings, Fredrick Whitehurst, Elliott Whitehurst

Roads, Joshua 4 February 1828 Bond No. 24
Ward: George Roads orphan of Joshua Roads deceased
Guardian: Abner Williams Bond amount: $1,000
Bondsmen: Abner Williams, James Scott, Edmund Trueblood

Roads, ___ 9 March 1831 Bond No. 178
Ward: George Roads orphan of ___ Roads deceased
Guardian: Abner Williams Bond amount: $1,000
Bondsmen: Abner Williams, John C. Ehringhaus, Edmund Trueblood

Rose, William 2 June 1829 Bond No. 100
Wards: Andrew Rose & Nancy Rose orphans of William Rose
Guardian: Benjamin Markham Bond amount: $2,000
Bondsmen: Benjamin Markham, John James, Demsey B. Pendleton

Rose, William   7 September 1830   Bond No. 145
Wards: Andrew Rose & Nancy Rose orphans of William Rose
Guardian: Demsey B. Pendleton   Bond amount: $500
Bondsmen: Demsey B. Pendleton, John James

Sanderlin, Asa   8 December 1829   Bond No. 111
Ward: Asa Sanderlin orphan of Asa Sanderlin deceased
Guardian: William Sanderlin   Bond amount: $2,000
Bondsmen: William Sanderlin, Henry Pendleton, Robert Pendleton

Sawyer, Enoch   8 March 1831   Bond No. 173
Ward: Ann Elizabeth orphan of Enoch Sawyer deceased
Guardian: Daniel Spence   Bond amount: $1,000
Bondsmen: Daniel Spence, Jonathan Brite, Lodwick Williams

Sawyer, John   1 September 1828   Bond No. 49
Ward: Charles Sawyer orphan of John Sawyer deceased
Guardian: Robert Morgan   Bond amount: $500
Bondsmen: Robert Morgan*
          *(*Note: no other bondsmen are listed and there are no
          signatures on the bond)*

Sawyer, John   2 September 1828   Bond No. 50
Ward: Charles & Thomas Sawyer orphans of John Sawyer
Guardian: Joseph Stokely   Bond amount: $500
Bondsmen: Joseph Stokely, Elisha Draper, Joseph Davis

Sawyer, Thomas   8 March 1831   Bond No. 177
Ward: William Sawyer orphan of Thomas Sawyer deceased
Guardian: William Weaver   Bond amount: $2,000
Bondsmen: William Weaver, Arthur Heath, Joseph Palin

Scott, Marmaduke   2 February 1830   Bond No. 126
Ward: Sophia Scott orphan of Marmaduke Scott deceased
Guardian: Allen B. Jones   Bond amount: $1,000
Bondsmen: Allen B. Jones, Jeremiah Sawyer, Ammon Scott

Guardian Bond Book 1827 - 1831

Scott, Marmaduke 2 February 1830 Bond No. 128
Ward: George W. Scott orphan of Marmaduke Scott deceased
Guardian: Allen B. Jones Bond amount: $5,000
Bondsmen: Allen B. Jones, Jeremiah Sawyer, Ammon Scott

Scott, Robert 7 December 1829 Bond No. 108
Wards: Eliz. Scott, Sylphia Scott & Samuel Scott orphans of
    Robert Scott deceased
Guardian: Caleb Scott Bond amount: $300
Bondsmen: Caleb Scott, John Scott, Hollowell Scott

Scott, Stephen 2 December 1828 Bond No. 63
Ward: Samuel Scott orphan of Stephen Scott deceased
Guardian: Ann Pendleton Bond amount: $1,000
Bondsmen: Ann Pendleton, William Wilson

Scott, Stephen 2 February 1829 Bond No. 78
Wards: Stephen Scott's heirs*
Guardian: William Scott Bond amount: $300
Bondsmen: William Scott, James Scott, Peter Cartwright
    (*Note: the word orphan was scratched out)

Sexton, John 8 March 1831 Bond No. 176
Wards: Olly, John & Tamer Sexton orphans of John Sexton
Guardian: Asa McCoy Bond amount: $1,000
Bondsmen: Asa McCoy, David Sharborough, Isaac Casey

Simpson, Evan 7 June 1831 Bond No. 185
Wards: Mary & John Simpson children of Evan Simpson*
Guardian: Evan Simpson Bond amount: $500
Bondsmen: Evan Simpson, Stephen Scott, John Hinds
    (*Note: the word orphan was scratched out)

Simpson, Jno. 2 December 1828 Bond No. 52
Ward: George orphan of Jno. Simpson deceased
Guardian: Abner Williams Bond amount: $500
Bondsmen: Abner Williams, Asa Rogerson, Asa McCoy

Simpson, Joab 2 March 1829 Bond No. 85
Ward: Robert Simpson orphan of Joab Simpson deceased
Guardian: Zachariah Brothers Bond amount: $300
Bondsmen: Zachariah Brothers, Caleb Brothers, John White

Small, Joseph 6 September 1830 Bond No. 139
Ward: Joseph Small orphan of Joseph Small deceased
Guardian: Thomas Lister Bond amount: $1,000
Bondsmen: Thomas Lister, John Lister, Elisha Lister

Smithson, Elisha 4 February 1828 Bond No. 25
Wards: Mary & Charity Smithson orphans of Elisha Smithson
Guardian: James Scott Bond amount: $1,000
Bondsmen: James Scott, Abner Williams, Robert Casey

Smithson, Elisha 7 February 1831 Bond No. 165
Wards: the heirs of the Elisha Smithson; Mary & Charity
Guardian: James Scott Bond amount: $400
Bondsmen: James Scott, James Cartwright, Caleb Scott

Spence, James 8 March 1831 Bond No. 174
Wards: Nancy, Renchir, Almond, Enoch, Polly, Daniel, David &
    Sarah Spence orphans of James Spence deceased
Guardian: Caleb Spence Bond amount: $500
Bondsmen: Caleb Spence, Daniel Spence, David Nichols

Spence, Mark 4 February 1828 Bond No. 27
Wards: Martha Spence, William Spence & Nancy Spence orphans
    of Mark Spence deceased
Guardian: Parthenia Spence Bond amount: $500
Bondsmen: Parthenia Spence, Joel Sawyer, David Nichols

Spence, Mark 8 March 1831 Bond No. 172
Ward: Nancy Spence orphan of Mark Spence deceased
Guardian: Parthenia Spence Bond amount: $500
Bondsmen: Parthenia Spence, Joseph Stokely, David Nichols

Guardian Bond Book 1827 - 1831

Squires, Demsey 9 September 1829 Bond No. 105
Wards: Mackey Squires, Nancy Squires, Martha Squires & John
    Squires orphans of Demsey Squires deceased
Guardian: Carter Barnard Bond amount: $200
Bondsmen: Carter Barnard, Thomas Barnard

Stott, Thomas S. 5 March 1828 Bond No. 42
Ward: Elizabeth Stott orphan of Thomas S. Stott deceased
Guardian: William Charles Bond amount: $300
Bondsmen: William Charles, Stephen Charles, Reding Banks

Stott, Thomas 5 March 1828 Bond No. 43
Ward: William Stott orphan of Thomas Stott deceased
Guardian: Thomas Banks Bond amount: $2,000
Bondsmen: Thomas Banks, Reding Banks, Exum Trueblood

Symons, John 4 February 1828 Bond No. 22
Ward: James W. Symons son of the said John Symons*
Guardian: John Symons Bond amount: $100
Bondsmen: John Symons, Rix Perry, Jacob Symons
    (*Note: the word orphans was scratched out)

Temple, Burtan 7 February 1831 Bond No. 164
Wards: James Temple, Turner Temple & Burtan Temple orphans
    of Butan Temple deceased
Guardian: Edward Williams Bond amount: $6,000
Bondsmen: Edward Williams, James Williams, John Williams

Thornton, James 8 December 1830 Bond No. 149
Ward: Abner W. Thorton orphan of James Thorton deceased
Guardian: Adolph C. Ehringhaus Bond amount: $2,000
Bondsmen: Adolph C. Ehringhaus, John McMorine, Exum Newby

Tooley, John 10 December 1830 Bond No. 160
Wards: Jethro Tooley, Richard Henry Tooley & John Tooley
    orphans of John Tooley deceased
Guardian: John C. Ehringhaus Bond amount: $2,000
Bondsmen: John C. Ehringhaus, Abner Williams, Thomas Jordan

Trueblood, Aaron   2 February 1829   Bond No. 79
Ward: Isaac O. Trueblood orphan of Aaron Trueblood deceased
Guardian: Thomas Trueblood   Bond amount: $400
Bondsmen: Thomas Trueblood, Joshua Trueblood, Thomas Bell

Trueblood, Samuel   3 December 1828   Bond No. 75
Ward: Mary Trueblood orphan of Samuel Trueblood deceased
Guardian: Robert Bailey   Bond amount: $2,000
Bondsmen: Robert Bailey, John Bailey, John C. Blatchford

Trueblood, Samuel   6 June 1831   Bond No. 183
Ward: Mary Trueblood orphan of Samuel Trueblood deceased
Guardian: Benjamin Bailey   Bond amount: $1500
Bondsmen: Benjamin Bailey, John L. Bailey, John S. Brothers, Grandy Cartwright

Trueblood, Thomas   10 December 1830   Bond No. 159
Wards: Morris, Mary, Elizabeth & Nathan Trueblood orphans of Thomas Trueblood deceased
Guardian: John C. Ehringhaus   Bond amount: $2,000
Bondsmen: John C. Ehringhaus, Thomas Jordan, Abner Williams

Twine, William   2 June 1829   Bond No. 99
Wards: Margaret Twine, William Twine & Jesse Twine orphans of William Twine deceased
Guardian: Elizabeth Twine   Bond amount: $2,000
Bondsmen: Elizabeth Twine, Stephen White, John Hollowell

Warrington, John R.   3 December 1828   Bond No. 76
Wards: Mary Warrington, Thomas Warrington & James Warrington orphans of John R. Warrington deceased
Guardian: Thaddeus Freshwater   Bond amount: $600
Bondsmen: Thaddeus Freshwater, William F. Banks

Warrington, John R.   7 September 1830   Bond No. 144
Wards: Thomas Warrington & James Warrington orphans of John R. Warrington deceased

Guardian Bond Book 1827 - 1831

Guardian: Mordecai Gregory   Bond amount: $100
Bondsmen: Mordecai Gregory, James Palmer, Palin Jackson

White, Benjamin   2 December 1828   Bond No. 53
Ward: Samuel White orphan of Benjamin White deceased
Guardian: William W. Freshwater   Bond amount: $400
Bondsmen: William W. Freshwater, Thaddeus Freshwater,
    Lemuel Snowden

White, Benjamin   3 March 1829   Bond No. 88
Ward: Thomas White orphan of Benjamin White deceased
Guardian: Thomas Bailey   Bond amount: $1500
Bondsmen: Thomas Bailey, Caleb White, Thomas Wilson

White, John   4 March 1828   Bond No. 37
Wards: James & Sarah Ann White orphans of John White deceased
Guardian: William I. Hardy   Bond amount: $100
Bondsmen: William I. Hardy, William W. Freshwater

White, Joseph   7 March 1831   Bond No. 168
Ward: Jeptha White orphan of Joseph White deceased
Guardian: David White   Bond amount: $3,000
Bondsmen: David White, Thomas Elliott, Joseph Elliott

White, Josiah   3 March 1828   Bond No. 32
Ward: Martha White orphan of Josiah White deceased
Guardian: David White   Bond amount: $2,000
Bondsmen: David White, Thomas Elliott, Aaron White

White, Josiah   3 March 1828   Bond No. 33
Ward: Jepthia White orphan of Josiah White deceased
Guardian: David White   Bond amount: $2,000
Bondsmen: David White, Thomas Elliott, Aaron White

White, Nathan   2 February 1830   Bond No. 123
Ward: Miriam White orphan of Nathan White deceased
Guardian: Thomas White   Bond amount: $200
Bondsmen: Thomas White, Caleb White, Cader Munden

White, Stephen 8 September 1829 Bond No. 103
Ward: Matthew White orphan of Stephen White deceased
Guardian: Josiah Perry Bond amount: $800
Bondsmen: Josiah Perry, Nathan Small, Nathan Bagley Jr.

Williams, David S. 2 December 1828 Bond No. 60
Ward: John T. Williams orphan of David S. Williams deceased
Guardian: Thomas Jordan Bond amount: $3,000
Bondsmen: Thomas Jordan, John C. Ehringhaus, Josiah Jordan

Wilroy, Nathaniel 2 December 1828 Bond No. 54
Ward: Nathaniel Wilroy orphan of Nathaniel Wilroy deceased
Guardian: William Martin Bond amount: $1,000
Bondsmen: William Martin, Lemuel C. Moore

Wood, Joseph 3 December 1828 Bond No. 74
Wards: Joseph Wood deceased orphans
Guardian: Sally Wood Bond amount: $400
Bondsmen: Sally Wood, Elliott Whitehurst, Fred. Whitehurst

Wood, Joseph 9 September 1829 Bond No. 104
Ward: Spence Wood orphan of Joseph Wood deceased
Guardian: Miles Smithson Bond amount: $100
Bondsmen: Miles Smithson, Frederick Whitehurst, Lemuel Jennings

Wood, Joseph 7 June 1831 Bond No. 190
Wards: Sally & Parthenia Wood orphan of Joseph Wood deceased
Guardian: Elliott Whitehurst Bond amount: $400
Bondsmen: Elliott Whitehurst, Fredrick Whitehurst, Lemuel Jennings

Pasquotank County, North Carolina
Guardian Bonds
Book 1827 - 1831

STATE OF NORTH-CAROLINA,
Pasquotank County.
KNOW ALL MEN BY THESE PRESENTS, That we

of the County of Pasquotank, in the State aforesaid, are held and firmly bound unto

Esquires, and the rest of the Justices assigned to keep the peace for Pasquotank County, in the just and full sum of
pounds, current money of the State aforesaid, to be paid to the said Justices, their successors or assigns: To which payment well and truly to be made, we do bind ourselves, each of us, our and each of our heirs, executors, administrators, and assigns, jointly and severally, firmly by these presents. Sealed with our Seals, and dated this   day of   , in the year of our Lord, Anno. Domini, one thousand eight hundred and twenty

THE CONDITION OF THE ABOVE OBLIGATION IS SUCH, That whereas the above bounden   is constituted and appointed Guardian to   Orphan of
deceased.   NOW if the said,
shall faithfully execute his said Guardianship, by securing and improving all the estate of the said Orphan, until   shall arrive at full age, or be sooner thereto required, and then render a plain and true account of   said Guardianship on oath, before the Justices of our said Court, and deliver up, pay to, or possess, the said
as Orphan ought to be possessed of, or to such other persons as shall be lawfully empowered or authorized to receive the same, and the profits arising therefrom, then this obligation to be void, otherwise, to be and remain in full force and virtue.

Signed, Sealed and Delivered
in presence of

This was a left over guardian bond book that was originally printed and used for the 1822 to 1824 bonds.

In this book, the word twenty was scratched out and thirty one or 31 was then hand written on all but one of these bonds. The date of 1821, which is only on the first bond in the book, was probably a mistake made by the clerk of court when the bond was originally issued. It was probably issued in 1831 the same as the rest of the bonds in this book.

Brite, Malachi   6 December 1831   Bond No. 8
Wards: Wilson Brite, Able Brite, Polly Brite, Timothy Brite &
    Ephriam Brite orphan of Malachi Brite deceased
Guardian: Jeremiah Stokely   Bond amount: $100
Bondsmen: Jeremiah Stokely, Joseph Stokely

Carver, Elias A.   6 December 1831   Bond No. 7
Ward: James S. Carver orphan of Elias A. Carver deceased
Guardian: Job Carver   Bond amount: $1,000
Bondsmen: Job Carver, Evergin Carver, Thomas Temple Jr.

Casey, John   7 December 1831   Bond No. 20
Ward: John Casey orphan of John Casey deceased
Guardian: William A. Pritchard   Bond amount: $500
Bondsmen: William A. Pritchard, Frances Ackiss, John C.
    Ehringhaus

Deale, Daniel   7 December 1831   Bond No. 19
Wards: Stephen, Patsy, Jno. Wesley, Winney & Henris Deale
    orphans of Daniel Deale deceased
Guardian: William Deale   Bond amount: $500
Bondsmen: William Deale, James Harris, Martin Harris

Fletcher, Aaron   7 December 1831   Bond No. 18
Wards: Malachi & Elizabeth Fletcher orphans of Aaron Fletcher
Guardian: William F. Banks   Bond amount: $20,000
Bondsmen: William F. Banks, Thaddeus Freshwater, William W.
    Freshwater

Fletcher, William   6 December 1831   Bond No. 16
Wards: Aaron & Mary Fletcher orphans of William Fletcher
Guardian: Francis Fletcher   Bond amount: $5,000
Bondsmen: Francis Fletcher, Thomas Banks, Abner Williams

Grice, Charles   _ September 1821*   Bond No. 1
Wards: Elizabeth M. Grice, Warren D. Grice, Sarah Ann Grice &
    Mary S. Grice children of said Charles Grice*

Guardian Bond Book 1821 - 1831

Guardian: Charles Grice   Bond amount: $2,000
Bondsmen: Charles Grice, William Rogerson, James M. Grice
(*Note: the words orphan and deceased were scratched out; the date on this bond probably should have been recorded as 1831)

Lowry, Benjamin   6 December 1831   Bond No. 17
Ward: Robert Lowry orphan of Benjamin Lowry deceased
Guardian: John Lowry   Bond amount: $3,000
Bondsmen: John Lowry, Benjamin Lowry, Frances Fletcher

Manyard, John B.   6 December 1831   Bond No. 9
Wards: *(Nepilian?)*, Ann & *(Jenil?)* Manyard orphans of John B. Manyard deceased
Guardian: Exum Newby   Bond amount: $1,000
Bondsmen: Exum Newby, Hezekiah Lockwood, Thomas Jordan

Overman, John   1 September 1831   Bond No. 2
Ward: Elisa Overman orphan of John Overman Esq. deceased
Guardian: Nathan Morgan   Bond amount: $1500
Bondsmen: Nathan Morgan, John Weeks, Seth Morgan

Overman, John   1 September 1831   Bond No. 3
Ward: Benjamin N. Overman orphan of John Overman Esq.
Guardian: Nathan Morgan   Bond amount: $1,000
Bondsmen: Nathan Morgan, John Weeks, Seth Morgan

Perry, Kader   6 December 1831   Bond No. 5
Ward: Sarah Perry orphan of Kader Perry deceased
Guardian: Doctrine R. Perry   Bond amount: $1,000
Bondsmen: Doctrine R. Perry, John B. Perry, John Winslow

Perry, Noah   6 December 1831   Bond No. 6
Wards: Margaret Perry, Mary Perry, Julian Perry, Allen Perry & Doctrine Perry orphans of Noah Perry deceased
Guardian: Josiah Perry   Bond amount: $1,000
Bondsmen: Josiah Perry, Doctrine R. Perry, Nathan Morgan

Simpson, Robert   5 December 1831   Bond No. 4
Wards: Joseph, James, Josiah, Matthew & Elizabeth Simpson
    orphans of Robert Simpson deceased
Guardian: Jesse L. Pool   Bond amount: $1,000
Bondsmen: Jesse L. Pool, Nathan Raper, Joseph Pool

Wilcocks, Jeremiah   6 December 1831   Bond No. 10
Ward: James Wilcocks orphan of Jeremiah Wilcocks deceased
Guardian: Elliott Whitehurst   Bond amount: $1,000
Bondsmen: Elliott Whitehurst, Lemuel Jennings, Fredrick
    Whitehurst

Wilcocks, Jeremiah   6 December 1831   Bond No. 11
Ward: Susan Wilcocks orphan of Jeremiah Wilcocks deceased
Guardian: Elliott Whitehurst   Bond amount: $1,000
Bondsmen: Elliott Whitehurst, Lemuel Jennings, Fredrick
    Whitehurst

Wilcocks, Jeremiah   6 December 1831   Bond No. 13
Ward: Jeremiah Wilcocks orphan of Jeremiah Wilcocks deceased
Guardian: Elliott Whitehurst   Bond amount: $1,000
Bondsmen: Elliott Whitehurst, Lemuel Jennings, Fredrick
    Whitehurst

Wilcocks, Jeremiah   6 December 1831   Bond No. 14
Ward: Stephen Wilcocks orphan of Jeremiah Wilcocks deceased
Guardian: Elliott Whitehurst   Bond amount: $1,000
Bondsmen: Elliott Whitehurst, Lemuel Jennings, Fredrick
    Whitehurst

Wilcocks, Jeremiah   6 December 1831   Bond No. 15
Ward: Louisa Wilcocks orphan of Jeremiah Wilcocks deceased
Guardian: Elliott Whitehurst   Bond amount: $1,000
Bondsmen: Elliott Whitehurst, Lemuel Jennings, Fredrick
    Whitehurst

Index

Ackiss
  Francis... 49, 63, 126, 153, 155, 163, 182
  James... 79
  Margaret... 35, 49
  Nancy... 49
  Thomas... 35, 49, 63, 126, 153

Adams
  Andrew... 64
  Elizabeth ... 64
  Letty ... 64
  Mary... 64
  Nancy... 64
  Thomas... 64
  Willoughby... 64

Albertson
  Benjamin...43, 44, 58, 64
  Emmaline... 64
  Joseph... 135
  P... 20
  Penelope... 64
  Phineas... 16, 26
  William... 16, 20, 64

Albright, William... 20

Allen
  James P... 91
  Lucy... 91
  Mary... 91
  Nancy... 91
  Thomas... 15, 91
  William... 15, 61, 63, 70, 79, 83, 91, 121

Avery, Thomas... 171

Aydlett
  Betsy... 50
  Eliza... 36
  Polly... 36, 50
  Sally... 50
  Sarah... 36
  (S or D)edima... 36
  Thomas... 35, 36, 50
  Wilson... 36, 50

Bagley
  Nathan Jr... 180
  William... 141
  William S... 101

Bailey
  Alexander... 64
  Ann... 50, 153, 154
  Benjamin... 37, 38, 63, 64, 76, 79, 83, 88, 91, 92, 99, 104, 111, 114, 121, 126, 135, 140, 144, 150, 151, 153, 154, 157, 158, 163, 167, 170, 178
  Cassandra... 153, 154
  Charles... 64, 79, 83
  Charles Harvey... 64
  Clarkey... 64
  David... 36, 50, 64, 65
  Gabriel...6, 9, 13, 25, 27, 39, 41, 43, 44, 47, 48, 55, 58, 59
  George ... 63, 65, 79, 87, 92, 121, 153, 154
  George W... 132, 137
  Henry...2
  Jack... 64
  John...6, 36, 44, 63, 64, 65, 70, 79, 87, 92, 121, 126, 127, 130, 131, 135, 143, 144, 149, 153, 156, 159, 166, 167, 170, 178
  John L... 98, 121, 127, 135, 154, 157, 158, 163, 178

Bailey cont.
  Joseph... 64, 91
  Mary... 65, 92, 126, 154
  Mary C... 92
  Maynard... 50
  Nancy... 64, 92
  Penelope... 153, 154
  Polly... 36, 92
  Rebecca... 64, 92, 126
  Robert... 63, 65, 79, 83, 87, 92, 99, 121, 130, 131, 146, 149, 154, 159, 178
  Salina... 154
  Sally... 36
  Sarah...2
  Tamer... 92
  Thomas... 36, 65, 92, 126, 179
  William... 36, 65

Banks
  Ann(a) (e) ... 65
  Benjamin... 126
  Frederick S... 154
  James... 25
  John... 93, 154
  Jonathan...9, 29, 30, 50, 65, 92, 93, 94, 120, 126, 136, 149, 154
  Joseph...4, 5, 6, 7, 16, 17, 18, 19, 20, 21, 23, 25, 28, 29, 32, 34, 44
  Joseph D...11
  Luook... 25
  Margaret... 154
  Martha... 92
  Patsy... 65, 93
  Rebecca... 126
  Reback... 25
  Reding... 50, 93, 94, 126, 177
  Sarah... 126
  Susannah... 25

  Thaddeus... 65, 93, 126
  Thomas...9, 12, 18, 20, 30, 41, 50, 51, 61, 65, 93, 94, 126, 154, 177, 182
  William...7, 9, 13, 17, 18, 30, 44, 65, 92, 93, 94, 126, 154, 156
  William C... 51, 126
  William F... 126, 154, 155, 178, 182
  William G... 50, 65

Barclift
  Cassandra... 127, 155
  Julian... 155
  Juliet... 127
  Juliet Ann... 154
  Rowan... 49, 69, 77, 83, 127, 154, 155

Barnard, Bernard
  Carter... 68, 70, 90, 91, 98, 130, 132, 137, 142, 152, 158, 177
  Jesse... 90
  Robert...6, 13
  Thos... 158
  Thomas... 53, 58, 98, 111, 130, 136, 152, 177

Barnes, Barns
  Ann(a) (e)... 36, 50, 65
  Clarkey... 36
  James...2, 62
  Silas Fountain...2, 25
  Stephen...2, 5, 32, 36, 50, 65
  Steven... 20
  Thomas...2, 25
  William... 54, 64, 90, 98, 104, 106, 130, 152

Index

Barron, John N... 84

Bartlett, William... 127

Bedgood, Will... 171

Bell
  Bailey... 127
  John...7, 8, 127
  (Majae?) ... 127
  Southey... 127
  Thomas... 136, 178

Benton
  James... 94
  Lemuel... 94
  Margaret... 94

Biddle, Cader... 131

Blatchford, John C... 178

Blount
  Edmund... 98, 104, 108, 122, 163
  Frederick... 28, 33
  James... 18
  Joseph C... 163, 165
  Wilson... 19

Boswell, Isaac... 36

Boushall
  Penelope... 94
  Thomas... 94

Boyce, John... 37

Boyd, John... 18, 29, 30, 40, 41, 47

Bray
  Mary... 26

  James... 26, 135, 147, 162, 165
  John... 26, 102, 103, 117, 135, 161, 162, 173
  Sarah... 26
  William... 26, 102

Brent
  Charles P. ... 16
  John... 16
  William... 16

Brite, Bright
  Able... 182
  Charles... 31, 36, 38, 42, 94
  Charles L... 155
  Ephriam... 182
  Jabez... 94, 127
  Jesse... 94, 127
  Jonathan...45, 116, 143, 146, 169, 174
  Louisa... 155
  Malachi... 182
  Mary... 94, 127
  Polly... 36, 182
  Nathan... 80
  Susan... 155
  Timothy... 182
  Wilson... 182

Brooks
  George A... 155
  Joseph L. ... 22
  William C. ... 74, 104, 136, 155, 164

Broshir
  Ann... 36, 51, 66, 95, 128, 155, 156
  Benjamin... 66, 95, 128, 155, 156
  Betty... 51

Broshir cont.
 Elizabeth... 37, 66, 127, 155
 Fernon L... 65
 John... 36, 51, 66
 John L. ... 22, 36, 51, 94
 Joseph... 36, 66, 95, 128
 Joseph L... 29, 32, 51, 66, 155
 Joseph (P or R)... 51, 127, 155, 156
 Joseph S... 37
 Mary... 66
 Nancy... 51
 Polly... 37, 51, 66
 Simon... 65
 Simon L... 36, 37, 44, 51, 66, 127, 155, 156
 Thomas... 66
 Thomas L... 154, 156
 William... 36, 51, 66, 94, 127, 155, 156, 164

Brothers
 Andrew...2, 12, 15, 45
 Ann (a) (e)...2, 15
 Benjamin... 26
 Betsy... 67
 Briant...12, 26
 Caleb... 67, 148, 160, 176
 Clark... 95
 Clarkey... 67
 Demsey... 75
 Durant... 67
 Elizabeth... 95
 Enoch...2
 Henry...3, 48
 Isaac C. ...2
 James... 26, 95
 Jas... 67
 Jesse... 26
 Job...3, 67
 John... 2, 15, 26, 51, 126, 143, 144, 154
 John S... 153, 154, 163, 167, 178
 Jonathan...2, 26, 37, 51
 Joseph...2
 Joshua...2
 Louis... 67
 Mabel...2
 Mary...2
 Micajah...2
 Miles...2, 15, 18, 45
 Millicent... 26
 Nancy... 67, 95
 Peggy...2
 Polly... 26, 51
 Reuben... 52, 80, 82
 Richard... 67, 95, 128
 Robert...2
 Ruth...2
 Samuel...2, 37, 72, 80, 97, 111, 134, 143
 Susannah... 67
 Tamer... 67
 Zachariah... 148, 176

Brownrigg, Thomas...47

Bundy
 Benjamin... 37, 51, 67, 95, 96, 128
 Caleb... 37
 Charles... 26
 Elias... 37, 51, 67
 George... 37, 43, 44
 James... 95
 Jesse... 37, 51, 67, 95
 John... 37, 51, 67, 128, 156
 Jonathan... 37, 51
 Joseph... 51, 67, 95, 96, 128, 156

Josiah...9, 16, 26, 37
Martha... 67, 128, 156
Mary... 67, 128, 156
Milly... 51
Miriam... 16, 26
Nancy... 51, 96, 128
Nathan... 67, 78, 114, 128, 137, 144, 156, 169
Peninah... 37
Ricks... 95
Rix... 37, 51, 67, 128
Thomas... 51
William... 51, 67, 95, 128, 156

Burcher, Robert H... 105

Burnham
Nancy... 68, 96
Sabra... 68
Thomas... 68, 96

Burton, John...14

Butler
Elizabeth... 156
Mary... 156
Penelope... 156
Rebecca... 156
William C... 156

Butt
Barshaba... 27
Christopher... 27
James... 27
Wilson... 27

Ca_u, William... 32

Caman, John... 98

Carey, John... 107

Carter, William... 30, 40

Cartwright
Ahaz...3, 16
Benoni... 55, 65, 78, 84, 93, 128, 129, 157
Christopher... 30, 37, 66, 72
Darias... 37
Deborah... 27, 52, 68
Elizabeth... 128
Enoch...3
Grandy... 157, 178
Hezekiah... 21, 27, 33, 53, 54, 58
Isaac... 33
James... 27, 52, 68, 69, 96, 99, 157, 163, 176
James Sr... 68, 69
Jehu... 67, 81
Job(e)... 16, 20, 22, 24, 27, 33, 52, 157
John...3, 27, 37, 52, 68, 73, 80, 96, 157
John M... 52
Jos... 68
Joseph... 32, 37, 68
Josiah... 16, 24, 31
Lancaster... 157
Lodwick... 157
Malachi... 27, 52, 68, 96
Marmaduke... 27, 52, 68
Matilda... 157
McKeel... 27, 37, 52, 96
Miriam... 27, 37, 52, 68
Nancy... 27, 37, 52, 68, 96
Pendleton... 157
Peter... 157, 175
Rebecca... 27, 52, 68
Sally... 157
Samuel... 52
Sarah... 128

Cartwright cont.
  Susannah... 27, 52, 69, 96
  Thomas... 27, 33, 52, 68, 69, 96, 157
  William... 128, 157
  Wilson... 37

Carver
  _ucky... 97
  Alfred...3, 27, 69, 97, 129, 157
  Betsy... 69
  Elias... 69, 97, 129
  Elias A... 129, 182
  Eliza... 69, 129, 157
  Elizabeth... 96
  Everga(i)n...3, 182
  James...3, 27, 28, 33, 34, 37, 40, 41, 42, 46, 97
  James S... 182
  Job...3, 27, 129, 132, 143, 146, 162, 164, 172, 182
  John...3, 27, 69, 160
  Mary...3, 69, 97, 129, 157
  Nancy... 97
  Olia... 96
  Polly... 69, 96

Case, Casse, John... 26, 33, 46, 59, 68, 74, 80, 81, 82, 99, 107, 117

Casey
  Bathia... 157
  Charity... 130
  Enoch... 157
  Frederick... 157
  Isaac... 157, 175
  James... 163, 171
  John... 129, 130, 158, 182
  Maria... 157
  Robert... 129, 147, 176

  Sarah... 129, 158
  Thomas... 157

Chalk, William...12

Chamberlin
  James... 19, 31, 33, 36, 45, 52, 53, 69, 97, 130
  Margaret... 52, 53, 97, 130
  Mary... 52, 53, 69, 97, 130
  Nancy... 52
  Peggy... 69
  Sarah... 52

Chancy, Chancey
  Edward...2
  Edmund... 38
  Micajah...2, 38
  Polly... 38
  Robert... 58, 129, 159

Charles
  Stephen... 80, 83, 142, 154, 177
  William... 154, 169, 177

Clark, Clarke
  Barney... 100, 102
  Cornelius... 33, 46
  Ephriam...3
  Isaac... 24
  James... 16
  Micajah...3
  Sally... 158
  Timothy... 158
  William... 158

Cobb
  Samuel...12
  Thomas R... 131

Index

Cock, John... 57

Coen *see* **Koen**

Collins
Janetta... 158
William... 158

Commander
Aylsberry... 16, 18, 27, 38
Carter... 98
James... 98
John... 10, 27
Joseph...4, 16, 24, 27, 28, 38, 70, 98, 158
Joseph Sr.... 28
Mary Elizabeth... 130, 158
Miles... 123
Parthenia... 98, 130, 158
Thomas... 16, 90, 91, 98, 100, 106, 123, 130, 137, 152, 158

Connor
Cader...4
Crawford...4
Demsey... 16
Fanny... 16
George A... 16, 31
John...4
John L. ... 16

Copeland
Ira... 69
Martha Nancy... 69
John Andrew... 69

Copper, John... 158

Coppersmith, John...41, 130

Cory
Benjamin... 28

Davidson... 28
Eleanor... 28

Cotter
Hamilton... 53, 69, 101
Hamilton W... 158
Hannah... 53
Margaret... 69
Timothy...2, 5, 7, 11, 12, 17, 18, 20, 21, 24, 28, 29, 30, 31, 34, 36, 40, 45, 46, 47, 53, 69, 98, 159
Wilson... 69, 98, 159

Cox
Jacob... 98
William... 98

Crocker, John...4

Crutch
George... 130, 159
John... 159
William... 53, 69, 71, 101, 130, 159

Dailey, Thomas... 54, 72

Davis
_ay... 159
Alfred C... 159
Andrew...40
Ann... 159
Anthony...4, 135, 164
Archibald...4
Arthur... 115, 159
Bailey...2, 4, 26, 36, 39, 44, 51, 64, 70, 88
Benjamin...2, 11, 23, 30, 65, 70
Catherine... 16

Davis cont.
  Christian... 53
  Clarkey... 36
  D... 120
  David...4, 100, 111, 115, 159
  Davis... 70
  Devotion... 10, 14, 130, 159
  Devotion Jr....2, 12
  Durant...2, 38, 70, 130
  Edmund... 37, 54, 130, 159
  Elizabeth... 53, 99, 130, 159
  Evergen... 159
  Frederick...9, 10, 38, 159
  Iara... 84
  Isaac... 38
  James... 159
  Jesse... 53, 124, 135, 147
  John...5, 35, 36, 38, 50, 54, 64, 70, 171
  Josephine... 130, 159
  Joseph...2, 4, 70, 135, 164, 174
  Lovey...4
  Lydia...4, 16
  Mabel... 38
  Malachi... 53, 56, 70
  Martha... 38
  Mary... 159
  Mary Clark... 70
  Mary Elizabeth... 159
  Miles...4, 26, 36, 38, 39, 44, 56
  Patsy... 70
  Rebecca... 38
  Reuben...46, 70
  Reuben M... 156
  Ruben Jr ...13
  Ruben Sr...13
  Ruth...4
  Sally... 70
  Samuel...4, 16
  Shadrack... 53, 99, 151, 162, 165
  Susannah...14
  Thomas...5, 16, 37, 38, 39, 44, 50, 51, 54, 57
  William... 146, 167
  William H...39, 64, 65, 70, 73, 74, 91, 92, 93, 97, 103, 104, 126, 130, 139
  Willis...13, 38
  Wilson... 155, 159

Deale
  Daniel... 182
  Henris... 182
  Jno. Wesley... 182
  Patsy... 182
  Stephen... 182
  William... 182
  Winney... 182

Delon
  Anne...39
  Elisha... 149
  Enoch...39
  Francis...39, 99
  Henry... 160
  Jesse... 99, 159
  Jonathan... 160
  Josiah... 160
  Margaret...39
  Mark...39
  Mark Anthony... 160
  Mary... 160
  Miriam...39, 99
  Nancy...39, 99, 160
  Nathan... 160
  Penelope...39
  Samuel... 160
  Simon...39, 95, 96, 99
  William...39, 99

Dozier
  Dennis... 160, 161, 172
  Willoughby...6

Draper
  Elisha... 119, 120, 143, 145, 160, 174
  Joseph...6, 28
  Lovey... 28
  Mary... 28
  Sarah... 28

Early, Miles... 117

Ehringhaus
  Adolph C... 177
  John... 84
  John C. ... 67, 74, 85, 86, 94, 102, 124, 131, 152, 173, 177, 178, 180, 182

Elliot, Elliott
  Abigail... 160
  Hannah... 138
  John A... 160
  Joseph... 170, 179
  Miles... 64
  Mordecai... 160
  Thomas... 56, 98, 123, 179

Etheridge
  Harriot... 70
  James... 70, 99, 131
  Matthias... 70, 99, 131
  Morris... 70, 99, 131, 160
  Richard... 70, 99, 100, 106, 131, 160
  Seth... 70, 99, 131, 160
  William... 70, 100, 131

Evans
  Ann(e) ... 71, 100, 131
  Benjamin... 71, 100, 131
  Elizabeth... 71
  Evan... 16, 71

  Mary... 71
  Rebecca... 71
  Sarah... 71
  Susanna...44

Fearing, Isaiah... 150

Ferebee
  Alfred... 100, 131
  George... 83, 97, 115, 116, 145, 172
  James... 100, 131
  Peter... 159

Fletcher
  Aaron... 65, 67, 70, 74, 95, 128, 182
  Elizabeth... 182
  Francis... 67, 99, 100, 106, 149, 182, 183
  Malachi... 182
  Mary... 182
  William... 67, 95, 128, 182

Forbes
  Evan... 84
  Jeremiah... 84
  Peter...12

Forehand
  Anthony... 28
  Esther... 28
  James... 28
  Parthenia... 28
  Rebecca... 28

Fox
  George... 71
  Joseph... 71
  Mary... 71
  William... 71

Freshwater
 Thaddeus...7, 9, 17, 22, 23, 37, 65, 66, 71, 73, 74, 78, 84, 92, 93, 94, 95, 99, 100, 105, 111, 112, 126, 127, 128, 131, 134, 135, 137, 140, 147, 149, 154, 155, 160, 164, 178, 179, 182
 Thaddeus Jr... 105
 W. W... 65
 William... 66, 105, 110, 126, 140
 William W... 66, 71, 72, 73, 74, 78, 89, 92, 93, 94, 95, 96, 100, 104, 105, 111, 123, 126, 130, 131, 132, 139, 140, 150, 164, 179, 182

Gale
 Cornelius... 17
 Elizabeth... 17, 53
 John... 17, 53
 Sarah... 17, 53
 William S... 17, 53

Gambling, Gamberling
 Jesse... 52, 59, 68, 71, 75, 100, 131
 John... 100, 131
 Lazarus... 52, 53, 71
 Polly... 71

Gaskins
 Fanny... 100, 132
 George... 94
 Nancy... 71, 100, 132
 Patsy... 71
 Thomas... 61, 71, 100, 132
 William... 20, 41, 51, 66, 100, 101, 132

George
 Ann... 132
 David...5, 132
 John...5
 William...5
 William C... 68, 75, 84, 87, 89, 97, 101, 110, 112, 118, 123, 129, 132, 152

Gilbert
 Aaron Lancaster...5
 Jeremiah...5
 Joel...5
 John... 101, 132, 160
 Joseph... 160
 Josiah Jr. ...5
 Rhoda... 132
 Susan... 132
 William... 101, 132

Glasgow
 Caleb...39
 Keziah...39

Godfrey
 Clarkey... 133
 Edmund... 133, 165, 167
 Edmund B... 134, 139, 157, 160, 165
 G. W... 157
 George... 160
 George W... 133, 160
 Jacob... 133, 160
 Nancy... 133

Gordon
 Dozier... 53, 71
 John... 28
 John D... 101
 Joseph... 28, 53, 71, 101
 Lydia... 53
 Mary... 28
 Nathaniel...44
 Sarah... 28
 William... 28, 53, 71, 101

Index

Grandy, Charles... 16

Graves, Greaves
James...5
Jeremiah...5
John... 101
John William... 101

Gray
_aney... 133
Dorcas...6
Elizabeth...6, 133, 160
Fanny... 133, 160
Griffin... 133, 160
James... 124, 133, 134
Jean...6
John...6
Jordan... 146, 160
Joseph...4, 6, 14, 46, 60, 61, 133, 160
Julian... 133, 161
Mary...6
Nancy... 133, 161
Polly... 28
Robert...6, 29, 34
Thomas...6, 28
Thorton... 133, 160, 161

Gregory
James... 84, 93, 134
Lemuel... 134
Miles... 146
Mordecai... 179
Morris... 134
William... 31, 94

Grice
Charles... 24, 39, 40, 42, 45, 58, 84, 161, 182, 183
Elizabeth M... 161, 182
Francis... 31, 40, 45
Harriet...40
James M... 161, 183
Joseph...40
Mary...40
Mary S... 161, 182
Sarah...40
Sarah Ann... 161, 182
Warren D... 161, 182
William...40

Griffin
David...40, 78, 79
Isaac... 161
James... 29, 161
John... 17
Joseph...40
Josiah... 26
Mary... 161
Moses... 101
Moses H... 72, 134
Robert... 161
Samuel... 17
Sarah...40, 161
Sophie... 161
Thomas... 72, 101, 134
Thomas W... 161
William... 156

Hain, George J. ... 30

Halstead
Benjamin... 17
John... 17, 24
Thomas... 17

Hamilton, John...46

Hardy
William... 92, 93, 94, 95, 100, 105, 126, 150
William I... 110, 134, 140, 147, 179

Index

Harkins, Thomas... 33, 48

Harrell
David... 59, 62
Jos... 69
Joseph... 68, 160, 161, 162

Harrington, Isaac... 56

Harris
Davis... 53, 102
Ephriam... 158
Grandy... 72, 102, 161, 162
Isaac... 53, 72, 102, 161, 162
James... 32, 59, 86, 102, 182
John... 102, 134, 162
John Jr... 158
John Sr... 158
Joseph... 84
Martin... 182
Martha... 53, 102
Maxey... 144
Reuben... 102
Ruben T... 72, 102, 144
Susan... 102
Susannah... 134, 162
Thomas... 53, 102

Harvey
Benjamin Hardy...40, 102
Julian... 102
Thomas...40, 102, 139
William M...40

Haskins, Thomas...46

Heath, Arthur... 100, 115, 174

Henley, Hinley
Abraham... 29
Elizabeth... 29
George R...6, 56

James... 29
Joseph...6, 17
Lucinda... 29
Nancy... 17
Sarah... 29

Herring
John... 72
Patsy... 72

Hewett, Hewitt
Benjamin...41, 57
Richard...41, 57

Hinds, John... 175

Hinton
William L. ... 31
William S. ...3, 17, 18, 27, 28, 33, 34

Hoffmire
Alex... 54
Alexander... 54, 72
Fanny... 72
Franny... 54
George W... 54
Joseph... 54, 72
Penelope... 72
Penniah... 54
Penny... 54
Sally... 54, 72
Sarah... 54
Washington... 54, 72

Holloway, Jesse... 162

Hollowell
Ambrose... 72, 134
Edmund... 134
John... 72, 134, 178
Margaret... 134

Index

Mary... 134
Noah... 99
Samuel... 72, 134
Zachariah... 134

Hooker
Anne...40
Milly...40
Stephen...40

Hornett, Benjamin... 72

Hos
George... 102
Joseph... 102
Mary... 102
William... 102

Howell
Benjamin...6
Rowan...6

Humphries
Betsy... 162
Jonathan... 26, 45, 102, 135, 162
Mourning... 102, 135
Nancy... 162
Richardson R... 102, 135, 162
Thomas... 26, 120, 162
William... 162

Jackson
Arthur...40, 45, 54, 72, 103
Asa... 15, 121
Bailey...5, 10, 13, 17, 19, 27, 40, 42, 46, 54
Barnes B... 73, 103
Benjamin...40, 131
Benjamin F... 162, 163
Benjamin M... 52, 55, 59, 96, 162, 163
Corbin... 54, 58

Elizabeth...40
Hezekiah... 79
James... 23, 32, 40, 73
Joab... 23, 40
John... 170
John M... 162
Jos... 73
Joseph...40, 54
L. Joseph... 171
Labray... 54
Lemuel... 33, 85, 154, 155, 162, 163, 169, 170
Louise(a)...40, 54, 72, 103
Lowry... 135, 163
Mala... 104
Malachi... 16, 36, 41, 50, 64, 65, 70, 73, 88, 89, 92, 103, 122
Mary...40, 54, 113, 114, 135, 163
Maximilian... 103
Maxy... 72
Miles... 135, 163
Milly...40, 54, 72, 103
Palin... 73, 103, 104, 179
Peggy... 54
Peleg... 54
Penny...40, 54
Polly...40, 54, 72, 103
Reuben...40
Seth... 54
Sophia... 103
Stephen... 103, 104
Stephen B... 73
Susanna(h) ... 54
Tamer...40
Thomas... 23, 40
William... 54, 135, 163
William L. Quincey... 163
Zachariah... 54
Zacharias... 163

James
  Benjamin... 54, 73, 104, 135
  John... 137, 173, 174
  Lemuel... 59
  William... 54, 73, 104, 135

Jarvis
  Caty... 29
  Elizabeth... 29, 41
  John... 29, 41
  Penelope... 29, 41

Jennings
  David...9, 10, 72, 84, 102
  Elizabeth... 29
  Frederick... 163
  James... 73, 104, 135, 163
  Jarvis...46
  John... 17, 41, 68, 72, 155, 163
  John Jr. ... 36
  Joseph... 29
  Lemuel... 82, 88, 102, 117, 134, 135, 144, 147, 161, 162, 163, 172, 173, 180, 184
  Mary... 17, 73, 104, 135, 163
  Miles... 163
  Polly...41
  Samuel... 82, 135
  Thomas... 16, 17, 19, 135, 163

Jones
  Allen B... 117, 147, 174, 175
  Benjamin...7
  Frederick... 145
  James... 23, 27, 90
  James I... 135
  John...3
  John R... 135
  Joseph E... 135
  Malachi W... 145, 173
  Samuel... 135, 164

  Senith... 33
  Smith... 90

Jordan
  Elizabeth...6
  Isaac... 29
  John A. ...6
  Joseph... 36, 54
  Josiah... 180
  Richard... 29, 71
  Thos. S... 72
  Thomas...4, 21, 29, 38, 53, 55, 57, 69, 70, 73, 77, 84, 104, 118, 132, 134, 152, 177, 178, 180, 183
  Thomas L... 104
  Thomas Jr. ...4, 9, 24, 52, 53, 59, 65, 89
  Thomas Sr. ... 19, 21, 33, 38, 48, 54

Keaton
  Anthony... 55
  Anthony M... 73
  Benjamin F... 164
  Benoni... 73
  Elizabeth... 29
  Fanny... 164
  Joseph... 10, 73, 89, 122
  Joseph L... 164
  Polly... 55
  Rebecca... 164
  Ruben...5, 7, 8, 9, 29, 55
  William...9, 10, 55, 73, with 64
  Winifred... 29, 73

Kenyon, Kinyan
  David... 159
  David A... 167
  David H... 159, 169, 171
  Joseph... 10

Index

Kinney, Charles R... 157

Kirby
Abraham...6, 13
Betsy...6
James...6
Lucinda...6
Sarah...6

Knight, Samuel... 108, 109

Knox
__le... 104
Ambrose... 53, 54, 57, 59, 64, 65, 67, 70, 71, 74, 77, 86, 88, 91, 92, 93, 94, 97, 100, 102, 104, 111, 112, 114, 115, 121, 126, 128, 129, 130, 136, 139, 145, 147
Andrew...13, 16, 20, 52, 74
Hugh...13, 55, 74, 136, 164
Hugh B... 68, 75, 112
Margaret... 74
Patsy... 55
Thomas A. ... 104
Thomas D... 74, 136, 164

Koen, Coen
Caleb... 18
Jonathan... 18
Joseph... 18
Murden... 164
William R... 164

Kote, William... 33

Lacy
Ann (a) (e) ... 29
Josiah... 29

Lane, John...2, 5, 6, 10, 13, 14, 17, 18, 41, 47

Lawrence, James... 104

Leigh, James... 122

Leonard
Benjamin...41
James... 75

Lister
Elisha... 18, 41, 148, 176
Israel... 18, 130, 158
Jacob... 18, 28, 41, 130, 136, 148, 158, 164
John... 176
Polly... 18, 41
Sarah... 136
Susanna(h)... 136, 164
Thomas... 18, 41, 118, 130, 136, 148, 158, 164, 176
Winifred... 18

Lockwood
Abner... 30
Armwell...7
Elizabeth...7
Hezekiah... 183
Holland...7, 30
James... 30
John... 30
Nancy...7

Long
Bray B... 140
Daniel... 136
Jesse... 136
Lowry... 136

Low, Lowe
Alfred... 164
Ann... 164
Arron...4, 134, 141

Low, Lowe cont.
  Christian... 164
  Elizabeth... 164
  Joshua...41
  Nancy...41
  Patsey...41
  Priscilla...41
  Sarah... 164
  Thomas...41
  Zachariah...41

Lowry, Lowrey
  Benjamin...7, 17, 22, 23, 30, 41, 74, 105, 183
  Benjamin B... 126, 165
  Jno... 74
  John...7, 41, 54, 76, 90, 105, 183
  Patsy... 30, 55
  Polly...7
  Robert... 30, 55, 105, 183
  Thomas... 74
  William... 74, 105
  William F... 149

Lucas
  George...41
  William...41

Lufman
  John...7
  Miles...7
  William...7

Luten, Luton
  Constantine... 30, 105
  Harvey... 30, 36, 37, 51, 52, 55, 59, 61, 73, 74, 105
  John... 30
  (Maryh?)... 105
  Milly... 30
  Nancy... 30

  Polly... 30
  Susannah... 30, 105
  Thaddeus... 74, 105
  William... 30

Madison, Matthias... 105, 106, 136

Madren, Madrin
  John... 37
  Mary...42
  Matthias...42, 74
  Miriam...42, 74
  Nancy...42
  Rebecca...42
  Thomas...42, 62

Mann
  Sarah...7
  Thomas...7

Manyard
  Ann... 183
  (Jenil?) ... 183
  John B... 165, 183
  (Nepilian?) ... 183

Markham
  A. R... 122
  Anthony... 61, 75, 106, 107, 165
  Anthony A... 101
  Anthony R... 87, 106, 136
  Anthony S... 136
  (_uckey) ... 55
  Benjamin... 55, 106, 173
  Charles... 55, 106
  Demarcus... 106
  John... 75, 107, 136, 165
  Keziah... 55
  Margaret... 55, 106

Index

Marlen... 55
Martha... 106
Millicent... 55
Nancy... 106
Penelope... 75, 136
Penny... 75, 107
Thomas... 55, 61, 70, 75, 80, 99, 100, 104, 106, 107, 127, 128, 131, 135, 136, 165
Thomas Jr. ... 55
Thos. R... 136
William... 75, 107, 136, 154

Martin
Leonard... 69, 80
William... 85, 90, 124, 152, 180

Matthews, Samuel... 90

McAdams, James... 19, 48

McBride, James...45

McCoy, Asa... 148, 149, 161, 168, 169, 175

McDon(n)ell, M(a)cDonald
Elizabeth... 75, 137, 165
(Grizzle?) ... 75, 137, 165
Johanna... 137, 165
John...4, 5, 8, 18, 21, 25, 29, 31, 32, 35, 37, 38, 39, 40, 41, 42, 47, 53, 55, 57, 58, 68, 69, 71, 73, 75, 84, 97, 112, 129, 134, 137, 140, 141, 157, 160, 165, 167
John W... 137
Nancy... 75

McMorine
John... 17, 150, 177

Robert...12, 16, 19, 20, 23, 34, 40, 47, 118

McPherson, McPerson
Daniel... 26, 53, 75, 85, 96, 99, 107, 118, 119, 124, 147
David... 53
Noah... 19, 22, 40, 60
Peter... 51

Meeds, Meads
Alfred... 18, 30
Benjamin...42, 137
Deborah... 18
Elijah... 137
John... 18
Nancy... 18
Rhoda...42
Robert... 18
Stanton... 137
Thaddeus... 18
Timothy... 18, 30

Milby
Polly...42
Susanna...42
Zadock...42

Miller
James... 75
Jamy... 165
John... 75
Willi... 165
William... 75, 107

Mitchell
Carrey... 165
Cealah... 165
Doretta... 165
Elizabeth... 30
Francis... 165

Mitchell cont.
  John... 30
  Mary... 165
  Tillmon... 165

Moore
  Lemuel... 74, 152
  Lemuel C. ... 67, 90, 131, 180

Morgan
  Benjamin... 67, 89, 107, 137, 166
  Beoni... 108
  Charles... 75, 76, 137
  Chloe... 30
  Christopher... 137
  Claudius... 24, 30
  David... 108
  Isaac... 108
  James... 56, 72, 75, 76, 101, 108, 122, 134, 144, 145
  Jonathan... 108
  Lemuel... 76
  Matthew... 79
  Nancy... 108
  Nathan... 67, 75, 76, 88, 101, 107, 108, 114, 122, 123, 128, 137, 139, 140, 141, 150, 164, 183
  Robert... 174
  Samuel... 56, 108, 109
  Seth... 183
  Uria... 137
  Urih... 75, 76

Morris
  Aaron... 18
  Aaron Jr...7, 8, 18, 19, 56, 58
  Aaron Sr. ...7, 8, 32, 42
  Anderson... 74, 76, 77, 87, 105, 108, 109, 110, 113, 121, 123, 128, 138, 139, 142, 156, 166, 169

Anna...8
Benoni... 57, 108
Caleb... 51, 67, 95, 123, 128
Christopher...7, 8, 16, 30, 56, 137
Elizabeth... 19
Hannah... 56, 76, 108, 138
Isaac... 31
James ... 56, 76, 109
Jehoshaphat...7, 18, 42
John...7, 8, 81
John B... 108
John W... 138, 166
Joseph...8, 56, 76
Joseph H... 108, 138, 166
Joseph Sr...8
Josiah... 56
Joshua...8, 17, 21, 26, 37, 38, 56, 58, 76, 77, 95, 108, 109, 110, 122, 138, 166
Lemuel C... 148
Margaret...8, 19, 56, 76, 77, 109, 110, 137
Mark... 31, 42, 56, 76, 108, 109, 138
Mary... 19
Millicent...8
Mordecai... 26, 56, 76, 77, 108, 110, 138, 139, 156, 166
Mordicai Jr ... 38, 51, 52, 56, 105, 108, 109, 113, 121, 138, 166
Mordecai Sr ... 56
Nathan...5, 8, 56, 67, 76, 87, 89, 138
Nathan O... 72, 74, 90
Penelope ... 56
Penniah...8, 76
Pritchard...8
Sarah...7, 18, 42, 56, 76, 108, 109, 138

Index

Sarah Ann... 77, 109, 110, 139, 166
Susanna... 138
Thomas... 19, 38, 51, 52, 56, 76, 77, 108, 109, 110, 138, 139, 166
Thomas Sr. ... 24

Mullen
Ambrose... 139
Catherine... 139
Elizabeth... 139
John... 38, 85, 139
Joseph... 57, 139
Louise Francis... 139
Margaret Ann... 139
Stephen ... 63, 69, 73, 77, 139

Munden, Cader... 107, 137, 156, 166, 179

Murden
Jeremiah... 19, 31
Robert... 19, 31
Silvanus... 19, 31

Muse
Richard... 58, 67, 68, 71, 77
William...3, 12, 19, 29, 34, 64, 66, 72, 77, 78, 79, 80, 84
William (F or P)... 13, 14, 18, 19, 21, 33
William T. ...3, 11, 20, 27, 28, 29, 31, 32, 34, 38, 40, 47, 50, 53, 57, 59, 64, 66, 68, 69, 70, 73, 74, 75, 77, 83, 84, 86, 89, 91, 92, 93, 97, 98, 110, 111, 113, 114, 115, 118, 121, 122, 124

Nash
Demsey...6, 56

Dundly...42
James... 56, 118, 119, 127, 157, 163
John...42, 56
Samuel... 53

Newbold
Elizabeth...42
Grizzle...42
John...42
Samuel...42
Thomas...42, 139, 166
Thomas J... 70
Will... 159
William...42, 126, 139, 151, 166

Newby
Ann... 77
Exum... 64, 177, 183
James... 77
John... 51
Mary Ann... 77

Nichols
Abner...3
Benjamin... 19, 31
Betsy... 31
David... 19, 43, 145, 146, 172, 176
Elizabeth... 19
Hezekiah... 31
John...43
Joseph... 19
Keziah... 19
Kiddy... 19
Polly... 19, 31

Nicholson
Christopher...4, 19, 77
Eliza... 56, 57

Nicholson cont.
  Elizabeth... 77
  George...8, 31
  Henley... 56, 57, 77
  Jane... 19
  Jean... 77
  Jerusha...8
  John...8, 31
  Mary... 56, 57, 77
  Nancy... 31
  Polly...8, 31, 77
  Thomas...42
  William... 37, 41

Nixon
  Emily K... 166
  James...43, 77, 110, 139
  John...13, 14, 20, 21, 57
  Lavinia S... 166
  Margaret...43, 77, 110
  Mary...43
  Mary Ann... 139
  Morris... 57
  Thomas...43
  Samuel...43, 77, 110, 166
  Samuel R... 57
  Sarah... 57
  William... 57, 151
  William Muse... 57
  William R... 142
  Zachariah...13, 14

Overman
  Ann(e)...44, 78, 110
  Benjamin... 23, 24, 43, 58, 78
  Benjamin N... 183
  Benjamin S... 21, 26, 167
  Berey... 31
  Charles...4, 9, 16, 23, 43, 44, 57, 58, 77, 78, 79, 110, 111, 134, 139, 140, 150

Daniel...9
Demsey... 79
Eli...43, 58
Elisha... 183
Elizabeth... 31, 43, 78, 110, 111, 139, 140
Isaac...3, 10, 14, 26, 27, 48, 58, 121
George... 78, 110
George F... 59, 87
George W... 140
Grandy... 58, 111
Henry... 65, 71, 80, 110, 111, 140
Henry P. ... 20, 32, 50, 51, 55, 61, 64, 65, 66, 68, 69, 70, 73, 78, 88, 89, 110, 139, 167
Isaac... 84, 87, 111, 115, 116
James... 23, 167
(Jas. or Jos.) ... 31
John...4, 9, 23, 24, 31, 36, 43, 49, 131, 149, 151, 183
Joshua... 20
Josiah... 116, 170
Lewis... 20
Martha... 78, 111, 140
Mary... 78, 111, 140
Matthew... 31, 76, 108, 109
Mekale... 167
Miriam...43, 57
Mordecai... 20, 78, 110, 140
Nathan... 20, 41, 43, 65, 78, 79, 111, 139, 140
Othniel... 20
Ozier...9
Pet. O... 167
Polly... 79
Reuben...9, 141
Rhoda...9
Robert... 79, 111

Index

Sally... 20
Samuel...9, 79
Sarah... 79
Simon... 163
Susannah...43, 77, 110
Thomas...9, 58, 79, 111, 140, 167
Thomas Jr ... 56
William... 20

Overton
Archibald... 80, 111
Betty... 80
Delilah... 80
John... 80
Lemuel... 73
Lucy... 80
Mary... 80

Padrick, Jonathan... 20

Palin
Henry... 80, 112, 140
John... 80, 112, 140
Joseph... 80, 111, 161, 174
Keziah... 31
Lemuel...9
Mary... 31
Nancy...9, 80, 112, 140, 167
Sarah... 80, 112
Susannah...9
Thomas...4, 9, 31, 32, 58, 80, 111, 112, 140, 146, 167

Palmer
Asena... 80
(Grizzy?) ... 80
James... 71, 100, 131, 139, 150, 165, 179
Thomas... 17, 36, 37
Willis... 17, 80

Parisho, Joshua... 16, 26

Parker, Joseph... 20, 21, 42, 47, 57, 77, 78, 110, 139, 140, 141

Parr
Milly... 80
Noah... 80

Pendleton
Abner...9, 20, 80, 111, 112, 140, 161, 167
Ann... 175
Andrew...14
Angelica... 112
Benjamin... 167
Charles S... 112
Clarky...44
Demsey... 159
Demsey B... 72, 130, 132, 140, 159, 162, 167, 173, 174
Elcey... 20
Elizabeth... 21, 44
Frederick... 72, 74, 99, 111, 112, 130, 132, 140, 159, 161, 167
George... 80, 110, 139
George W... 66, 112, 140, 141, 167
Henry... 20, 32, 164, 174
John... 10, 11, 20, 22, 25, 27, 80
John F. ...9, 10, 20
John T... 80
Joseph... 20, 32, 44
Joshua...44
Maranda... 80, 141, 167
Meke_... 167
Nancy... 80, 140
Nehemiah...9, 28, 32, 139

Index

Pendleton cont.
Robert... 20, 21, 164, 174
Samuel... 20
Thaddeus... 32, 44
Thomas... 14
Timothy... 72, 80, 84, 111, 112, 141

Perkins
Caleb... 66, 127
Edmund... 72, 129, 134, 137
Edmund H... 65, 66, 80, 89, 112, 127, 139, 140, 141, 155, 157, 165, 167
Joseph... 66, 84

Perry
Abner... 168
Alexis... 168
Alexis A... 142
Allen... 183
Cader... 81, 141, 167
Davis... 142
Davis W... 141
(Deacel?) Elizabeth... 168
Doctrine... 183
Doctrine R... 183
Druzilla... 168
Elizabeth... 142
H... 75
Hardy... 141, 167, 168
Israel... 168
Jacob... 141, 168
Jacob H... 168
John... 141, 168
John B... 81, 168, 183
Jonah... 168
Joshua M... 168
Josiah... 123, 151, 166, 180, 183
Josiah W... 168
Julian... 183

Kader... 43, 49, 168, 183
Margaret... 183
Mary... 167, 183
Matthew... 142, 168
Mill_... 168
Nelson... 142
Noah... 183
Polly... 141
Rix... 139, 141, 162, 167, 168, 171, 177
Robert... 78, 89, 90
Robinson... 81
Sab_na... 141
Sally... 141
Sarah... 77, 81, 110, 139, 141, 142, 167, 168, 183
Sarah E... 141
William... 81, 88, 141, 142, 168

Pike
Benjamin... 58, 127
Ferbee... 81, 142, 168
Jesse... 58, 81, 142, 168, 169
John... 22, 58
Jonathan... 58, 127
Joseph... 58
Pharibe... 81
Wilson... 58, 81, 127, 142, 169

Pipen
Nathaniel... 58
Thomas... 58

Pool, Poole
Alfred... 142
Ann... 142
Broshir... 93
Eliza... 113
Elizabeth... 44, 142
Emaline... 113

Index

Isaac... 81, 112
James... 10, 15, 21, 50, 71, 82, 83, 86, 88, 91, 94, 98, 100, 101, 113, 114, 120, 142, 144
James A... 113
James Jr... 60, 86
Jesse... 169
Jesse L... 171, 184
John... 10, 21, 38, 41, 50, 55, 57, 58, 59, 61, 69, 71, 82, 83, 98, 113, 114, 120, 121, 132, 136, 144, 155, 160, 164, 173
John Jr... 98, 100, 101, 113, 114, 142
John Sr... 60, 64, 73, 81, 82, 86
Joseph... 10, 184
Joseph H... 160, 167
Joshua... 10, 84
Joshua A. ... 77, 81, 87, 115
L. B... 89, 128, 129, 136
L. B. Jr... 65
Margaret...44
Maria... 113
Mary... 142
Nancy...44
Patrick... 10, 21, 44, 81, 112, 142
Richard... 60, 71, 72, 77, 81, 82, 83, 86, 94, 104, 110, 112, 113, 114, 120, 126, 144, 145, 169
Robert... 10, 34, 113, 142, 154, 169, 171
Simon B... 66, 80, 127, 154, 155, 156
Solomon... 10, 21, 94, 98, 100, 101, 113, 141, 142, 149, 166, 169, 171
Solomon Jr... 84, 87, 132, 142, 159, 161, 167, 169
Solomon P... 133
Tamer... 10, 44

Thomas...48, 81, 113, 142, 169
Thomas Jr. ... 81, 94, 112, 120
William... 10

Powers, Benjamin... 55, 154

Poyenter
John... 10
Joseph... 10
Thomas... 10

Price
John... 21
Samuel... 21, 28, 34
Sarah... 21

Pritchard
Abigail... 170
Ann... 58, 82, 113, 143, 169
Aseneth... 170
Arthur... 36
Benjamin...7, 8, 9, 21, 22, 36, 40, 44, 56, 58, 77, 81, 94, 104, 109, 112, 113, 114, 123, 127, 138, 142, 150, 151, 169
Benjamin Jr... 67, 82, 89
Caleb... 50, 56, 81, 113, 142, 169
David... 10, 54, 58, 85
David Jr...42, 58, 59
Enoch... 74
Hugh... 143, 169
Isaac... 21
James... 58, 82, 113, 143, 169, 170
Jane... 143, 169
John ... 32, 53, 58, 82, 143
Joseph... 36, 63, 81, 89, 104, 108, 109, 111, 114, 120, 121, 122, 123, 135, 137, 143, 144, 151, 169, 170

Index

Pritchard cont.
  Josiah... 82, 102
  Lacy... 143
  Malachi... 32
  Margaret... 82, 113, 143
  Mary... 58, 82, 113
  Mary Ann... 170
  Peggy... 32, 58, 82
  Pennia(h) ... 170
  Peter... 82, 143
  Philip... 82, 144
  Richard... 82, 143, 144
  Sally... 58, 82, 143, 170
  Samuel... 21, 127
  Sarah... 82, 114, 144
  Susanna(h)...14, 44 170
  Thomas... 21, 56, 67, 82, 109, 114, 137, 144
  William... 58, 82, 113, 127, 154, 155, 169, 170
  William A... 130, 143, 155, 158, 163, 170, 182

Proby
  Paul... 82, 144, 170
  Paul S... 114
  Sally... 170
  Sarah... 10, 82, 114, 144
  William... 10, 11, 17
  William Jr....11

Proctor, Samuel... 97

Raper
  (_olrey) ... 59
  Ann... 83
  Bailey...44
  Caleb... 83, 113, 114, 134, 144, 145, 170
  Cornelius...44, 83, 114, 144
  David...44
  Davis... 170, 171
  Davis D... 170
  F(r)anny... 83, 114
  Henry... 49, 59, 61, 83, 114, 144
  John... 59, 83, 114, 144, 145, 170
  John Robert... 83
  Joshua... 83, 144
  Mary... 170, 171
  Nathan... 184
  Nathan M... 170
  Patsy... 83, 114, 144
  Rebecca... 59
  Robert... 59, 83, 114, 144, 145, 170
  Samuel... 83, 114, 144
  Thomas... 170, 171

Rayner
  Elizabeth... 59
  John... 59
  Sally... 59
  William... 59

Redding, Reding
  Henry Palin...11
  Jesse...2, 6, 9, 10, 11, 13, 14, 17, 18, 25, 28, 30, 44, 48
  Keziah...44
  Paul... 21
  Thomas...11
  William... 21

Relfe
  Anna Drew...11
  Blakely... 171
  Decatur... 171
  Enoch...11, 12, 115
  James Shaw...11
  John...12

Joseph...6, 10, 12, 31, 36, 38, 45, 83, 115, 171
Josiah...2, 21, 28, 30, 33, 34, 36, 38, 45, 48, 58, 83, 115, 145, 171
Malachi... 83, 115, 171
Margaret... 115, 171
Mary Ann... 115
Montgomery... 171
Nancy... 83
Nathan...12
Stephen... 83, 114, 171
Thomas T...11
Thomas...12
William... 61, 103, 171
William T. ...7, 19, 41, 44, 55, 72, 73, 103, 166, 171

Rhodes, Roads
George... 115, 173
Joshua... 173
Linkham... 115

Richardson
Benjamin... 83, 116, 145, 172
Daniel...43, 145, 171, 172
Demsey... 145, 171, 172
Elizabeth... 83
Fanny... 145, 172
Ferebee...45
Gabby... 145
Ivy... 172
Jacob... 19, 31, 32, 43, 73, 85, 102, 103, 117, 172
James... 119, 172
John...45, 90, 101, 145, 172
John Sr... 116
Joseph... 172
Josiah... 32
Lancelot...45
Levi... 145, 172
Levy...43
Miles... 17, 83, 115, 116, 145, 172
Olly... 172
Polly... 83
Richard... 145
Rite... 172
Sally... 83, 115, 172
Samuel... 172
Stephen... 32
William... 145, 171
Winifred...45

Riggs
James... 84, 173
Reddick... 84, 173
Samuel... 84, 173

Roads *see* **Rhodes**

Roberts
Joshua... 84
Patsy... 84

Robertson, J. H... 87

Robinson
Elizabeth Matilda... 32
John C... 60
Margaret Anne ... 32
Martha Jane... 32
William... 21, 26, 32

Rogerson
Asa... 148, 168, 169, 175
William... 161, 183

Rose
Andrew... 173, 174
Nancy... 173, 174
William... 55, 106, 122, 173, 174

Rowe, John... 21, 27, 35, 37, 49, 59, 84, 85

Russell
Elizabeth...45, 84, 116
James...12, 45, 84, 116
John... 20, 22
Malachi...45, 84, 116
Mary...12
Thomas...12

Saltenstall
Chaprin... 146
Dudley... 146
Louisa... 146

Sanderlin
Asa... 28, 67, 116, 174
Bridget... 116
Elizabeth... 116
Maximilian... 116
Patsy... 116
William... 116, 164, 174
Wilson... 22, 116

Sanders, Saunders
Abi... 22
Ann (a) (e)... 22
Elizabeth... 32
Evan... 32
Hosea...12
Jacob... 167, 168
Jacob Winslow... 142
Mary... 32
Richard...12, 22
Simson... 32

(Sapell?)
Benjamin... 116
Margaret... 116
Mary... 116

Sawyer
Abel...12, 60, 68, 69, 96, 129, 132, 146
Ann Elizabeth... 146, 174
Benjamin... 10, 22
Caleb...45, 84
Charity... 146
Charles... 69, 174
Clarkey... 146
Daniel... 146
David... 159
Demsey... 19
Ebenezer...7, 13, 45
Enoch... 146, 147, 174
Fanny... 146
Ferebee...45
Frederick... 26
Frederick B. ...6, 10, 13, 19, 28, 29, 32, 34, 42, 60, 61
Griffith... 19
Hollowell...6, 45, 116, 146
Ira...45, 116, 146
Isaac... 159
James...6, 18, 20, 21, 45
Jeremiah... 82, 102, 117, 134, 144, 147, 174, 175
Joel...42, 45, 46, 85, 103, 117, 119, 120, 129, 135, 143, 149, 164, 176
John...45, 146, 174
Joseph... 22
Julian... 146
Kiddy...46
Lot...12
Malachi... 38, 45, 48
Mark... 146
Margaret... 146
Martha...12
Mary...12, 45, 84
Matthias E. ...4, 10
Nancy...12

Index

Nichols...46
Noah...42, 45, 54, 62, 152, 165, 172
Polly... 84
Spence... 146
Spencer... 148, 149
Susannah...45
Thomas...45, 84, 146, 174
William... 84, 146, 174
William Templeman... 146
Wilson...46, 146

Scaff
David... 31, 59, 119, 148
James... 119, 148
John... 59, 148

Scarborough, Sharborough
David... 22, 46, 72, 131, 175
Hillgrove...46
Jehu... 22, 46
John... 22, 46
Joseph... 22, 46
Luke...46

Scott
_hen... 158
Anna... 85, 117
Armon... 85, 117, 174, 175
Benoni... 147
Caleb... 175, 176
Charity...46
Charles... 59
Dorcas ... 32, 46
Edward... 33, 46
Eliz... 175
Elizabeth...46, 147
Enoch...46, 59
George... 85, 117
George W... 117, 147, 175
Hollowell... 129, 175

James...46, 85, 117, 129, 147, 149, 173, 175, 176
Jarvis... 59
Jeremiah... 117
Jesse...46
John... 175
Joseph...2, 4, 5, 9, 147
Lemuel... 147
Malachi...46
Margaret... 85
Marmaduke... 17, 27, 42, 85, 117, 147, 174, 175
Milly... 85
Miriam... 85
Nancy... 85
Peggy...46
Robert... 27, 33, 34, 85, 86, 175
Reuben... 85
Ruth... 147
Sally... 147
Samuel...12, 26, 46, 59, 117, 147, 175
Simpson ... 32, 33, 46
Sophia... 85, 117, 147, 174
Stephen... 85, 86, 129, 147, 175
Stephen Jr.... 34
Stephen Sr. ... 34
Susan... 85
Susannah... 85, 147
Sylphia... 175
Thomas... 85, 86
William... 54, 75, 82, 119, 129, 147, 149, 155, 157, 163, 170, 175

Sewell, Ambrose... 141, 146

Sexton
Elizabeth... 147

Sexton cont.
John... 59, 175
Mary... 147
Olly... 147, 175
Samuel ... 62, 147
Tamer... 175
William... 147

Shakespeare
George...12
Martha...12
Samuel...12

Shannon, John... 75, 107

Shannonhouse
Eleanor L... 117
James...3
James L... 21, 37, 117
Thomas... 70, 77, 78, 79, 118

Sharber, David... 96, 100, 105, 115, 116, 120, 136, 142, 148, 149

Sharborough *see Scarborough*

Shaw
John...2, 47
William...48

Sheppard
Ann... 86
Ciperan...11, 14, 29, 86
John... 86
Margaret... 86
William... 26
William B. ... 29, 147

Shirley
Ann... 59
Daniel...11, 33, 118
David... 15, 59
John... 59, 118
Nancy... 118

Simpson
_lly... 148
Caleb...12, 33
Catherine... 148
Elizabeth... 184
Evan... 175
George... 118, 148, 175
Harriet... 118, 148
Hezekiah... 72, 75, 148
James... 184
Jesse... 149
Jno... 175
Joab...12, 33, 148, 176
John... 20, 118, 148, 175
Joseph... 184
Josiah... 184
Marius... 148
Mary... 175
Matthew... 184
Robert... 75, 81, 85, 86, 118, 131, 143, 148, 170, 176, 184
Sarah... 118
Willis... 26, 75, 80, 82

Skinner, John M... 122, 136, 155, 158, 163, 164, 165

Small
Elizabeth... 22
Joseph... 33, 118, 148, 176
Joshua... 22
Nancy... 33
Nathan... 22, 70, 130, 133, 139, 143, 153, 155, 167, 180
Obadiah... 22
Samuel... 33

Index

Smith
 Abraham ... 62
 James...6, 86, 124
 Joseph... 59, 119, 148, 149
 Lydia... 59, 119
 Mordecai...12
 Robert... 59, 119, 148, 149
 Robert H...48, 64
 Sally... 59, 119, 148
 Tamer... 59
 William...46

Smithson
 Bathsheba...13
 Caleb... 33
 Charity... 119, 149, 176
 Elisha... 119, 149, 176
 Lovey... 33
 John...2, 12, 33
 John Jr. ...7
 Joseph...12
 Malachi... 30, 47
 Mary... 176
 Matthias... 34, 47, 83
 Miles...13, 30, 46, 47, 180
 Milly... 33
 Miriam... 33
 Penelope... 33
 Polly...13, 119, 149
 Ruben...13
 Sally...13
 William...13

Snowden
 Lemuel... 22, 52, 73, 86, 93, 96, 102, 104, 111, 127, 128, 131, 135, 147, 179
 Thaddeus... 23, 59, 86
 William... 22, 23, 55, 59, 86

Spence
 Almond... 176

 Alson... 133, 146, 160, 162
 Betsy... 60
 Caleb... 176
 Daniel... 132, 145, 146, 169, 172, 174, 176
 David... 176
 Edmund... 33
 Edward... 23
 Elizabeth... 60, 119, 149
 Enoch... 176
 James...4, 6, 12, 24, 176
 James Jr. ... 22
 James Sr. ... 28, 29, 33, 34
 Joseph... 60, 86
 Mark... 22, 23, 33, 60, 119, 132, 145, 149, 173, 176
 Martha... 119, 149, 176
 Miles... 23, 33
 Nancy... 23, 60, 119, 149, 176
 Parthenia... 60, 119, 149, 176
 Patsy... 60
 Polly... 176
 Renchir... 176
 Reuben... 60
 Samuel...3, 22, 23, 60, 86
 Sarah... 176
 Susannah... 60
 Thornton... 60, 129
 William... 23, 33, 38, 60, 119, 149, 176
 Willis... 86
 Wilson... 23, 33

Squires
 Demsey... 177
 John... 177
 Mackey... 177
 Martha... 177
 Nancy... 177

Index

Stafford
 Adam... 106
 John... 86
 Stephen... 74

Stamp
 Richard...13, 47
 Thomas...13, 47

Stokely
 Alford... 60
 Betsy...47
 Elizabeth... 34
 Emmy... 60
 Harvey... 34
 Isaac... 22, 28, 60
 Jeremiah... 60, 182
 Joseph... 33, 34, 47, 146, 151, 152, 160, 161, 162, 164, 171, 172, 174, 176, 182
 Joshua... 60
 Lydia... 60
 Peggy... 60
 Polly... 34, 47
 Rhoda... 60
 Sally... 33, 47
 Susannah... 33

Stone, Robert... 107, 118

Stott
 Elizabeth... 60, 120, 149, 177
 Thomas... 60, 86, 120, 149, 177
 Thomas S... 177
 William...9, 12, 34, 61, 86, 120, 149, 177

Sutton, Benjamin... 118

Swann
 John...13
 Rebecca...13

Symons,
 Abraham...47
 Benjamin... 16, 19, 29, 34, 47, 48
 Ferebee...13
 Jacob... 52, 67, 95, 96, 128, 156, 177
 James W... 177
 Jehoshaphat... 56
 John...23, 23, 61, 167, 168, 177
 John Sr....13, 14
 Mary...14, 23, 61
 Penelope... 23
 Sarah...13, 23
 Thomas...14, 23
 William...13, 23

Taylor
 David... 170
 Gabriel... 50
 John... 50
 Joseph...14, 23, 34
 Nancy...14, 23, 34
 Steven... 81

Temple
 Burtan... 177
 David... 120
 Dozier... 86
 James...14, 61, 86, 90, 177
 Joseph...14, 86, 120
 Robert... 86, 90, 120
 Thomas... 61, 68, 69, 83, 86, 96, 132, 145, 169, 171, 172
 Thomas Jr... 132, 182
 Turner... 177

Thomas
 John... 107
 William... 53, 117

Index

Thompson
 Henry... 87, 120, 149
 John... 87, 120, 149

Thornton
 Abner W... 177
 James... 177

Tooley
 Adam... 23, 34, 47
 Elizabeth... 23, 34, 47
 Jethro... 177
 John... 23, 34, 47, 64, 75, 104, 105, 106, 107, 108, 122, 136, 149, 154, 177
 Richard Henry... 177
 Sarah... 23, 34
 William... 23, 34, 47

Trueblood
 Aaron... 120, 178
 Alfred... 61
 Andrew... 87
 Ansalem... 121
 Clarkey... 87
 Edmund... 74, 87, 96, 105, 106, 107, 115, 120, 136, 142, 148, 149, 171, 173
 Edward B... 58
 Elizabeth... 178
 Ephriam... 120
 Exum... 87, 121, 177
 Fred B... 87
 Isaac... 120
 Isaac O... 178
 James...14, 17, 27, 87, 120, 121
 Jesse...47
 John...14, 23, 31, 87
 Jonathan... 27, 48, 61
 Joshua...3, 6, 12, 13, 14, 56, 57, 58, 87, 120, 121, 170, 178
 Josiah... 87
 Malachi... 87, 120
 Margaret... 121
 Mary... 47, 87, 121, 149, 178
 Maynard... 61
 Millicent...47, 120, 121
 Morris... 178
 Nancy...47
 Nathan... 31, 37, 43, 44, 57, 178
 Peggy... 121
 Rebecca... 23
 Samuel...14, 17, 87, 121, 149, 178
 Sarah... 87, 120
 Stephen... 87
 Thomas... 116, 120, 130, 170, 178
 Timothy... 61, 121
 William... 74, 77, 87, 104, 105, 109, 110, 121, 123, 138
 Wilson... 87, 121

Tubbs
 William... 150
 William D... 150

Turner
 Agathy...47
 Fanny... 121
 James... 86, 88
 James W... 110, 121, 122
 (Janug?) ...47
 John H...47
 Joseph...8, 10
 Peggy...47
 William... 121

Twine
 Elizabeth... 178
 Jesse... 178
 Margaret... 178
 William... 178

Varden, Tully... 90

Warner, Warnier
(Auget?) ...47
Caroline...47
Lydia...47
Margaret... 87, 122
Mary... 87, 122
(Muhuly?) ... 87
Nicholas... 122
Paloey... 61
Peggy... 61
Polly... 61
Priscilla... 61, 87, 122
S... 118
Sally... 61
Samuel... 61, 87, 122
Samuel R... 101
William... 87, 122

Warrington
James... 178
John R... 62, 71, 178
Mary... 178
Thomas... 22, 178

Weaver, William... 141, 159, 174

Weeks, John... 78, 79, 90, 158, 164, 183

Weymouth
Amos... 24
Miriam... 24
Robert... 82, 88, 106
Thomas...39, 88
Wilson... 88

Whaley, John... 146

Whidbee
Addison... 139
James... 73, 77, 104, 135, 151, 163
James Jr... 163

White
Aaron... 67, 81, 122, 123, 128, 150, 179
Abraham...47, 61
Alfred... 122, 150
Ann (a) (e)...14, 48, 89, 123
Benjamin... 16, 18, 19, 24, 29, 40, 41, 43, 47, 56, 61, 88, 89, 122, 141, 150, 179
Caleb... 108, 127, 138, 139, 156, 169, 179
David... 89, 123, 151, 179
Devotion... 10, 12, 48
Edmund... 89, 122, 123, 150
Eli... 72, 88, 101, 122, 123, 140, 150
Elizabeth... 24, 88, 89, 122
Francis... 23, 24, 40, 48
George... 88, 122, 150
Henry...47, 61, 121
James... 24, 89, 150, 179
Jenetta... 89
Jepth(i)a... 89, 151, 179
Jepethih... 123
John... 24, 48, 104, 110, 134, 146, 148, 162, 168, 176, 179
Jordan...48
Joseph... 179
Joseph Sr... 142
Joshua...47
Josiah... 24, 34, 41, 47, 48, 50, 61, 89, 123, 151, 179
Josiah Jr... 18, 19, 89
Lydia... 88, 122
Margaret S... 123, 150

Index

Martha... 34, 48, 89, 123, 151, 179
Mary... 34, 48, 89, 123, 150
Matthew... 90, 123, 151, 180
Miles... 142
Miley... 88
Milly... 122
Miriam... 151, 179
Nancy...47, 89
Nathan... 151, 179
Nehemiah... 34
Patsy... 89
Peggy... 34
Rebecca... 89, 123
Reuben... 34, 151
Richard...48
Robert... 23, 61
Robertson... 76
Robinson... 111, 141
Samuel... 88, 89, 150, 179
Sarah... 24
Sarah Ann... 179
Stephen... 56, 61, 89, 90, 110, 123, 126, 138, 139, 151, 153, 168, 170, 178, 180
Thomas... 108, 151, 164, 166, 179
Toms...9
William...48

Whitehurst
Elliott... 124, 151, 161, 162, 173, 180, 184
F... 115, 116
Fred... 180
Fred R... 53
Frederick... 36, 52, 53, 88, 134, 144, 151, 161, 162, 163, 172, 173, 180, 184
(Fruterin?) ... 124

Whitney
Abner... 29, 33, 34, 151
Franklin... 151
William... 162
William D... 151

Wilcocks
Eliz... 151
James... 151, 184
Jeremiah... 151, 184
Jesse... 151
Louisa... 184
Stephen... 151, 184
Susan... 184
Susannah... 151

Williams
A... 146
Aaron...7
Abner... 68, 71, 74, 77, 80, 81, 87, 96, 100, 105, 115, 116, 117, 120, 129, 136, 142, 148, 149, 154, 155, 168, 169, 170, 173, 175, 176, 177, 178, 182
David L... 90, 123
David S... 180
Demcy... 152
Edward... 133, 134, 146, 177
Elisha... 62, 124
Elizabeth... 152
Evan... 90
Harvey... 116, 133, 134, 146, 151
Horatio N... 150, 157
James... 96, 146, 152, 177
James H... 158
John... 157, 177
John T... 152, 180
John Thomas... 90, 123

Williams cont.
Lodwick...14, 23, 90, 143, 146, 174
Lurana ... 62
Lurancey... 124
Mark... 86
Mary... 90, 124
Maxey... 124, 147
Maxwell... 62
Mejiah... 152
Owen... 27, 62, 124, 152
Sarah... 152
Seth ... 62, 96, 124
Shadrack Owen ... 62
Susannah... 124

Wilroy, Nathaniel... 90, 152, 180

Wilson
Edward E... 133, 154
Francis... 37, 41, 90, 152
Jeremiah...14
Jesse... 170
Milly... 90
Nathaniel... 124
Ruth...14
Stephen...14
Thomas... 153, 170, 179
William...3, 8, 11, 23, 25, 28, 29, 31, 32, 35, 42, 44, 47, 57, 61, 69, 70, 79, 83, 88, 94, 104, 111, 114, 115, 116, 121, 126, 128, 129, 130, 133, 136, 145, 154, 155, 170, 175

Wilson... 152

Winberry, Winbury
Enoch... 24
Milly... 24
William... 24

Winslow, John... 77, 89, 90, 98, 110, 132, 134, 141, 162, 168, 169, 183

Wood
Evan... 34
Gray... 124
James... 24
John... 24, 124
Joseph... 24, 124, 180
Molly... 34
Parthenia... 180
Polly... 124
Sally... 124, 180
Sarah... 124
Spence... 124, 180
William... 24, 60, 76, 107, 124

Wyatt
Isaac...48
Richard...48

Young
David... 24
William Proby... 24

ABOUT THE AUTHOR

JEAN WOOD PASCHAL has devoted over thirty years to researching her own family history. When the she stumbled across the Pasquotank County Guardian Bond Books which identified the family of one of her "difficult" ancestors, she realized what a wonderful source for information they are. Unfortunately, a researcher would have to go through these books page by page and decipher the names on each bond to locate possible ancestors. Some of the Guardian Bond books did have an index, but there were errors and many names were simply not recorded in the existing indexes. Since this information has never been printed in any form and the Bond Books can only be viewed in the North Carolina State Archives or by microfilm, the author decided to try and make this available to others by abstracting all the bonds which are presented in this two-volume series.

www.ingramcontent.com/pod-product-compliance
Lightning Source LLC
Chambersburg PA
CBHW051048160426